1st

35 —

D1601678

No. 0347

Lola Montez

The California Adventures of Europe's Notorious Courtesan

Study of Lola Montez
From sketchbook of Wilhelm von Kaulbach
Courtesy, California State Library

Lola Montez

THE CALIFORNIA ADVENTURES OF EUROPE'S NOTORIOUS COURTESAN

by

James F. Varley

THE ARTHUR H. CLARK COMPANY
Spokane, Washington
1996

Copyright, 1996 by
JAMES F. VARLEY

———————

All rights reserved, including the rights to
translate or reproduce this work or parts
thereof in any form or by any media.

———————

LIBRARY OF CONGRESS CARD CATALOG NUMBER 95-22922
ISBN 0-87062-243-9

Library of Congress Cataloging-in-Publication Data

Lola Montez, The California Adventures of Europe's Notorious
    Courtesan /by James F. Varley
    269 p. cm. —   ISBN 0- 0-87062-243-9 (alk. paper)
1. Montez, Lola, 1818-1861. 2. Courtesans—Europe—Biography.
3. Mistresses. 4. Montez, Lola, 1818-1861—Homes and haunts-
-California. 5. California—Social life and customs—19th century.
6. California—History—1850-1950. I. Title.
DD801. B383M6938 1995
979.4' 04'092—dc20
[B]   95-22922
                                                        CIP

To Sarah and Leona—
And to their progeny, my girls—
Kirstin, Karin, Sarah, Deanna and Elena

Contents

Illustrations

Preface

When one thinks of the fast-paced, burgeoning state of California, folklore is usually the last thing to cross the mind. Denizens of the Golden State seem to have little time for recollection of the past. This notwithstanding, there are two traditions which have managed to survive down through the years since their emergence in 1853. One is the legend of the illusory bandit, Joaquin Murrieta, and the other concerns the subject of this history—that divinely-eccentric dancer and tamer of men, Lola Montez.

In 1939, a play by Robert Craig entitled *Red Bumblebee* opened at San Francisco's Curran Theater. It was called a comedy of early California, and Craig's principal characters were Murrieta, the Mexican Robin Hood of the new world, and Lola Montez, courtesan of the old world. Leo Carrillo, a popular romantic comedian of Western movies, played Murrieta, opposite dancer Tamara Geva as Lola, the colorful "bumble bee." The play's thin plot wove a tale of the romance that might have been, had the two ever actually met, and it reflects a curious desire on the part of people even unto this day that the paths of the fabulous Irish beauty and the infamous robber might have crossed. Perhaps this is because, for a brief period, they were the two most exciting characters ever to come to early California.

I became interested in the Montez story while doing

research for my first book, *Brigham and the Brigadier.* It took little convincing to get this project started, inasmuch as the enigmatic woman's life is such a colorful and fascinating study. Her brief span on earth was remarkable in its variety and excitement; only rarely has a person made such an impact with so little talent and so much derring-do as did Lola Montez.

When the thirty-five-year-old Irish woman first appeared in San Francisco, the Gold Rush had just passed its peak—and so had she. But Lola still had great appeal; she retained a surfeit of overwhelming beauty, a cocky spirit and a quick wit, and she was well-known in the world at large for the distinguished male scalps she had collected, and for her scandalous antics all across Europe.

The few years Lola spent in northern California engendered a whole host of stories to which the passing of time has lent widespread credence. Some say, for instance, that she came as the principal stockholder of Grass Valley's famous Empire Mine and, while living there in the Sierra Nevada foothills, she and a group of Southerners plotted a revolt which, had it succeeded, would have established her as empress of the slave state of California. There are others who have claimed that she shocked a prim old Grass Valley minister by coming, uninvited, to dance before him in his parlor, that she might demonstrate how proper and tasteful was her art.

Indeed, with the exception of Murrieta, more exaggerated and dubious history has been written about Lola Montez than any other historical personage in California. Seemingly, every "old timer" to have been there had known her, and all were quick to recollect their personal anecdotes concerning her eccentric behavior. The fabrications and exaggerations of these pioneers were abetted greatly by the free-wheeling newspapers of the second half of the nineteenth century.

Separating fact from fancy has been difficult. Nearly all previous Montez biographies have been based largely on the aforesaid anecdotal information, and they portray Lola simply as a wild, but heroic, much misunderstood woman. Through extensive research of contemporary newspapers, genealogical records and other fresh sources perhaps I have been successful in my goal of presenting a more balanced and accurate story of Lola's life. Certainly no attempt has been made to ignore or gloss over her warts—the intense sexuality, her probable contraction of syphilis, and her incessant prevarication, for instance.

My thanks for the assistance of librarians throughout the West. I am particularly grateful to the personnel of the California State Library, Sacramento, and to Mary Joerger of the College of Southern Idaho for her unflagging help in obtaining research materials.

Mackay, Idaho   JAMES F. VARLEY
1995

Lola Montez in 1846
From a painting by Josef Steiler in the Residenz Museum, Munich.
Courtesy, California State Library

CHAPTER ONE

She Dances As The Birds Sing

Such is the social and moral fabric of the world, that woman must be content with an exceedingly narrow sphere of action, or she must take the worst consequences of daring to be an innovator, and a heretic.   Lola Montez, *Autobiography*

There was never any shortage of dynamic men to add mystique and myth to California's earliest history. Who today in that land of everlasting sunshine and smog—except, perhaps, the most recent arrival—has not heard of John Fremont, Kit Carson, Sam Brannan, the chimerical bandit Joaquin Murrieta and others of similar fascination? But, of the few women who first came to the nascent Golden State, all left but little imprint—all save one, that is.

When she felt the need to impress or intimidate, the woman called herself Marie Elise Rosanna Dolores, Countess of Landsfeld de Heald, Baroness of Rosenthal and Chainqinnese of the Order of St. Therese—or some slight variation thereof. But the world knew her better as the dancer and courtesan, Lola Montez. In 1853 she came to spend a few brief years in California and, despite a flagging spirit and fading beauty, her coming created all the excitement and upheaval of one of the state's major earthquakes.

She was an accused bigamist, an insatiable amorist, the classic *femme fatale*. Word had it she had taken so many lovers that a centipede couldn't count them on its legs. Best known had been her liaisons with Franz Liszt, Alexandre Dumas the elder, and King Ludwig I of Bavaria. The latter had lost his crown, at least in part, because of the influence she wielded in Bavarian politics.

Moralists never hesitated to use all the veiled synonyms in their dictionaries in pronouncing Lola Montez a prostitute. She was compared most often to Aspasia, Pericles' mistress and advisor, whom tradition says instigated the Peloponnesian War. At other times she was labeled a Pompadour, a modern cyprian, and worse. She lived, after all, in the age of Victoria, wherein brazen sexuality such as hers was not to be openly tolerated.

As the most bohemian woman of her time, Montez achieved a world-wide notoriety. Her activities filled more newspaper columns and spawned more biographies than had those of any woman before her. She was a sort of demi-goddess among a class of young Poles, Frenchmen, and Germans. Horace Vernet used her as a model for the classic woman in his huge painting of "The Taking of the Smala of Abd-el-Kadir"; Dumas, Francois Joseph Mery and Auguste Barthelemy all celebrated her in odes.[1]

Normally soft-spoken and gracious to those around her, and possessing natural and simple manners, she was invariably kind to children and those in need, sharing her bounty unostentatiously. But the Montez temper was legendary. When thwarted or attacked—or simply when the notion took her— she could become an imperious, sometimes violent termagant,

---

[1]*Sacramento* (CA) *Daily Union*, July 4, 1853: New York *Herald*, Jan. 13, 1852. Vernet (1789-1863) was a well-known painter of military and Arab subjects. Mery (1797-1866) was a journalist and man of letters who, with his compatriot, Barthelemy, published satirical pamphlets, epic poems, plays and vaudevilles.

pitching fearlessly into her tormenters. This mercurial woman was also as capricious in her affections and interests as the wind, and she was easily influenced and imposed upon, despite her boasted knowledge of the world.

The detractors of Lola Montez always credited her with a bold, masculine aspect but, in fact, she was one of the most beautifully feminine women of her day. Her perfectly oval, sensuous face, with its flawless complexion and prominent cheek bones, was intensely expressive, and her raven-black hair, said one fellow performer, "a mermaid might envy." Her small feet, thought another hopelessly-stricken man, supported "fine, shapely calves" which were "the lowest rungs of a Jacob's ladder leading to Heaven."[2] Although as a younger woman she had been more full-figured, during her years in California, Lola was much lighter in form and of sparer features, carrying perhaps 110 pounds on a frame of medium height—quite slender for that era of voluptuous heavyweights.

But everyone seemed to agree that the chief attraction of this enchantress lay in her unusually large and clear, deeply-blue eyes. So dazzling and expressive were these dark-ringed orbs that they were described by different observers at various times as being grey, blue-grey, black, blue by day and dark by night, and as combining the varying shades of the sixteen varieties of forget-me-not. One of her close associates said they had an "unaccountable color, which varies with the hours, the emotions, the interior blaze that lights them."[3]

It is difficult from this distance in time to recognize Lola as an unusual beauty, but it is apparent that there was more to her attraction than could be captured in a mere painting or photograph. She seems to have exuded an impression of beauty—a

---

[2] Walter M. Leman, *Memories of An Old Actor*, 251; Edmund B. D'Auvergne, *Lola Montes, An Actress of the Forties*, 51.

[3] [John Richardson?] *Lola Montez; or a Reply to the "Private History and Memoirs" of That Celebrated Lady*. Other descriptions of the Montez eyes can be found in New Orleans *Daily True Delta*, Dec. 25, 1852; *N.Y. Herald*, Apr. 17, 1852.

certain *je ne sais quoi*—which she retained even into her later years, as an Australian miner who saw her attested:

> In person she is rather slight, with very slender arms, and very sym-metrical "determinations downwards." Her feet are about the size of full-grown mice, and her ankles about as large as a baby's wrist. Her hair is like the raven's plumage; her lips like rosebuds; her teeth like ivory; and oh! my stars, what eyes...large, dark, liquid and veiled eye lashes which, like mist before sun, prevent them from dazzling one entirely...Her movements are graceful, her smile bewitching...she is a lost Peri, a stray angel, a star unsphered, a Cleopatra without a throne...[4]

There is little certainty about the beginnings of this enig-matic woman. Late in life, Lola would say of herself that, while seven cities had claimed Homer, the biographers had given her to more than twenty-one. One placed her birth in Spain, another in Cuba, and others in India and Turkey. One "fugitive from the gallows," she said, had her being born of a washer-woman in Scotland; another author made her the child of a Spanish Gypsy, and still another the daughter of Lord Byron, and so on until they had given her "more fathers than there are signs in the Zodiac."[5]

What Montez neglected to say is that much of the confu-sion surrounding her origins came from false information she herself parceled out over the years, giving revised birth dates and claiming less noble parentage as she aged, and as more and more of her true history was exposed. The facts in the matter seem to be—as Montez would finally fully reveal as her death approached—that she was born out of wedlock, in 1818, at Limerick, Ireland, as Eliza Rosanna Gilbert. Only a year before

---

[4]Roslyn Brereton, "The Glamorous Gold Rush," *Pacific Historian*, 13:3, 10.

[5]Lola Montez, *Lectures of Lola Montez...Including Her Autobiography*, 16. There is much uncertainty about Lola's real origins. A search of Limerick, Ireland, birth records shows no evidence that an Eliza Gilbert was born there in the years surrounding Lola's supposed birth date. But the register of St. Michael's Church lists an Eliza Watson born on Dec. 11, 1817, to Henry and Lucinda Watson. (Birth Record Registers, Genealogical Library, Church of Jesus Christ of L.D.S., Salt Lake City, Utah.) The name Watson recurred with tantalizing frequency during Lola's life.

siring Eliza, her father, Edward Gilbert, had been appointed an ensign in the 25th Regiment of Foot, the King's Own Borderers, which was garrisoned at Limerick. Soon after the birth, he evidently married Eliza's fifteen-year old mother, Elizabeth Oliver.

In October 1822, Gilbert was transferred to the 44th Regiment of Foot, and he and his little family were shipped out to India. Shortly after arriving, he died of cholera but, happily, a close friend, Lieutenant Patrick Craigie, stepped forward to marry six-year old Eliza's attractive mother. Lola-Eliza would always admit to having acquired her wild (but harmless) ways as a little girl in India. When old enough to begin her education, the somewhat wayward child was sent back to Montrose, Scotland, to Lieutenant Craigie's parents. But they too had trouble handling her, so Sir Jasper Nichols, the major-general commanding Bengal forces, was asked to raise her along with his two daughters. Under the tutelage of the Nichols family, young Eliza received a good education, including some training in music and the social graces.

While Eliza was at a finishing school in Bath, England, her mother returned from India in company with Lieutenant Thomas James of the 21st regiment of Bengal Native Infantry, who was on sick leave. James—probably infatuated with Mrs. Craigie—accompanied her to Bath to give nineteen-year old Eliza the news that a match had been made for her with a very rich old nabob in India, a supreme court judge who apparently wanted a young wife shipped to him with his next batch of London newspapers.

Eliza, quite naturally, revolted at these arrangements. To avoid the match, she turned her embryonic charms of seduction on Lt. James, and persuaded him to elope with her. After some difficulty, the bolting couple obtained Mrs. Craigie's consent—but not her blessing or her presence—and they were married at Meath, Ireland on July 23, 1837, by James' brother, a Catholic priest. Mother and daughter would be forever estranged as a result of this incident.

The newlyweds lived in Dublin until the fall of 1838, when James was ordered back to India. What little is known of the ensuing period has come from Montez herself, except for the observations of one woman who saw the couple briefly at the east Punjab resort town of Simla in 1839. The youthful, lively Mrs. James was deemed to be the prettiest of a bunch of army wives, and the writer accurately predicted that "if she were ever to fall into bad hands, she would soon laugh herself into foolish scrapes."[6]

Although it would prove to be her most successful attempt at connubial bliss, Eliza's marriage to James, alas, didn't long endure. As she later commented, "Runaway matches, like runaway horses, are almost sure to end in a smash-up."[7] While living in Karnal—so Eliza would come to assert—her husband ran off with a certain Mrs. Captain Lomer and, soon after this, she, a poor grass widow, had no choice but to return, against her will, to her mother and Patrick Craigie in Calcutta. Once there, she said, they locked her in a room until a certificate could be obtained to the effect that she was in ill health and must be sent home to England.

One suspects that Eliza was the philandering party in her marriage. At all events, Lt. James wrote Sarah Watson, his sister in England, saying his wife had fallen from a horse and was otherwise so out of health that her return home was necessary. An old army friend in England was asked to take charge of her when she arrived, and see that she got safely to Patrick Craigie's sister in Edinburgh.

These arrangements completed, James and Patrick Craigie gave Eliza some money and saw her on board the East India

---

[6]M. Cannon, *Lola Montes: the Tragic Story of a "Liberated Woman,"* 5, quoting Emily Eden, *Up the Country: Letters from the upper provinces of India.* Also see *A List of Officers of the Army and Royal Marines...* (London, 1819), 187.

[7]Montez, *Lectures*, 22.

trader *Larkins* at Calcutta on a day in late September 1840. James stayed with his estranged wife until the ship was some distance down the Ganges delta, perhaps to attempt a reconciliation, but, more likely, to ensure that she didn't fly the coop. A certain Mr. and Mrs. Sturges, passengers who were friends of the family, had been asked to look after her during the voyage, and Lt. James undoubtedly disembarked confident that his wife was in good hands. But, events would prove the Sturgeses to be miserable chaperons.

Larkins touched briefly at Madras to embark more passengers, returning home from the arduous duties of Empire. In just a few days, one of them—Lt. Charles Lennox—was engaged with Mrs. James in what was described as "violent flirting"[8] by the ship's captain. During the remainder of the five-month trip, the lieutenant was seen entering Eliza's cabin at all hours of the day and night; a maid observed him lacing Eliza's stays, kissing her, and even boldly watching while she put on her stockings. After the captain and his wife reproached Eliza, and were told impertinently that she would be her own mistress, they quickly washed their hands of her.

Upon arriving at Portsmouth in February 1841, Eliza and Lennox traveled to London together. Here, Patrick Craigie's army friend called, as had been arranged, but Eliza declined his help. Instead, for about a month, she lived in a boarding house in St. James, where Lennox visited her daily. When her husband's sister came to urge that she go to the Craigies, she continued to adamantly refuse, letting it be known that she would soon be divorced so as to marry Lennox.

But Charles Lennox would have no place in our heroine's future. Just what became of him can't be said. Perhaps Eliza tired of him. More likely, he soon abandoned her even though she had risked everything on his behalf. In any case, the offended husband, Lt. James, applied to the Catholic ecclesiastical

---

[8]*London Times,* Aug. 7, 1849.

court in London and, by December, 1842 he had won a judi-
cial separation from his wife, based on the evidence recounted
above. As to Eliza, after the bad marriage, the bullying by her
mother and the soured relationship with Lennox, she sought a
means of becoming financially independent.

The career choices available at the time to women, particularly those with a free spirit like Eliza, were slim. The performing arts were a notable exception, and this is the path she chose.
In her fiction-filled autobiography, the now-independent but
scarlet woman would come to claim that she had studied acting until, because of her poor English, it was decided she might
be better suited as a dancer. One can suppose that she was actually motivated toward a dancing career by having seen the
immense success of the notorious Fanny Elssler, who was then
at the peak of her popularity, and whose specialty was numbers
with a Latin flavor, such as *La Cachucha* and *La Tarantule*. However she may have come to choose it, Eliza said she learned the
basics of her art in London from a Spaniard named Espa, and
then went on for further training to Spain, traveling by herself
throughout that country.

Armed with her new skill, Eliza began boldly representing
herself to be "Doña Lola Montez," a Spanish dancer. The surname "Montez," or "Montes" as it is sometimes spelled, she
probably stole from the then-famous Spanish matador of that
name. As to "Lola," she would explain, it was the diminutive of
her supposed name, Maria de Los Dolores. As an accessory to
the fiction that she was Spanish, she henceforth adopted a foreign accent, which many throughout her life would correctly
assess as being affected.

"Doña Montez" returned to England on April 14, 1843.
The Earl of Malmesbury, years later, would admit having
made her acquaintance when the consul at Southampton asked
him to take charge of a Spanish lady who had just landed.

Lola Montez by Wilhelm von Kaulbach
Grace Greenwood visited Munich in 1853 and wrote: "In a rose-
embowered studio of [Kaulbach] we found another portrait of the
Countess of Landsfeld. It was a full length, in an antique Spanish
Dress...[a] statuesque picture after the style of Van Dyke."
From the author's collection

Malmesbury agreed—eagerly, no doubt, once he had laid eyes on the attractive woman—and the two traveled by carriage to London. Lola, who was dressed in black and seemingly in deep mourning, told the earl, in fractured English, that she was the impoverished widow of a Spanish officer lately assassinated by the Carlists. She was bound for London to sell some of her possessions and to give singing lessons. Once arrived, Malmesbury said, he invited the poor, bereaved woman to a party where she sang for his guests and sold them mantillas and other articles, and that, thereafter, she received a good deal of assistance.

Within weeks, with the help of an unnamed English nobleman—perhaps Malmesbury—Lola had convinced Benjamin Lumley, the director of Her Majesty's Theatre, to allow her to perform. Billed as a native of Seville, and the daughter (not widow) of a noted Spanish patriot, she appeared on stage for the first time on Saturday, June 3, 1843, between acts of *The Barber of Seville*. Castanets in hand, the audacious Montez danced something she called "El Olano," or "El Olle," and thoroughly conned a house crowded with England's upper crust. Even the stuffy old *London Times* was fooled, as one can see from this review of the debut:

> There was a solemnity in the whole affair...a gloominess in the music...The few bars that preceded the rising of the curtain sounded forebodingly; and when the curtain was removed, we saw...a few little ladies of the corps de ballet on each side of the stage; but the principal object was a mysterious folding door in the centre of the scene at the back. This opened slowly, and a figure completely muffled in a black mantilla stepped forward. A few moments and the mantilla was cast aside, leaving visible the tall and commanding person of Dona Montez, attired in a black bodice, the skirt terminating in dark red and blue points. In the most stately fashion she wound round the stage, executing all her movements with the utmost deliberation...the bending forward and drawing back, the feat of dropping on the knees, the haughty march forward. But in the style which

Lola Montez
From an engraving in the *Illustrated London News*, March
20, 1847, whose caption reads: "The character of the
Spanish dancer, whose pas and poses have been more
than a match for a Ministry, upheld by all the influence of
the Jesuits, is better known than her history...Wherever
she appears, she is in the midst of an imbroglio."
From the author's collection

Dona Montez went through these movements there was something
entirely different from all that we have seen.

The *Times* conceded that Montez wasn't a very polished
dancer, but there was, nevertheless, an impressive "national
reality" and intensity about her:

The haughtiness with which she stepped, the slow play of the arms, the air of authority...with hands resting on the hips all gave an air of grandeur to the dance...The whole soul of the artist seems worked up to a stern purpose—we do not believe Dona Montez smiled once throughout. As she retired from the stage showers of bouquets were thrown, but the proud one of Seville did not deign to return to pick them up.[9]

But, unnoticed by the *Times*, Lola was hissed by a small group of men, led by Thomas Heron, the Viscount Ranelagh, who recognized that "Doña Montez" was really Betty James, the runaway wife of an army officer. So great was the scandal in subsequent days that Montez felt obliged to write a letter to the *Times*, defending her identity. The paper printed the missive, but—no doubt embarrassed by the gushing review already published—allowed it only as an advertisement.

During her short, turbulent life, Lola would pen many lying letters to justify her actions. In this, her first, she expressed annoyance at reports that she had long been known in London as a disreputable character, and insisted that this was her first visit to the city. In fact, she claimed, the only time she had ever been in England was as a ten-year old, in 1833, when her parents had sent her to live for seven months with a Catholic lady at Bath. "The imperfect English I speak," Lola said unblinkingly, "I learnt at Bath...from an Irish nurse who has been many years in my family." The recent misfortunes of her parents had obliged her to earn a living, Lola explained, and she had come to Albion hoping its people might appreciate her "native dances."[10]

But, with the cat out of the bag, manager Lumley adamantly refused to let the imposter appear again on his boards, despite

[9] *Ibid.*, June 5, 1843, Aug. 11, 1849; Philip Vandam, *An Englishman in Paris.* 102-03; Sacramento *Placer Times*, Apr. 22, 1850; *New York Times*, Jan. 22, 1861; San Francisco, *The Wide West*, May 30, 1858; S.F., *Daily Evening Bulletin*, Mar. 22, 1858; S.F. *Daily Alta California*, Mar. 21, 1858; *N.Y. Herald*, Oct. 31, 1851; Apr. 6, July 17, 1852.

[10] *London Times*, June 13, 1843.

knowing that she would have drawn large audiences. He confessed many years later that this "strange and fascinating
woman," who in fact was an "English adventuress," had totally
taken him in. All those who had seen her dance, Lumley
remembered, were rapturous about her, in spite of her being a
rank novice. He laid this strange infatuation to her singular
beauty, and her new, piquant and provocative style.[11]

Another observer would describe Lola's captivating style in
this way:

> One may have seen the dancing of Taglione, Carlotta Grisi, Fanny
> Elssler, and Cerito, and not know the dancing of Lola Montes. It is
> something bizarre and unforeseen, that has no analogy in any other
> choreography...[Her] dancing is not an art; it is a phantasy, it is a
> passion; it is the dream of her spring and the caprice of her summer.
> She dances as the birds sing, without knowing why.[12]

In her autobiography, Lola would credit the abrupt end of
her debut in London to a disagreement over terms. Some have
said she went next to Brussels and was soon reduced to singing
in the streets; others say she became a prostitute there. But
these theories seem unlikely since, by early October 1843, she
was reported to have been dancing for some time at Berlin,
with great success. It was an escapade in the Prussian capital
that month, in fact, which first brought Lola's violent temper
to the public's attention.

Somehow, Montez had finagled an invitation to observe a
grand review given by King Frederick William to honor the
visiting Nicholas I of Russia. Astride a horse, she was assigned
a position at some little distance from the royal cortege. But, as
luck—or perhaps design—would have it, the firing of salutes
caused her animal to bolt, carrying her straight into the suite of
the two sovereigns. A startled policeman who ordered her to
fall back, and struck her horse with the flat of his saber, was no

---

[11]*Alta California*, Aug. 27, 1864; San Jose (CA) *Sunday Mercury*, Feb. 3, 1867.
[12]*N.Y. Herald*, Oct. 28, 1851.

doubt even more alarmed when Lola responded by whacking him across the face with her whip.

Next day, she disdainfully tore up a police summons for the offense. But, although she was arrested and could have been jailed for five years, for some reason the matter was quietly dropped. Perhaps it was because poor Lola, as the press reported, was the daughter of a deceased Spanish general, and only nineteen years old. Her ploy to attract royal attention, if that is what is was, apparently worked. Nicholas invited her to visit St. Petersburg, and she readily agreed to come after she first fulfilled a scheduled engagement at Warsaw. It is from a well-publicized incident in this Polish city that we get the first of the many stories Montez would fashion to demonstrate the staunchness of her virtue.

Accounts at the time—which undoubtedly originated with Lola—relate that, after her first performance in early December, she was visited by Colonel Abrahamowicz, one of the Russian functionaries then governing occupied Poland. He made indecent proposals, Lola said, causing her to have him shown out. So humiliated was the colonel at being rejected that he laid plans to have the dancer hissed at her second performance. But Lola got wind of his intentions from some of her Polish literary friends, one of whom was Lesniowske, editor of the Warsaw Gazette. Thus forewarned, when next she danced and was, indeed, hissed from the gallery, Montez came forward to deliver a defiant footlight speech. After thanking the audience for its applause, she pointed directly at Abrahamowicz's box, and said, "It is that dastard who thus attempts to revenge himself on a defenseless woman, who would not permit him to realize his infamous projects."[13]

Lola was reported to have then left the theatre, under the protection of Lesniowske and others, with the police close on

---

[13] *London Times*, Jan. 16, 1844; also Oct. 12, 1843.

her heels. At her hotel a cluster of police attempted to examine her papers but, when she drew a poniard from her garter and threatened to kill anyone who dared come near her, the inquisitors were so cowed that they contented themselves with escorting her to the frontier. There, in a final argument, Lola was said to have drawn her dagger once again, and to have torn up and thrown in the faces of the Russian agents some letters they wanted to examine, one of which was from the Queen of Prussia. In the aftermath of this blowup, the hated Russians reportedly jailed and whipped several of Lola's protectors, including Lesniowske.

Eight years after the event, in America, S. M. A. Walowski, a Polish refugee pianist, would recount a variation on this anecdote which portrayed Abrahamowicz as merely a messenger boy for old Field Marshal Ivan Fedorovich Paskevich, the Russian viceroy of Poland. It was the viceroy, not the colonel, who was infatuated with Montez. But, he was a repugnant old man who, when he spoke, threw his head back and opened his mouth so wide as to expose the artificial gold roof of his palate. So repulsed was Lola during a private interview by this "death's head" making advances, that she disdainfully rejected his offer of a splendid country estate and jewels. Then, after Paskevich had her performance disrupted, and she made her plucky speech exposing his vile actions, the Poles became so agitated against the Russians that police came to arrest her. She barricaded herself in her room with a pistol, Wolowski said, until finally rescued by the French consul.[14]

What actually happened at Warsaw we may never know, just as there is no inkling of Lola's relationship with Czar Nicholas. But, of her affair with Franz Liszt, there is no doubt.

---

[14]New Orleans *True Delta*, Jan. 10, 1850; S.F. *The Wide West*, May 30, 1858; Montez, *Lectures*, 45-45; *N.Y. Herald*, Apr. 6, 1852. Russian Field Marshal Paskevich (1782-1856) commanded the army which suppressed the revolt for independence in Poland; afterwards he was designated viceroy of the Kingdom of Poland.

She and the great pianist-composer first met at Dresden, where both were performing. Liszt, then at the height of his fame, already had a mistress of some nine years—the Comtesse d'Agoult, who wrote under the pen name Daniel Stern. But no matter. For a week he and Montez rutted together in his hotel; he wrote her a sonata and took her to a special performance of Wagner's new opera *Rienzi*. And then, just as quickly as it had flared, the flame of passion sputtered out, and Liszt somewhat relievedly fled from Lola's overpowering presence.

Montez went after this to Paris, where she was dismissed by the manager of the Opera following a single appearance on the evening of March 30, 1844. Her offense in this case was taking off "certain portions of costume" that were considered *"de riguer"*[15] for dancers—some said her garters—and tossing them into the boxes to be pounced upon by wildly-cheering men of fashion.

Lola stayed on in the French capital, and eagerly sought out the company of intellectuals and artists. One of these, the novelist and dramatist Alexandre Dumas, *pere,* is said to have fallen passionately in love and engaged her in a brief affair of perhaps a few nights. Dumas, like Liszt, was then at the height of his popularity and in his sexual prime. He was also an admitted and notorious womanizer, who had quickly deserted, in turn, each of the women who had born his several illegitimate children.

The claim has been made that Dumas said of Lola, "She has the evil eye and is sure to bring bad luck to any one who closely links his destiny with hers, for however short a time...If ever she is heard of again, it will be in connection with some terrible calamity that has befallen a lover of hers."[16] Certainly, the death and disaster that henceforth followed Montez would prove this prediction correct.

---

[15]London *Illustrated London News,* Mar. 20, 1847.

[16]Vandam, 105-06; D'Auvergne, *Lo la Montez,* 65-66, 106-07.

The first of her lovers to die would be a young Parisian, Alexandre Henri Dujarrier, part-owner and editor of *La Presse*. Montez would always credit this avid republican with teaching her to hate tyranny and oppression. What started in the fall of 1844 as a mere affair, blossomed into a full-blown romance of the heart and flesh—one of perhaps only two deep loves Montez would ever experience during her checkered life. The carefree pair laid plans to marry in the spring, and it was arranged that Dumas and the poet Mery would accompany them on a honeymoon tour through Spain.

But fate canceled these idyllic plans. At a wild party, Dujarrier was challenged to a duel by his long-time enemy and rival journalist, Jean de Beauvallon. Poor Dujarrier, who had absolutely no experience as a duelist, nor any desire to fight, asked his friend Dumas to intercede, but the Creole writer merely braced the editor to the deadly task at hand. Montez had been told her lover was to fight a bad marksman like himself and, when she learned at the last minute that his opponent was to be Beauvallon, she said, "then he is a dead man." And, indeed he was. Like a lamb led to slaughter, Dujarrier succumbed to a pistol wound received on the duelling ground in the Bois de Boulonge on March 11, 1845. When he was carried home, observers said, Lola flung herself on his dying body and covered his face with kisses.

Despite such a touching display of grief, within weeks of Dujarrier's death Lola had once again reverted to her wild ways. She was hired to dance at Paris's Theater Porte St. Martin, but only managed to survive a few evenings. On the first night she engaged in a backstage brawl with a girl of the ballet company; on the second, she attempted to stab another of that company with the dagger she reputedly always carried on her person. When she tried to dance a third time she was hissed off the stage. Once more on tour, Lola is supposed to have seen

Liszt again at festivities for the Beethoven monument in Bonn where, after making a scene at the hotel, she forced her way into an all-male banquet and leaped on the table to dance a *fandango*.

A full year after killing Dujarrier, Beauvallon was tried for murder on charges of having test-fired the pistols prior to the duel. Lola went to Rouen to testify against him, along with Dumas, and the trial gave great impetus to her growing notoriety. If it was her design to create a sensation, as some have suggested, it certainly worked. She appeared in mourning dress —nothing severe, mind you, but soft masses of silk and lace— and when she lifted her veil and removed a glove to take the oath, a murmur of admiration ran through the court. "I was a better shot than Dujarrier," she declared from the stand, "and if Beauvallon wanted satisfaction, I would have fought [him] myself." Despite her testimony, the accused was acquitted, but in a second trial for perjury eighteen months later, he was found guilty and jailed for eight years.[17]

Not long after the trial, in early 1846, Lola traveled to the Grand Duchy of Baden, where she met Henry LXXII of Reuss. She became the prince's mistress and accompanied him to his estate, but their brief affair ended farcically—Lola was expelled from the tiny principality, for having walked across one of Henry's favorite flower beds, and then striking a servant who admonished her for the infraction.[18]

Unarguably, Lola Montez's greatest amatory conquest was King Ludwig I of Bavaria. As with so many other men in her life, she would run this ruler to ruin like a beggar on horseback. When they first met, Montez was still a beautiful woman of

---

[17]Montez, *Lectures*, 60-62; S.F. *Alta California*, Dec. 13, 1879; *N.Y. Times*, Jan. 22, 1861; *Illustrated London News*, Mar. 20, 1847; D'Auvergne, *Adventuresses and Adventurous Ladies*, 216-20.

[18]D'Auvergne, *Adventuresses*, 221. The principality of Reuss touched Bavaria on the south, and Prussia-Saxony on the north. The princes of both branches of the Reuss family were all named Heinrich (Henry), which explains why there could be 72 of them.

twenty-nine, but Ludwig was a 60-year old physical wreck, longing to be young again. He stuttered, and had been hard of hearing since an attack of scarlet fever in his youth. When Lola first met him, a disfiguring cyst had begun to form on his not-too-handsome brow. And, like Montez, Ludwig was quick-tempered, impetuous, moody and obstinate.

The lifelong ambition of the Bavarian king had been to make his capital the most beautiful city in Germany—a new Athens, a center of art—and he is responsible for many of the public works and buildings which comprise today's Munich. This lover of beauty spent a great deal of his time collecting paintings and sculpture, but even more effort went into amusing himself with gorgeous women.

His marriage to the attractive Saxon princess, Therese of Hildburghausen had produced nine children. She was apparently an understanding woman, for it was hardly any secret that, since even before assuming the Bavarian throne in 1825, her husband had engaged in liaisons with at least a half-dozen actresses and singers. Then too, he had coupled with the notorious Lady Jane Ellenborough when she visited Munich in 1832, and he had maintained a lifelong relationship with an Italian woman, the Marchesa Maria Florenzi.

Thus was the old sensualist ripe for plucking when Montez arrived in Munich in October 1846 on a professional tour she had begun at Paris in June. Knowing the king's reputation, it is probable that she came there deliberately to catch him. Now calling herself "Señora Maria Dolores de Porris y Montez"— the daughter of a Carlist officer and a Cuban lady—she applied to the director of the Munich court theater for permission to perform. Having been refused, she used her wiles to arrange an audience with Ludwig.

There would be stories that, during her interview, Lola ripped open her bodice to display her delicious bosom for the king, but no one could say for sure, since they met in private.

All we know for certain is that the interview went far beyond its allotted time, and the cleverly-brazen woman obtained the regal authorization she sought.

Dazzlingly arrayed in a Spanish costume of black silk and lace, with here and there a glittering diamond, Montez danced a *cachucha* and a *fandango* on October 10 at the court theater, between acts of another production. A lady who witnessed it said "she danced after the fashion of her country, swaying on her hips, and changing from one posture to another, each exceeding the former in beauty...Fire seemed to shoot from her wonderful blue eyes, and she bowed like one of the Graces before the King, who occupied the royal box."[19]

Captivated, licentious old Ludwig allowed Lola to perform once again four days later. If one can believe Montez, the king had been so impressed with her political ideas during the initial audience that he invited her to remain in Munich for a few days as his guest. When she asked what people would think, Ludwig said he had absolutely no fear of scandal. So, Lola stayed on as his mistress and, though all the world came to know of their relationship, the pair would always maintain the facade that it was platonic in nature—an attraction of the mind, not the flesh. Ludwig so insisted even on his deathbed.

Lola would further allege that, soon after she arrived, the king took her before his court, in the presence of his wife, and introduced her as "My best friend in the world." That it was more than mere friendship, however, can be seen in Ludwig's letters to his longtime confidant, Heinrich von der Tann. Despite his age, Ludwig told Tann, he had "inspired the first passion in the heart of a beautiful 22-year old daughter of the South, an aristocrat by birth." Lola had wept at the thought of leaving Munich. Passion, such as he had "never experienced

---

[19]*Unter den Vier Ersten Kinigen Bayerns*, in Cannon, 19; also Count Corti, *Ludwig I of Bavaria*, 280-81.

before" had also possessed him, Ludwig gushed. He "had grown young again."[20]

Ludwig's Christian name was Louis, after his godfather, Louis XVI of France. Soon Lola was calling him by the familiar appellation, and he, in turn, spoke adoringly to her as his "Lolita." As he had with previous mistresses, the aging monarch wrote impassioned, sentimental verse to and about her. Within just weeks, he had ordered several portraits to be painted of his new plaything. One was done by Wilhelm von Kaulbach; another, by Josef K. Steiler, would come to be displayed in Ludwig's Schonheitsgalerie—a hall containing portraits of European beauties, both famous and obscure.

Kaulbach was apparently quick to detect the unsavory influence Montez was gaining over his king, and one of his later paintings would show, with stark, unflattering imagery, Lola mounting a scaffold, whip in hand and with a serpent girdling her waist. Still later, the artist would draw a bitter and cynical pencil sketch showing Ludwig kneeling submissively in front of Lola. In it, her beautiful face is but a mask covering a grinning death's head; the king's crown and scepter lie broken on the floor beside him, and a cat is shown playing nearby with his orb of the realm.

Unconcerned about what his subjects might think, the king gave his new "friend" a substantial annual income and amended his will to bequeath her 100,000 gulden, plus a generous annuity, provided she hadn't married by the time of his death. She was also accorded a magnificent carriage, a theater box adjacent to his own, and a fine house at No. 7 Barenstrasse, just an easy stroll from the royal palace.

Lola had two wings made of white marble added to the house, and she furnished the place lavishly. A gilded fountain

---

[20]Corti, 284-85, Ludwig to Tann, Nov. 17, 1846; also *N.Y. Herald*, Jan 15, 1852.

was installed, and a crystal staircase built, the steps of which were so constructed as to be elastic and easy on the feet. Purportedly to manage the affairs of the household she named as her "chamberlain," a certain Auguste Papon, whom she had known before in Geneva and Baden. Papon, one of the first of several penniless charlatans that Lola would take up with during her lifetime, was a onetime panderer who wore a bogus uniform and posed as a marquis and captain of the Croatian guard. Later, Lola would also allow Papon's parents to come and live in the little palace the king had given her.

Lola's arrival in Bavaria coincided with a pivotal time in the politics of that country. There had been a constitution in place since 1819 and, early in Ludwig's reign, he was enthusiastic about its more liberal provisions, including those allowing a free press. But his pleasure with the document began to wane after attacks were mounted against him by left-wing writers, and because his first Landtag failed to pass most of the bills he gave them. Then, when in 1830 the autocratic Charles X of France was deposed, causing liberal factions to grow bolder, a startled Ludwig became a stanch adherent of that most conservative of all the Germans, Austria's prime minister, Clemens Lothar von Metternich. Fearing democratic anarchy, the headstrong king became more and more imperious.

Bavaria was a country whose population was two-thirds Roman Catholic. Ludwig himself was one, and, in 1837, he appointed a Jesuit priest, Karl von Abel, as his Minister of Interior and principal advisor. Abel was a hot-tempered conservative, totally in harmony with Ludwig's inclinations. Under his leadership, a new epoch was loosed in Bavaria, in which the constitution was tightly interpreted and, one by one, its more liberal provisions were modified or annulled. Catholic ecclesiastics came flocking in, and Protestants began to be harried and repressed by new laws and by Abel's decrees. Eventually, the reactionary, ultramontane party, through Abel, assumed control of all aspects of Bavarian temporal life.

Lola would take credit for changing all of that. She molded the king's mind to a love of political freedom, she later said, and got him to promise a course of steady improvement. A correspondent, who interviewed Montez in Munich not long after she arrived, confirmed her claim, noting that she held breakfast levees with ministers, artists and foreigners from all over the world. He said the king visited her nearly every morning and sometimes would summon her to his palace "to consult with him...on state affairs." This observer thought Ludwig's relationship with his dancer-turned-minister was not at all of a vulgar character.[21]

But nearly everyone else did. Shocked at the scandal the king's behavior was causing, Ludwig's sister, the Empress Karoline Auguste of Austria, severely reproached her brother. Ludwig's queen, in receipt of anonymous and accusing letters, confronted Ludwig with them. Most remarkably, even one of Ludwig's former mistresses, a Spanish actress, felt obliged to verbally attack Lola's reputation.

What alarmed Abel and his clerical ministry most was just how quickly Montez had been able to gain political influence over the king. Inquiries were made and, from the publicity surrounding the Dujarrier duel, Abel learned that Lola was not of noble Spanish birth, but rather, merely the estranged wife of Lieutenant James. He also obtained details of the escapades in Berlin and Warsaw, and of her banishment from Reuss shortly before arriving at Munich.

Increasingly anxious over this stranger's influence, Abel and the other ministers, aided by churchmen and some of the nobility, hatched a plan whereby they might discredit Montez.

[21]N.Y. Times, Jan. 22, 1861; also Dr. Herman Dyer, The Story of a Penitent, 7; S.F. Alta California, Jan. 24, 1874; Fritz von Ostini, Wilhelm von Kaulbach, 110, Richardson, 10-11.

They induced a maid of Lola's, named Ganzer, to keep a diary of her mistress's movements and, within just a few weeks, they were able lay an accusative mass of evidence before the king.

Lola reacted to her enemies' charges by becoming cold and formal with Ludwig. When she threatened to leave Munich, the old monarch—now completely enmeshed in her web—took his courtesan's side against the conspirators. Interestingly, Lola would later be accused by a cast-off lover of subjecting the woman Ganzer to a mock trial in the presence of the king and his court, wherein Ganzer was burned in effigy and "convicted" of having killed her illegitimate child.

Having failed in their first attempt, Lola's opponents next asked a certain Protestant nobleman to plead with Ludwig to give her up. After the king refused him, the aristocrat approached Lola herself and offered her an annual income of 50,000 francs if she would only leave the country. But, playing for bigger stakes, Montez rejected the bribe out of hand. When she told Ludwig about it, the befuddled old man thought her refusal was a sure sign of her love for him.

Probably at Abel's request, the Catholic hierarchy was next to remonstrate with Ludwig. The Archbishop of Munich wrote the monarch to warn him of "devilish arts and sinful lips"; Pope Pius IX admonished him to return to the path of righteousness.[22] But, faced with all this unwanted clerical advice, Ludwig merely dug in his heels, insisting he was innocent of any immoral intercourse, and let it be known he wouldn't tolerate any interference in his kingly affairs.

Soon, nearly the entire populace was upset with the scandalous situation. Burghers, the upper classes, army officers, and even Ludwig's own sons were becoming disquieted. There were rumors in some quarters that the king was insane, and there began to be talk of deposing him and appointing Ludwig's son, Prince Maximilian, as regent of the kingdom.

[22]Corti, 299.

In succeeding years, Lola would become fond of boasting that Ludwig had once said of her, "She is King!"[23] With such power, as one might expect, she became exceedingly arrogant, feeling free to misbehave as the notion struck her. Dissatisfied with the royal theater, she caused the stage manager to lose his job; when the royal stable master objected to her choosing a horse that the queen customarily used, he got fired; after the police sent her a note regarding some minor infraction of the law, she tore it up and then complained to the king, who took her side. Most brazen of all, she acquired a Bavarian artillery officer, Lieutenant Nussbaumer, as a lover.

One memorable wrangle occurred when Lola was walking in Munich's St. Louis Street with her huge bulldog in tow, and the animal suddenly attacked one of the horses of a brewer's cart. While the king's mistress might have been amused by her pet's antics, the cart driver wasn't. In the ensuing argument, the Montez dignity was insulted, and she bashed the driver with her umbrella. When a crowd gathered and began abusing her, she sought refuge in a chemist's shop, slamming the door so hard as to break a great deal of glass. Venting their wrath for the hated woman, the mob threw stones through what few panes remained. Lola was finally able to return home after darkness but, on the following day, another crowd gathered to pummel her house with rocks. As a result, the king threw a cordon of police around his love nest for several days, while tempers calmed.

Thus despised, but determined to have some respect, Montez began badgering Ludwig to elevate her to the nobility. There were rumors that he intended naming her Countess of Starenberg, and would give her the fine estate of that name situated some twenty kilometers south of Munich. But, first, Abel and the ministers would have to cooperate by granting citizenship to Lola. This they refused to do when Ludwig

---

[23]*N.Y. Herald,* Jan. 15, 1852.

asked in February 1847. Worse yet, they sent the king a disrespectful response stating that Bavarians believed themselves to
be governed by a foreign woman with a bad reputation. After
their letter was printed in the papers, and Abel refused to back
down, Ludwig dismissed the entire ministry. "Things have
come to a pretty pass", he told Tann, "when there is a question
whether the King or the Jesuit Party is to rule."[24]

Montez was given all the credit for getting rid of Abel and
his unpopular ministry. One aristocrat reported that she had
caused the downfall of "the arch-Catholic Abel." The *London
Times* called her a "saltatory Pompadour," but nevertheless
applauded her influence in ending the "reign of black bigotry"
of the Roman church. The *Illustrated News* likewise decried the
shameful goings-on, but reminded Londoners that the Bavarian court had never been "remarkable for its morality." Ludwig's Mistress of the hour should be thanked, the paper said,
for having inspired in him the boldness to "carry his disposi-
tion to liberal measures into action."[25]

To commemorate Lola's victory, her supporters had a
medallion struck, engraved with the motto "Lola Castigit
Loyola" and showing her with a birch rod in hand pursuing a
Jesuit priest. And, presumably with her advice, Ludwig
appointed a new, more liberal "Dawn of Freedom" cabinet,
with a Protestant professor, Ludwig von Maurer, at its head.
But, although Lola was now granted a certificate of naturaliza-
tion, Ludwig put off the decision to give his mistress the title
she ardently desired, having been warned by von Maurer of
how the nobility would react to such a course.

Shortly after the change of ministry, Ludwig dismissed a
Jesuit professor at the university for speaking out in Abel's
defense, and this action impelled yet another jeering, stone-
throwing mob to gather at Lola's palace. She fearlessly presented herself at the window and, holding up a glass of champagne,

---

[24]Corti, 302; also *London Times,* Feb. 26, 1847.
[25]Corti, 306; *London Times,* Mar. 18, 1847; *Illustrated London News,* Mar. 20, 1847.

prepared to toast this latest throng, but was interrupted by a stone landing at her feet. She coolly finished her toast, drinking the health of those assembled below, then—so said the *Courier des Etats Unis*—she uncovered her bosom and "laughingly exclaimed that if they really wished to injure her, it was there they should direct the attack."[26] This audacious act is supposed to have disarmed the hostility of the crowd, giving the king time to arrive to stand beside her in a show of support. But, ominously, that evening for the first time, the royal palace was also beset with rioters.

French newspapers had been busily reporting the tumult in Bavaria while, at the same time, revealing details of Lola's background. To contradict these unfavorable reports, she penned several letters to the London journals, in which she continued to insist that she had been born in Seville to a Spanish father. But now, in order to explain why some papers were calling her an Irishwoman named Mrs. James, and others were saying she was "Betsy Watson," the illegitimate daughter of a Scottish washerwoman, Lola was obliged to reinvent her mother. While affirming that mama had been born in Cuba, Montez now declared that her dam was of Irish extraction, and was presently married, for the second time, to an Irish gentleman.

Montez freely admitted that she had been taught to hate Jesuitism since earliest childhood, but denied having influenced the recent ministerial change. She credited Abel and his fellow priests with having caused their own demise. They were the ones who had made the abortive attempts to get rid of her, and it was their money that had hired the rampaging mobs which had recently assaulted her home and the royal palace. Her letters reflect a sense of relief that she had won her battle for Bavarian citizenship, and could now abandon her dancing—which she admitted wasn't all that polished—and make Munich her permanent residence.[27]

---

[26] Richardson, 66.
[27] *London Times*, Mar. 2, 18, Apr. 9, 1847; Vandam, 108.

In the summer, Lola accompanied her patron to the resort of Bad Bruckenau, where she intensified her campaign to obtain a title. Alternately petulant, loving and imperious with Ludwig, the wily woman finally wore the monarch down. On August 14 he and a reluctant von Maurer signed letters patent making the Irish poseur Countess of Landsfeld, Baroness of Rosenthal and a canoness of the order of St. Therese, of which Ludwig's humiliated queen was the head. Along with these titles came with an impressive crest, an estate of importance— probably Starenberg—and certain feudal rights over some 2,000 people. Ludwig commanded his subjects to acknowl- edge their new Countess—who came from a "noble Spanish family"—and to treat her like one, or else face the threat of criminal prosecution.[28]

The king continued to pamper his pet. On his birthday he gave an extravagant party to celebrate her new, elevated status; he disclosed that Madame de Landsfeld would henceforth receive a lifetime income equal to 52,000 francs from the state; and, it was announced that five large houses in the Rue de Havart would be pulled down so that a lavish "Winter Palace" could be built there for her.

But Montez was still not content. Maurer and his ministers were guilty of having resisted the issuance of her patent of nobility and, now that she had it, they and nearly everyone else refused to pay her homage. In early September, preparing to present herself at court in her new role, she attempted to call upon some twenty of the first families of Munich, only to be coldly rebuffed by them all. When the queen declared that she would remain absent if the new countess were ever to be pre- sented at court, Ludwig decided he'd best not accord his mis- tress the honor.

While there was little Montez could do about the queen or

---

[28] *London Times,* Sept. 7, 1847.

the nobility, she certainly knew by now how to deal with recalcitrant ministers. As a consequence of their attitude toward her, on November 30—like Abel and his Jesuits before them—von Maurer and company were also dismissed, and an even more liberal "Lola Ministry" was appointed under Prince Oettingen-Wallerstein.

But, despite installation of these newest officials, widespread discontent continued to grow during the winter. Given such conditions, it seems almost inevitable that the Montez Bavarian adventure should have come to a tumultuous end. The people of that country, however phlegmatic and patient, could no longer bear the yoke of being ruled, in effect, by a Spanish dancer.

The final act began in January 1848. A few weeks earlier, Lola had acquired as a new lover a twenty-two year old Polish nobleman, Eustach Karwaski. Urged on no doubt by Montez, Karwaski organized an association of some twenty Protestant students, calling them the Alemannia. As with most other German universities, there had long been such groups at Munich. The established five, Pfalzer, Schwaben, Franken, Bavaren and Osarem, took their names from the provinces of the kingdom, and each proudly wore caps of a distinguishing color.

Lola Montez took this new, sixth student corps under her wing and fitted them out with their own caps of a deep red, trimmed with a colorful fringe, an alluring model of which she herself wore. The young men were given the run of her house, and soon the king was receiving reports from Tann and others that the place had become a den of orgies, with Karwaski said to be engaging with Lola in extensive sexual activities. Lola, of course, denied the tales, and blamed the Austrian minister for circulating them; she then persuaded the all-believing, pathetic Ludwig to have the minister recalled.

Now with her own devoted bodyguard, Montez grew even

bolder. On January 31, Jan Gorres, a former revolutionary who had turned mystic and ultramontane in his later years, was buried. The large procession of Catholic students carrying him to his grave ultimately resolved itself into a demonstration against the king's mistress and, when Lola learned of it, she went out straightaway to do battle, accompanied by a few of her Alemanni. She and her young men recklessly waded into the mourners, shouting for them to make way, only to be insulted and physically abused by the clerical students until police could arrive to offer her protection.

Several days afterward, when the odious Alemanni first presented themselves at the university, they were hooted at and insulted by the other students, and, in perhaps the worst slight of all for the perpetually-duelling German students, the Alemanni weren't to be allowed satisfaction for any insult, however gross.

Despite the efforts of authorities to make peace between the student factions, there were serious clashes at the university for several days running. Then, on February 9, after a large number of functionaries whom Lola disliked were removed from office, her students were once again pounced upon by their opposition. One of the Alemanni, Count Hirshberg, brandished a dagger to fend off those surrounding them, while his comrades retreated to safety in the cafe where they customarily ate and held their meetings.

Thus treed, the Alemanni sent word of their predicament to Lola who, heedless of any danger, snatched up a pistol and rushed to the scene. Once there, she was badly roughed up by the crowd. With all doors in the neighborhood closed to her, she found a temporary haven in the Church of the Theatine, whence gendarmes escorted her to the gate of the royal palace. Here, Ludwig came out, gave her his arm, and took her inside to safety. But, undaunted, Lola went out on the streets a second time to bait the crowd, until the king forced her back again into the palace. Even those who hated Montez were impressed with her courage and how magnificent she looked during the encounter.

In retaliation for the treatment accorded his mistress, Ludwig announced on the morning of February 10 that the university would be closed for a full year. This stirred up further unrest and, a few hours afterward, one of the large detachments of police patrolling the city charged into a crowd, shamelessly cutting and bayonetting until two students were wounded and a workman killed. Rumors flew that the commander of the detachment, Captain Bauer, owed his rapid advancement to Lola's protection.

With all classes of citizens now out of patience, the municipal council demanded of Ludwig, in the afternoon, that he punish Bauer, disband the Alemannia and reopen the university. The king equivocated, and, within a few hours, the entire city was in insurrection. A huge mob went to Lola's house and would have destroyed it, had it not been vigorously defended by police and soldiers.

On the eleventh, screaming crowds surrounded the royal palace. When the troops and police defending it showed no desire to drive off the people, the king, enraged by their refusal and by the demands which had been made on him, hurriedly sent to Augsburg for a reinforcement, by rail, of light cavalry. While he waited and fretted, some 2,000 of Munich's burghers met and sent a deputation to him demanding the expulsion of Lola and the reopening of the university. The burghers, the ministers of state, and even the princes, his sons, warned him of the imminent danger of civil war being caused by his obstinacy. So, suspecting that his troops couldn't be counted on, Ludwig at last yielded. His mistress would leave Munich within the hour, the decree suspending the lectures of the university would be repealed, and Captain Bauer would be arrested.

Lola was dumbstruck by Ludwig's capitulation. Even with crowds threatening her safety, she tried to delay her departure, and then drove to the palace in her carriage in an attempt to see the king. Finding the gates closed and guarded, she quickly departed for Starenberg castle outside Munich. Poor Ludwig, perhaps wishing to explain his actions, arrived at Lola's Munich palace some two hours after she had gone. He found his troops standing quietly by while the elated people wreaked havoc on the building and its contents. As Ludwig watched, his authority completely disregarded, he was accidentally struck by a stone. He turned and walked back to his palace with tears in his eyes.

Like a bad penny, Lola turned up again in Munich the next day, February 12, dressed in male attire and accompanied by some of her Alemanni. Unluckily for her, she was discovered before she could reach the king. Prince Wallerstein had her arrested and given a passport, after which she was unceremoniously placed in a post-chaise with three of her students and two policemen, and taken to the suburb of Pasing, where she was put on a train to Switzerland. On leaving, she predicted that Ludwig would abdicate and follow her into exile.

Even with Lola gone, Ludwig's problems were far from over. Throughout the German Confederation—indeed, all across Europe—liberating storms continued to brew. Soon Berlin would be enveloped in riots; in Vienna a revolution would force Metternich to resign and flee. In France, King Louis-Phillippe's July Monarchy would be overthrown. In Munich, with disorder continuing to prevail, Ludwig issued a proclamation on March 6 which agreed in principle with extensive new middle-class demands for reform, including complete freedom of the press and open administration of justice.

The king just might have survived after making these concessions had Lola not made a second flying visit from Bern to Munich, in company with a certain Baron Moller. On March

8, Ludwig met with her secretly, and gave her a check for 500,000 florins on the house of Rothschild in Frankfort. She left immediately for that city to get her money, and then returned up the Rhine to Bern. She spoke of buying a country house near Veray where she expected Ludwig—who, she said, wrote her every day—to pay her a visit during the summer.

When news of Lola's visit leaked to the populace, civil turmoil began anew in Munich. Ludwig was compelled on March 17 to issue a decree revoking Montez's citizenship and to order police to arrest her if she were ever again found in Bavaria. Three days later, his spirit broken by this final indignity, and unable to rule effectively, the old king abdicated in favor of his eldest son, Crown Prince Maximilian II. Said the *London Times* on March 27: "There is no doubt that his retirement is owing to an anxiety to regain his 'ladye faire.'"

But, though a hopeful Lola stayed on in Switzerland, she was never able to convince Ludwig to join her in exile. After the Munich interlude ended, in November and December 1848, Auguste Papon apparently made an attempt to extort 10,000 francs from Ludwig by threatening to publish letters detailing Lola's escapades, before and during her time in Bavaria. In his unanswered epistles to Ludwig, Papon thinly disguised the blackmail by calling it payment for his services as Lola's chamberlain. Though unsuccessful with Ludwig, Papon later published his titillating dirt in the "Private History and Memoirs" of Lola.

Since the deposed monarch believed Lola to be a part of Papon's skulduggery, the incident may well have convinced him, at last, to sever their ill-fated relationship. Their final meeting well have been on August 19, at Berchtesgaden, where he was spending the summer licking his wounds. Lola reportedly arrived there in a magnificent carriage, which the unforgiving citizenry pelted with stones and mud while shouting insults at her. During her brief stay in the little Bavarian resort

village, a cordon of troops had to be thrown around her lodgings for the protection of her and two female companions.[29]

The former royal counselor and comforter, now with a
worldwide notoriety, finally abandoned Switzerland for London, where she arrived on December 30, 1848. Most
observers thought her beauty had faded somewhat since last
she had been there but, as events would prove, what still
remained was more than adequate to attract a new sponsor. To
this end, Lola took a house in Mayfair and, calling herself
Marie, Countess de Landsfeld, began living ostentatiously.

The next to be seduced by the Montez charms would be 21-
year old George Stafford Heald, a sub-lieutenant of the 2nd
Regiment of Life Guards, who had just come into a substantial
annual inheritance of some five or six thousand pounds. In the
summer of 1849 Lola met Heald during one of her daily
horseback outings in Hyde Park. After several weeks, on July
19, she married the tall, juvenile-looking Oxford drop-out,
despite the fact that he was ten years her junior. A wedding ceremony was performed at the French Catholic Chapel in King
Street and then—perhaps to be doubly sure the marriage
would take—Protestant vows were exchanged at St. George's,
Hanover Square. But it would take more than dual, ecumenical
ceremonies to hold together a marriage made by Lola Montez.

First of all, she hadn't reckoned with rigid English society.
Until recently, a spinster aunt, Susanna Heald, had been the
guardian of her new husband's inheritance. A mere nineteen
days after the wedding, this aunt filed bigamy charges against
Lola, having discovered that she was still legally married to
Thomas James. When the police arrived at the Healds' house

---

[29]Regarding Lola's Bavarian adventure, also see *N.Y. Herald*, Aug. 29, Dec. 25, 1851,
Jan. 13, Apr. 30, 1852; *N.Y. Times*, Jan. 22, 1861; S.F. *Alta California*, Apr. 1, 1852, Mar. 2.,
1858; *London Times*, Sept. 9, 22, 1847, Feb. 17, 21, Mar. 25, 25, Apr. 4, 1848; S.F. *Bulletin*,
Mar. 22, 1858; New Orleans *Daily Picayune*, Oct. 27, 1848; Montez, *Lectures*, 63-76;
George S. Werner, *Bavaria in the German Confederation*, 201-09.

Lola Montez in 1848. As painted by C. Sohn. Lithography by Leon Noel in 1853.
Courtesy, California State Library

in Picadilly to arrest Lola, she asked, rhetorically, "What will the King say?"

The accused appeared at Marlborough Street police court for her preliminary hearing on August 6, dressed conservatively and leaning fetchingly on her husband's arm. The couple pushed their way through a huge crowd of onlookers to take their places near the bar, where she sat, "quite unembarrassed." During the whole proceedings, young Heald—his hormones no doubt raging—clasped Lola's hand in his. Occasionally he would give it a fervent squeeze or press it to his lips with "juvenile warmth" as he whispered fondly to his bride.[30]

The prosecution said it was prepared to offer proof that the decree of separation, which had been granted by the Catholic Consistory Court in 1842, was merely a separation from bed and board, prohibiting either party from marrying again, so long as the other lived. It could further prove that Thomas James was still alive and well in India as captain in command in the Kotah contingent—at least up until six weeks prior to Lola's marriage to Heald.

Real divorce was very unusual in England at the time. An aggrieved party had to bring a criminal action against his partner's paramour and, if successful, could then apply to the House of Lords for a private bill of divorce. The cost was well beyond the means of most people, and usually involved an embarrassingly-detailed examination by a committee into all alleged sexual transgressions.

Lola had no rebuttal to offer the court. Heald's lawyers, who represented her, could only argue that this was the first case of bigamy they had ever seen wherein one of the spouses wasn't the complainant. Montez didn't deny her previous marriage, but insisted that it was an illegal one, since she had used the false name, Rose Anna Gilbert. Moreover, she insisted that she believed Lord Henry P. Brougham had obtained an act of Parliament to divorce her from James.

Just prior to her arrest, on July 26, the new Mrs. Heald and Brougham had shocked all of London, in what may have been her first overt act of social consciousness. The eccentric old Brougham had escorted her into the peeresses' gallery of the House of Lords, to show support on the night a bill to protect women against prostitution was given the royal assent. Brougham, a former Lord Chancellor of England who was as

[30]*London Times*, Aug. 7, 1849, also Jan. 2, July 21, Aug. 11, 20, 1849; *Illustrated London News*, July 21, 1849; List of Officers of the Army...., Apr. 1849, Apr. 1850, s.v. "Heald, George Safford."

well known for his intellect as for his lack of sexual morality—his "would-be Don-Juanesque behavior"[31]—may have met Lola on one of his many trips to Paris in earlier years.

To be absolutely certain that Captain James hadn't died just prior to Lola's latest marriage, the court granted the prosecution time to obtain more recent information from India. The accused bigamist was released on bail, but, no sooner had it been posted than polite society dealt the newlyweds another blow—the Marquis of Londonderry, who commanded the Guards, recommended to Queen Victoria that Heald be compelled to resign his commission and leave the regiment before his "unfortunate and extraordinary act" could sully its name.[32]

Heald relinquished his commission and, a few days later, he and Lola put London, their tormentors and the terrible cholera epidemic which was then sweeping the city, behind them. They had intended making a belated honeymoon tour of the continent, but, at Naples, after just a short respite, a letter was received stating that Lola's bail would expire on September 11. So, leaving baggage behind, the extravagant Heald hired a steamer to take them to Marseilles, whence they sailed to arrive at London just before the deadline.

But Lola and her husband failed to appear in court. Since the prosecutor now could prove that Captain James had been alive as of six days before Lola's marriage, it looked more and more as if the bigamy charge might stick. Thus, as quickly as they had returned to England, Lola and Heald fled to Boulogne, France, forfeiting bail.

The couple lived for the next two years in a state of almost constant quarreling, much of which was unfailingly reported by the European press. Lola seemed to delight in keeping

---

[31]Vandam, 82; *London Times*, July 30, 1849; Sacramento *Placer Times*, Dec. 8, 1849. Brougham (1778-1868), an education and law reform advocate, served first in the Commons. He was raised to the peerage in 1830 and made Lord Chancellor of England for four years. After losing this office, he became a hard-drinking eccentric.

[32]*London Times*, Aug. 10, 1849.

Heald in the greatest fear of her. She even stabbed him during one memorable squabble in Catalonia, causing him to flee from her bed for several days before returning, tail between his legs. Again, on Christmas morning, 1849, just after they had arrived in Cadiz from Barcelona, Heald left her and went to Gibraltar to catch a steamer to England. A furious Lola tracked him down with the help of two male courtiers, and she and Heald reconciled, but continued to live in turmoil.

In March 1850, the Healds signed a long lease on magnificent apartments in Paris, and furnished them opulently, using what little remained of his money, and a great deal of credit. Heedless of the consequences, the pair continued living the high life. They rode about in a splendid carriage with two footmen in rich livery; for 4,000 francs the well-known portraitist, Jacquand, was commissioned to depict George, in uniform, offering Lola a gift of jewelry. Lola's lavish apparel was also the subject of much comment and, when she attended a ceremony at St. Quentin, the gossips accused her of trying to attract the attention of President Louis Napoleon in order to play him the same tricks she had played on Ludwig of Bavaria.

But soon the money was gone and it was once again time to cut and run. When their upholsterer appeared in mid-August to collect an overdue bill, Lola put him off for a few hours by explaining that her husband had departed Paris without leaving her any money. The tradesman returned later and was astonished to find Lola preparing to abscond with carts loaded full of his furniture and the remaining contents of the household. The police were quickly called to intervene, and the other creditors were informed of what was happening, but Lola was not easy to trap. She assured one and all that she would pay, but first needed to see a locksmith to obtain a key for her cash box. So, off she rode in a carriage, leaving her creditors to repossess all of the expensive trappings.

Lola joined Heald in Compiegne, and from there they traveled to The Hague. Then, after another notable fight, Heald deserted his loving wife and fled once again to England. Lola pursued him there, but was obliged to return to Paris, in September, alone and seemingly destitute. Quite unbelievably, Lola later said of this turbulent marriage: "He was unsuited to my character...instead of finding a quiet, domestic happiness, I found myself the wife of a dissipated and impoverished English spendthrift."[33]

Still married, and calling herself La Comptesse de Landsfeld Heald, Lola remained in Paris with the help of new sponsors. For a month or so, until he left France in early October, she was "very intimate" with Jung Bahadoor, the ambassador from Nepal. He had reportedly given his "pet," who spoke the "language of the Brahmas," many precious jewels, and an Indian shawl covered with gold and diamonds. Jung, who had womanized shamelessly with most of the Paris Opera's *corps de ballet*, took an unnamed English woman back to Nepal with him as consolation for having to leave Montez behind.

Although she was said to be disconsolate over Jung's departure, he had no sooner left than Lola moved to a hotel in the Rue Blanche, furnishing her rooms extravagantly at the expense of Michel de Coral, one of the leading *beaux* of that city, and with a large amount of money said to have been received from Ludwig. She and Coral held several elegant soirees for important Parisians and visitors to the city in December, at each of which the guests were provided a first-rate concert and supper. A description of Lola's appearance at one of these parties is evocative of Marguerite Gautier, the *Dame aux Camellias* immortalized by Alexandre Dumas, *fils*, two years earlier:

[33]*N.Y. Herald,* July 17, 1852, also Oct. 23, 1849, Apr. 22, Sept. 9, 12, Oc t. 7, 1850, Oct. 31, 1851; New Orleans *True Delta,* Dec. 5, 1849, July 18, 23, Sept. 14, 18, 1850, Mar. 19, 1851; Sacramento *Placer Times,* Apr. 22, 1850; *London Times,* Aug. 13, Sept. 8, 11-13, Oct. 25, 30, 1849, May 4, Aug. 16, 1850; Richardson, 28, 32; Christening records, St. Mary's Church, London.

Her lovely head was adorned with a simple gold chain twisted around her hair, and on the left side she wore a natural camellia which highlighted her dark hair. She was dressed in a white silk robe, upon which she had placed the grand cordon of the order of Therese...given to her by the King of Bavaria with her title.[34]

In ludicrous contrast to this image, it was revealed that the countess had that very morning fought with her milkman over a past due bill. The New York *Herald's* gossip monger in Paris said of this strange admixture called Lola Montez: "How curious to see in a woman such an assemblage of nobility of sentiments, and a low style of manner. How curious to meet, in a splendid attire a woman who possesses the most refined education in a parlor and who has been fighting...in the morning with her milk furnisher."[35]

So, while she may have had a small monthly pension from Ludwig, and another 500 pounds a year from Heald, it apparently wasn't enough to sustain such a lavish lifestyle. Perhaps in an attempt to raise money, in early 1851 Lola's memoirs, dedicated to King Ludwig, began being published serially in *Le Pays*. They were discontinued after just a short time, however, when Lamartine, the religious poet, took over editorial charge of that paper. Nearly every-one agreed that the memoirs were badly written, and a few detractors even accused Montez of having penned extortion letters to many of those she intended to mention in the account, before it went to press.

Stories continued to circulate that Lola was trying to insinuate herself with Louis Napoleon. It was said that after being refused an invitation to a ball at the Elysee Palace, she arrayed herself in her most brilliant and revealing black velvet dress and, concealing it under a large cloak, drove to the palace and asked to see the president. Colonel Edgar Ney, son of Bonaparte's great field marshal, was sent to speak to her, and she

---

[34]S.F. *Daily Herald*, Feb. 22, 1851; *N.Y. Herald*, Oct. 21, 26, 1850.
[35]*N.Y. Herald*, Dec. 23, 1850.

used her dazzling eyes and charming mouth to such advantage that he, without even knowing her name, admitted her into the president's presence to hear her "urgent petition."

As soon as she was alone with the president, so the story went, Lola threw off her cloak to display her "superb toilette," and, "falling at the feet of the president," began to speak. But, recognizing her, Louis Napoleon raised her gallantly but coldly to her feet and led her to the door where he asked Ney to see her to her carriage. Lola was reportedly planning to challenge the president to a duel for his insulting conduct towards her.[36]

There are those who say Montez's affair with Michel de Coral ended when she came close to dying in an influenza epidemic in early 1851, and that her hair had fallen out by the handful with the fever. Indeed, she herself admitted to being "shattered in fortune, and broken in health"[37] during this period, but, judging from subsequent events, the more likely cause of her illness was syphilis, contracted from either Jung Bahadoor or Coral. The most common symptoms of the secondary stage of the disease—a rash and fever—often mock those of a host of other ills and, frequently, hair will also fall out for a few weeks, until, finally, all of the symptoms disappear and the disease becomes latent. It is highly possible that Lola herself may not have realized the true cause of her illness at the time.

So, very likely infected with an incurable venereal disease, and her affair with Coral finished, in March 1851 Montez took up with a down-at-the-heels, young American dilettante, Edward P. Willis, who had been in Paris since November. Willis told Lola his impoverished state was due to delays in receiving his usual remittances from agents in New York City, so Lola good-naturedly replenished his scanty wardrobe, redeemed his watch, paid off some 2,000 francs in debts he

---

[36]New Orleans *True Delta*, Mar. 6, 1851, also Feb. 1, 19, Apr. 30, 1851; *N.Y. Herald*, Feb. 8, 21, July 30, Oct. 31, 1851.

[37]Montez, *Lectures*, 77.

had run up, and moved him from the tiny garret where he had been living into her own lodgings.

It was apparently Willis who sparked Montez's interest in resuming her dancing career. He offered to manage the details of a tour of America, and assured her of success under his tutelage. His brother, after all, was Nathaniel P. Willis, well-known editor of the *Home Journal*, which was one of the most influential papers in the United States.

Still financially pressed, Lola agreed to Willis' plan. She took up residence near the Tuileries Gardens, and set about regaining mastery of her art, lost during her long absence from the stage. Mabille, a ballet master of the opera, was hired as her teacher, and he drilled her twice daily in strenuous practice sessions for well over three months. She worked up a routine of six new dances, which included the *Tarantella* soon to become so very famous as her "Spider Dance."

Montez didn't let the hard work interfere with role as lioness of the Paris social scene. In mid-July she attended the races of Chateau de la Marche, attended by Louis Napoleon and a large crowd of wealthy sportsmen. When the jockey club there gave her a grand dinner at which she was the only female among 150 men, one commentator acidly referred to her as the "Countess of Mansfeldt," and accused her of renewing her dancing career merely to catch another monarch.[38]

James Gordon Bennett, proprietor of the New York *Herald*, was in Paris during this period, and, through a friend, finagled an invitation to one of Lola's Saturday soirees. As was usual at her parties there was a striking mixture of guests: three young East Indian princes, a few Hungarian and Italian refugees, English, French and Spanish diplomats, three Russian officers, a dozen young French noblemen, many literati and even a few ladies.

To amuse the East Indians, Lola showed them her pair of

---

[38]*N.Y. Herald*, Aug. 13, 1851; also Dec. 9, 1850; July 30, Aug. 29, 1851; Jan. 13, 1852.

inch and one-half long pistols, which were kept in a tiny jewel box along with all their accessories—bullet molds, ramrods, cap and ball box. The delighted young princes shot the pistols at a wax taper all evening long. Ices were served to the guests while a handsome young Neapolitan sang at the piano, and a German pianist rendered some Bach. Then Lola herself sat at the piano to play and sing a Spanish tune, and an old troubadour song, "The Duke of Guise."

Bennett was totally taken by it all. He thought his hostess had a grace and elegance "as sweet and natural as a thoroughbred" and he considered her most ladylike, even though, at dinner, he watched, fascinated, as the chain-smoking countess lighted a dozen or more cigarettes, never taking more than a few puffs from each. He was amazed by Lola's quick and brilliant conversation, her wit, and by her knowledge of the world and human nature, which he thought mere artifice could never have produced.

Montez, of course, liked people to think she spoke a variety of languages fluently, but the truth seems to have been that she merely spoke a smattering of quite a number. Bennett credited her with being fluent in seven, including Persian, and was sure that when she became bored with her dancing career, she could successfully lecture on European affairs, in any language.

Like most, the publisher seemed awe-stricken by the fabled Montez beauty, which, combined with her "air of good fellowship," rendered her "irresistible." Even though some considered Lola well past her prime, Bennett thought her still young and enthusiastic, and noted the "strange and startling brilliancy" of her eyes, the "harmony and proportion" of her form, and her graceful motions. He would remain her constant defender until she finally showed him her bad side after arriving in America.[39]

With rumors abroad that she intended returning to the

---

[39] *Ibid.*, Nov. 6, 1851; Feb. 16, 18, 1853.

stage, a good many theatrical managers evidently strove for the right to represent the resurgent dancer. Benjamin Lumley of London, who was scheduled to come to Paris and manage an Italian opera house, had supposedly engaged her; she was said to have refused a million francs from one agent in Paris for an eight-month contract, and 6,000 francs per night from another. Still another extravagant story had a committee of 500 men in Paris offering her 10,000 francs just for one evening's entertainment.

Whether or not these rumors had any basis, it is a certainty that P.T. Barnum, the noted American impresario, negotiated through his European agent, LeGrand Smith, to bring Lola to America. But, by early July, she had made it known that all offers had been rejected, including Barnum's, and she had instead engaged Edward Willis to be her agent and private secretary in America. After looking into Barnum's past promotions of freaks, oddities and obvious hokum, Montez declared that she was "humbug enough herself, without uniting her fortunes with the Prince of Humbugs."[40] Barnum insisted vehemently that he'd never had anything to do with the "notorious Lola Montes."[41] He was even threatening to sue Bennett of the *Herald*, who had revealed the negotiations, until Bennett published concrete evidence that they had, in fact, occurred.

With her work-up nearly complete, on August 26 Lola signed a contract with a theatrical manager named Roux for a six-month tour of various cities in Europe, the United States and other countries. How she explained this arrangement to Ned Willis, whom she had promised to let manage her affairs, is not known.

Montez began her comeback on September 15 with a sneak preview for newsmen in her Paris apartments. Her first appearance in public was at Boulogne, after which she visited Mar-

---

[40]*Ibid.*

[41]*Ibid.*, Nov. I, 1851; also July 18, 1851, Jan. 10, 1852; S.F. *Alta*, Dec. 14, 1851; *Nevada* (City) *Journal*, Sept. 29, Oct. 25, 1851.

seilles, Brussels, and Antwerp, playing everywhere to huge crowds at double prices. In Antwerp, her presence on election day was credited with helping the liberal party win decisively for the first time in memory. There was a commotion at one of her performances in that city between cheering liberals and hissing royalists, which ended with every one of the royalists being turned out of the theater. Afterward, Lola's carriage was escorted by the cheering populace to her hotel. The king of nearby Holland was so alarmed by these demonstrations that he prohibited the dancer from entering his country.

Liberal students at Aix-la-Chapelle also lionized Montez and, because of the tremendous excitement her presence caused there, the Prussian Minister of Interior sent her a dispatch saying she wouldn't be permitted to dance any longer in Germany. After all, theater audiences gone wild for a beautiful and politically-inclined dancer might just be the spark to incite further rebellion.

Lola toured southern France before returning to Paris about November 12. When her agent, Roux, learned suddenly that his client was about to leave for America with Willis, he brought a lawsuit claiming she had refused to fulfill dates he had arranged for her at several Paris theaters. Lola would afterward say she won the case by arguing that Roux had made no such arrangements and, furthermore, that he had completely exhausted her with an intense schedule, and had written an absurd biography of her which he distributed during performances.

More likely, however, knowing Lola, she simply skipped town. Willis in tow, she hurried to Le Havre to catch the November 20 sailing of the steamship *Humboldt* for the New World.[42]

---

[42]*N.Y. Herald,* Oct. 28, Nov. 29, Dec. 6, 8, 30, 1851; July 17, 1852; *N.Y. Times,* Oct. 11, 1851.

CHAPTER TWO

Coming To America

Shattered in fortune, and broken in health, she came with curiousity
and reviving hopes, to the shores of the New World; this stupen-
dous asylum of the world's unfortunate, and the last refuge of the
victims of the tyranny and wrongs of the Old World!

...Lola Montez, *Autobiography.*

And so, the resurgent and revitalized dancer crossed the
Atlantic to America, which was destined to become her
adopted country.

Sailing in the same ship was a European of even greater
notoriety, Lajos Kossuth, who boarded *Humboldt* with his family when it stopped at Cowes, England for passengers. As governor of Hungary, Kossuth had led a struggle for independence
from Austria during the revolutionary years of 1848-49. After
Czar Nicholas' Russian armies suppressed this uprising, Kossuth fled to Turkey, where he was made to endure a lengthy
internment. Released only a month before *Humboldt* sailed, and
still fearful of capture by the Austrians, Kossuth had hurried to
England to catch the ship. His mission was to secure help from
the United States in his country's cause.

Montez was accused by some of scheming to take the same
ship as Kossuth in order to bask in his reflected glory. Whether
true or not, the vessel certainly proved to be too small a con-

tainer for these two monumental egos. Perhaps Kossuth didn't want any truck with a courtesan; for certain, Lola didn't enjoy being upstaged. After having had just a few shipboard conversations with the Hungarian—as Ned Willis later revealed—Montez dismissed him as a humbug, and thenceforth devoted herself to amusing the other male passengers with her singing and a constant flow of witty repartee. But, during the remainder of the voyage, she was often seen sitting in the lee of the ship's funnel, puffing away at a cigarette, silently taking the measure of the famous Magyar as he paced the deck.

A huge crowd was on hand when the steamer arrived off Staten Island, New York on December 5, 1851. But the throng was there to greet the patriot, not the courtesan. While Kossuth was being honored with a 21-gun salute and an impressive welcoming ceremony, a neglected Lola stood in a corner of the ship's lounge as a mere witness to the proceedings. Completely overshadowed, all she could manage was a few sniggering remarks reflecting on the stupidity of the whole affair.

Earlier in the year, a spicy book had been published in New York City which purported to be a reply to a private history of Montez, previously written by Auguste Papon. While making a pretext of defending her, the reply nevertheless managed to reveal or substantiate many sordid details of Lola's background. The little opus is believed to have been written by Canadian-born author John Richardson, who probably knew Lola when she lived in France. If it was indeed his writing, Richardson's name can be added to the list of unfortunate fellows whose lives had been apparently been jinxed by Lola—he would die in abject poverty in New York City at age 56, within months of her arrival there.

Perhaps as a consequence of this book and the other tales which had reached America over the years, much of the New York press was against Montez from the start—most notably

Horace Greeley of the *Tribune* and Henry Raymond of the
Times. Even Bennett of the *Herald* occasionally showed animosity: on the very day *Humboldt* docked, his paper cruelly juxta-
posed a facetious schedule of events for Lola's "reception"
right alongside an authentic three-column program for Kossuth. Supposedly gotten up by residents of Staten Island,
Lola's welcome would consist of a tour of the island in an
omnibus, and a look at the new fence on Stapleton Dock, after
which the dancer would be put up at the Seaman's Retreat on
the island.[1] If this sort of attack bothered Montez she, at first,
showed no sign.

Arrangements had been made for E. A. Marshall, lessee of
the Broadway Theater, to handle Lola's billings in the United
States, and his original plan had been for her to open in New
York within a week or ten days. But, eclipsed by the commotion over Kossuth, her appearance was delayed until the Hungarian left town. During the three week wait she secluded
herself at a private residence on White Street and refused to see
sundry dignitaries, giving as her reason the need to recover
from the fatigue of an ocean voyage. Aside from waiting out
Kossuth, Lola may also have been dodging Roux, her former
agent, who had arrived from France and was searching high
and low for her, threatening a lawsuit. The Frenchman would
ultimately relent, but only after a lawyer hired by E. A. Marshall frightened him off with the threat of a counter suit.

Montez also used the long delay to rehearse her repertoire
of three elaborate ballets with the corps of five male and fifteen
female dancers Marshall hired to support her. No description
has survived of the first routine, which was called "Diana and
Her Nymphs," but one can imagine it was both diaphanous
and titillating.

The second ballet, entitled "Betley the Tyrolean," began

---

[1] *N.Y. Herald,* Dec. 5, 1851, also Oct. 31, Nov. 29; and Jan. 13, 1852.

with the entire corps standing frozen in tableaux as Montez, playing Betley, descended grandiosely to the stage on a staircase which simulated a path winding down a mountain. The star's first number was a solo Tyrolean dance, followed by a "festival dance" with one of the men. Next, while the corps did a "mountaineer dance," Lola changed into a stunning military costume consisting of a red and white-striped Hungarian skirt of satin, a jacket of black velvet faced with gold and, atop her lustrous tresses, a red hat with feather. Thus arrayed, she danced a military routine, which ended with her marching the ballet company off the stage in stirring fashion.

But Lola's tour de force was an extravaganza called *Un Jour de Carneval a Seville.* This piece consisted of several Spanish dances and a gallop by the corps, interspersed with Lola's dances—an Andalusian, a *pas de Sivigliana* and the *Pas de Matelot,* or "Sailor's Dance." It ended impressively with an elaborate grand tableaux.

Months later, after she had offended him, Thomas Barry, the Broadway Theater stage manager, would reveal exactly what he thought of Lola's dancing skills. While rehearsing, he said, she "danced through a certain routine of steps, without regard to time, music or anything else." To see that she and the orchestra ended together, Barry said he was obliged to instruct the conductor to follow Lola precisely, and to stop when she stopped, whether or not the music was finished. Barry further alleged that, later in Philadelphia, where the orchestra played the score without regard to her steps, one never knew who was going to finish first. This always greatly disturbed Montez, Barry said, causing her to stamp and storm and curse the music, swearing that there "were Jesuits...smuggled into the orchestra, either as a violin, bassoon, or clarinet player."[2]

After Lajos Kossuth finally left New York, Montez went to work and played three engagements at the Broadway, from

[2]*Ibid.,* May 5, Dec. 9, 1851; S.F. *Daily Herald,* Oct. 20, Dec. 30, 1851; Broadway Theater, NY, Advertising Broadside for Jan. 8, 1852 (Calif. Hist. Ctr., Sacramento).

Playbill for Montez performance in New York City. Courtesy, Eleanor McClatchy Collection, City of Sacramento, History and Science Division, Sacramento Archives and Museum Collection Center.

December 29 through January 16, 1852, her ballets drawing huge houses. Upon the advice of her handlers, Willis, Barry and Marshall, the productions were marked by an unusual modesty. Thus, while initially very few women came to see her, soon even some of the region's most fashionable ladies could be seen in the audiences.

One woman to witness a performance was Sarah Jane Clarke, who wrote for the Washington *National Era* as "Grace Greenwood." The correspondent recognized that Lola was by no means a nice or proper person; she knew that Montez lacked artistic finish as a dancer, and relied for success wholly on dash and dazzle, the piquant beauty of her face and the splendor of her costumes. Yet, Greenwood admitted, everyone was anxious to see "that dancing enchantress...that subduer of elderly kings and tamer of young husbands." Everyone went at least once, she said, and was "subject for one perilous evening to the spell of her dark, splendid, entangling eyes...blazing forth now and then from under heavy, long, drooping lashes— the masked batteries of passion—and her dark, soft, abundant hair, gathered back from her low forehead in lovely, shining ripples, and lit by some gorgeous tropical flower." Still, Greenwood thought, there was "something sad in her passionate, defiant, utterly unpeaceful face."[3]

Like her dancing, Lola's behavior off the stage was also unusually decorous during her first few weeks in America. As James Gordon Bennett said, she lacked only "the sanctification of the church and a pair of wings to make her a complete angel."[4] But, as we have seen, she found it quite impossible to stay completely out of trouble for long, and her libido drove her to change lovers almost as often as her petticoats. Soon, there was a spat with her landlord, during which she would

---

[3]San Jose *California Sunday Mercury*, Feb. 3, 1867.
[4]*N.Y. Herald*, Dec. 23, 1851.

have been ejected by the police had not her lawyer arrived to settle matters amicably. Then, within a month of her arrival and with the help of a "generous fire eater from the South," her "agent," Ned Willis, was inelegantly kicked downstairs and dismissed from Lola's service for the alleged reason that his accounts were unsatisfactory.

The Southerner who helped Lola, and whom she soon chose as her new money manager was the "Reverend" Joseph C. Scoville. In previous years, Scoville—alias Mr. Pick—had been associated with the New Orleans *Times-Picayune* and other papers, and had served as private secretary to John C. Calhoun. Most recently he had been writing for the New York *Picayune*, but had been fired just a few days before taking up with Lola. He was not a minister, of course, but had been accorded his sobriquet after once standing in for the parson of a Swedenborgian church. Scoville was also known as an eccentric, a ladies man and an alcoholic who had just taken the pledge.[5]

Another new member of Lola's retinue was Col. W. M. Bobo, the son of a Haitian aristocrat. Bobo—described by one malevolent New York editor as a "splendid-looking negro" who would make a "capital presidential candidate for the abolitionists"[6]—reportedly had come to New York to induce Lola to visit his country. After Willis had been booted, Lola gave Bobo written authority to act as umpire between the former agent and herself, to recoup some of the money she claimed he had pocketed. But, when Bobo investigated and certified that Willis' accounts were satisfactory, Lola was obliged to abide by his decision and withdraw all claims.

But, Montez had aptly demonstrated in Europe that she fully understood the power of the press and now, in America, her skills much improved, she used the pages of the *Herald* very effectively to vanquish Willis, and, for a time at least, her jour-

---

[5]*Ibid.*, Jan. 5, 1852; also Dec. 30, 1851, Mar. 20, Apr. 14, 1852; *N.Y. Times*, Jan. 15, 1852   [6]*N.Y. Herald*, Jan. 13, 1852.

nalistic foes. Simultaneously, she did much to redeem herself in the public eye for all the bad publicity, both past and present.

In a first letter, Montez accused Willis not only of financial irregularities, but also of attempting to enter her bedroom, and other unnamed actions, to compromise her with the inmates of her house. She said she had dismissed him from both her home and service as soon as possible after arriving in New York and finding friends she could rely upon.

Willis made an somewhat ineffectual reply in the same paper. The embittered man, still greatly enamored of his tormentor, denied ever having been Lola's business agent, and said he had never received a penny of hers that he hadn't spent in her interest. He had tried to secure her a successful reception in America, despite the many unfavorable reports she had spawned, but the dancer had always insisted on having things her own way, never willing to play second fiddle. If he weren't a gentleman, said Willis, he could have insisted on payment for his services, and might even have published her letters to make his case.

This gainsaying prompted a second missive from Lola—yet another of her famous "biographical letters." This would be the first of several exploiting a new theme: an appeal for gentlemanly conduct and fair play toward a humble and defenseless woman like her, alone in a foreign land. She told of being virtually forced to marry her first husband at the tender age of thirteen, and then, due to his unloving nature, of being divorced in the East Indies (not London), and thrown "upon the world friendless" without any means of support "except her own industry." She neglected to mention her affair with Lt. Charles Lennox, of course.

It was merely her profession, Lola explained, which exposed her to the approaches of licentious, bad men. Looking back on her tempestuous career, she admitted to having sometimes

Lola Montez as Mariquita
in "*Un jour de Carneval a Seville*," at Boston's Howard Athenaeum.
From *Gleason's Pictorial*, April 17, 1852.
Courtesy, California State Library

been "wild and wayward," but "never wicked." As to her relationship with Ludwig, with whom she still corresponded, she loved him as "she would love a father." It was "not a love that any woman need be ashamed of," she said; he was her friend.

Next came a tirade against Jesuits and Austrians. These were the villains who had pursued her through Europe, and now had come to America to foment the current troubles. They were the ones who had deprived her of what little property she had acquired through the years by "laborious study and incessant exertion," and of the gifts of her "kind benefactor," the Bavarian king. The letter concluded with an appeal to "high-souled, free, liberal and honorable" Americans to credit her "simple tale."[7]

Most thought this fervent, second letter did more for Lola's cause than 100 speeches had done in behalf of Kossuth's. Its eloquence even temporarily quieted criticism in the press, except for Monsieur Arpin of the *Courier des Etats Unis* who, being French, probably knew better than to believe her. Then too, there were a few doubters who thought the bewitching sensualist was incapable of such a dashing and caustic communication, and suspected that one of her many male friends—perhaps former Senator Wescott of Florida—had written it.

Her image thus buffed up a bit, Lola Montez began a hardworking and highly-successful tour of other Eastern cities, under the aegis of E. A. Marshall. He put together a company to support her, comprising six young ballet girls, a similar number of musicians and a male comic dancer, named Cane. Changes were made in *Un Jour de Carneval a Seville* which substituted Lola's more popular "Spider Dance" for one of the Spanish dances, and added a gymnastic and farcical *pas seul* by Cane. The first stop on the tour was Philadelphia's Walnut Street Theater on January 22. From there the troupe went to Washington, Richmond and Norfolk, and thence to Balti-

---

[7]*Ibid.*, Jan. 15, 1852; also Jan. 6, 7, 10, Mar. 22, May 23, 1852.

more's Holliday Street Theater, playing everywhere to good houses at double the prices most performers could command.

Though Ned Willis had been dismissed, and Joe Scoville remained behind in New York to start up a weekly paper of his own, Montez didn't lack male attention. In all the cities she visited, her salons were well attended by respectable men who danced eagerly in her train. She now felt free to behave as she had in Paris and Bavaria, surrounding herself with pomp, and receiving people every morning at her hotel, while reclining abed in state, much like the former kings of France.

The expenses of the Montez retinue were reportedly enormous. She freely dispensed wine, brandy and tobacco to all her friends, who lived, reporters said, in "extravagant dissipation, only equalled by the followers of Kossuth." She herself was now said to abstain from using liquor, although she chain smoked upwards of 500 cigarettes or cigarillos per day, employing her cavaliers in carrying and presenting them to her lighted.

All this pretension by the countess led, naturally enough, to a certain amount of old-fashioned Yankee ribbing, as in the instance when Lola had a brief, chance meeting with a group of Indian chiefs returning home from a pow-wow in Washington. What was apparently a simple exchange of gifts became greatly embellished at the pen of a reporter with a vivid imagination. He credited the chiefs with dubbing Lola "Cat-rat-tantarara" the great female war dancer—and making her an honorary member of their tribes by placing on her head a crown made of the plumage of rare birds. This journalistic nose-tweeker even alleged that the warriors had offered to make Lola their queen, if only she would come to live with them on the plains.[8]

In the nation's capital, highly-placed and somewhat randy officials clustered about Montez, vying for attention. Major William Hawkins Polk, a Tennessee congressman and brother

---

[8] *Ibid.*, Feb. 6, 1852, also Jan. 16, Feb. 9, 10, 12, 22, 23, May 1, 2, 1852; S.F. *Bulletin*, Feb. 14, 1861; S.F. *Alta*, May 12, 1852.

of former President James Knox Polk, shocked everyone by driving the notorious dancer in an open carriage in broad daylight down the great avenue of the capital. Even the "Hero of San Jacinto," 60-year old Senator Sam Houston of Texas, was rumored to have been among the Washingtonians who believed themselves irresistible, only to discover that the countess could be disagreeable, even to those of high position, if they had presented themselves in a too-familiar manner. In all, Lola must have been exceedingly pleased at having triumphed socially and artistically in the same city where the pretentious Lajos Kossuth had recently failed miserably in his attempt to win official support for his cause.

When Lola reached Boston with her troupe on March 13, excitement over her coming was at a high pitch. As one enthusiast remarked, young men, from "engineers to flapdoodles," went "almost mad in pursuit of a glance from her flashing, ravishing eyes, or a kiss from her fair...hand."[9] The favorable impression created by her sharp letters defending her character, and her reception into high society, particularly in Washington and Richmond, led the *Boston Times* to admit that she had become a "lofty intellectual and noble-hearted woman since leaving her enemies in Europe." Another Bostonian thought that half the reports about her weren't factual, and that she would be welcomed by all except "puritanic rogues," since she had only been guilty of an "amiable weakness" which had "rarely been allowed to weigh heavily against pretty women and gallant men" of intellect and high station.[10]

Notwithstanding the favorable welcome, Montez felt greater anxiety about visiting Boston than any other city, because of what she had heard of the strict piety of its citizens. But, despite her fears, for several weeks everything went exceeding well: she offered a matinee performance for families; was

[9] *N.Y. Herald,* Apr. 15, also Mar. 28, 31, Apr. 1, 1852; *N.Y. Times,* Apr. 1, 3, Nov. 12, 1852.

[10] *N.Y. Herald,* Mar. 12, 15, 1852; also Feb. 28, Mar. 3; Nevada (City) *Nevada Journal,* June 5, 1852.

feted by the Free Masons, and was presented to many distinguished citizens. But finally—just as had been the case nearly
everywhere else—a storm of controversy broke around her.

Her troubles began the moment she stepped outside her
assigned pale. Montez was certainly not highly-intellectual.
She would be quoted, in fact, as saying that, of 97 English sonnets she examined in Boston, ninety-five "commenced with the
bronchitis and ended with a newly-made grave."[11] But,
throughout her life, she had expressed a sincere interest in children, particularly those in need. So it was not unusual when, in
Boston, she asked for, and received, a tour of three of the city's
renowned model grammar schools.

Afterward, reproving reports abounded, stating that the
schools had accorded Montez high honors and pageantry, and
that she had interrupted classes to pompously lecture the students in a variety of languages. Such alleged presumption on
her part drew a fresh outburst of morality in the New York
papers and from Epes Sargeant, the Puritan poet and editor of
the *Boston Transcript.* These writers railed against the cast-off
courtesan and bigamist who dared play the part of Minerva to
Boston's students.

Robert E. Hudson of the Merchant's Exchange had made
the arrangements for Lola's tour with Frederick Emerson of
the school board. Afterward, the unfortunate Emerson had to
defend his actions to fellow board members, whom he hadn't
consulted beforehand, and who were terrified to think they
might be blamed for catering to such a fallen woman.

To his credit, Emerson explained that his guest had displayed great tact and exceedingly good manners in each of the
schools. There had been no pageantry, and no orations. The
reports of Lola making speeches in foreign languages had
sprung from her having exchanged a few remarks in French
with one of the teachers, and having quietly read a few lines

---

[11] *Nevada Journal,* Aug. 14, 1852.

from a Latin text. Emerson argued correctly that Lola hadn't forfeited her right to the same courteous treatment which had been given to so many others, simply because she was a dancer. Nonetheless, the school committee would go on debating the matter for another seven months before finally concluding that, in fact, no preferential treatment had been shown.

But Montez didn't need any help in defending herself against bothered Brahmins. By now an inveterate letter writer, she dashed off another of her amazing epistles, this one to Epes Sargeant. In it she managed to invoke the combined spirits of Daniel Webster, John Calhoun, Henry Clay, and even the Pilgrim fathers, all in support of her good name.

Lola asked Sargeant—whom she called a "good little fellow" who published a "good little paper," even though he had failed as a playwright—if he thought the school children would have had any impure thoughts connected with her visit if he, Sargeant, hadn't put them there. "There are men who would stand before the Venus of Medici and the Apollo of Belvidere," Lola pointed out, "and see nothing in them but their nudity." She reminded the journalist that Bostonians had previously allowed an equally-bohemian dancer, Fanny Elssler, to dedicate the capstone of the Bunker Hill Monument; she called his attention to the many contributions performing artists had made over the years to local charities.

There was no humbug in her makeup, the dancer told Sargeant. She had had offers which would have brought her to America in triumph, with flowers spread across her path, her carriage drawn by human hands to her hotel, and so forth, but she had turned them all down. Additionally, Barnum's proposal had been rejected because she was determined to return to the stage legitimately as an artist, not to be put on display "like a wooly horse or a white negro," even though it would have been more profitable.

When she announced her intent to come to the United

States, Lola continued, the American journals began heaping upon her all the epithets "in the vocabulary blackguard." It was stated that "she tamed wild horses, horse-whipped gendarmes, knocked flies with a pistol ball off the bald heads of aldermen, fought duels, threw people overboard for the sake of saving them from drowning," and a multitude of other such feats. These stories, she explained, were invented by her "Jesuitic enemies" who were trying to unsex her and deny her that protection normally accorded women. She defied, in boldface, "ANY MAN LIVING TO PROVE" the aspersions against her character.[12]

At least one Bostonian credited the feisty woman with having completely vanquished Sargeant, but confessed that his "staid, God-fearing community" had been completely shaken from its propriety. Satan had arrived in the form of a "charming danseuse, whose wit, appearance and effrontery had actually crazed the descendants of the sober Puritans." Montez—the embodiment of the spirit of discord"—had succeeded everywhere in stirring up trouble, while she presided over the "melee with the utmost grace and nonchalance." Regrettably, the "good days of witch-burning" were gone, this fellow complained.[13]

The editor of the New Orleans *Bee* failed to see what all the fuss was about in Yankee land. After all, the "private intrigues and doubtful morality" of a performer were none of the public's business. Montez only professed "the poetry of motion, not the purity of a saint"—and anyway, everyone knew that ninety-nine out of every one hundred dancers were women "of impure and depraved character" so, in the South, they weren't introduced to wives and families, nor escorted to the schools—they were kept "in their sphere."[14]

---

[12]In *N.Y. Times*, Apr. I, 1852, also Apr. 3, Nov. 12, 1852; *N.Y. Herald*, Mar, 21, 27, 31, Apr. I, 1852.

[13]*N.Y. Herald*, Apr. 6, 1852.

[14]*Ibid.*, Apr. 17, 1852.

Apparently unruffled by it all, Lola played intermittently at the Howard Athenaeum, and used Boston as a home base to fulfill dates in other nearby cities until mid-April. In her fashion, she continued to create controversy. Accompanied by her merchant friend and a highly-placed cleric, she visited Boston's House of Corrections. This led James Gordon Bennett, who was fast losing his fondness for the dancer, to comment that a jail was a very natural place for Lola to investigate, since no one could tell how soon she might be there herself. But what seemed to have been the final straw for Bennett and many other supporters was her reconciliation with former lover Edward Willis, whom she had earlier denounced as a liar and swindler. Back when Lola dismissed him, Willis had returned to Boston, his hometown, and then, about April 5, a mutual friend got the pair back together. During the separation, Willis had dropped heavy hints about the true nature of their relationship, and Lola didn't contradict him when the two made up. As she remarked, languishingly, "Well I suppose he loves me yet."[15]

There would be one final splash in the papers before Montez left Boston. On the evening of the day after she had finished playing the Athenaeum, Lola returned to the theater, accompanied by Willis, to search for a missing piece of her jewelry. When the prompter came into the property room to turn off the gas lights, Lola told him to leave them on so that she might continue looking. Unhappily for him, the man talked back, so Lola pulled him by the nose, slapped his face and, with the aid of her friends, ejected him.

Disparagers would accuse her of being in the theater only to hinder the performance of an old enemy, Julie de Marguerrittes, who was singing on stage at the time. Even though the vocalist denied having either been annoyed or insulted, the prompter still wasn't satisfied, and he obtained a warrant for Lola's arrest on assault charges. But, by then, the tempestuous

---

[15]S.F. *Alta*, May 12, 1852; also *N.Y. Herald*, Apr. 6-14, 1852.

Montez was performing in Salem. She returned to Boston by train April 13, fully expecting to be arrested, her friends ready with bail, but apparently the matter had been dropped.

Lola journeyed back once again to New York City after playing a single night at Hartford, Connecticut. She now had discarded Ned Willis for a second time and, though he would hover about for a while, attempting another reconciliation, his days with her were finished forever. Within twelve months he would die in Boston at age 36 of pleurisy, and all those who had heard of Dumas' prediction about Lola and her men were probably not at all surprised to learn of his demise.[16]

The famous American tragedian, Edwin Forrest, had been performing at the Broadway Theater ever since Montez had vacated that stage. Since his engagement still had ten days to run, Lola had some time on her hands in which to once again stir up trouble. This time she was at the center of an escapade which would become notorious as the "Battle of the Howard Hotel."

On April 29, the countess, as was her habit, entertained a party of gentlemen admirers at a soiree in her rooms at the Howard. Among these "whiskered panderers and fierce hussars,"[17] as James Gordon Bennett called them, were Count Wallowski, a refugee Polish nobleman and pianist; Wallowski's father; another Polish refugee, Count Kazinski; F. Manetta, the Italian Prince of Como (also known as Carissimo); and a certain Mr. Davis of Boston who was Lola's house guest.

That evening, cigars and champagne circulated freely, making the party a pleasant and jovial one. The topic of conversation drifted easily from the impending presidential election to

---

[16]Record of death of Edward P. Willis, Mass. State Archives, Boston; Sacramento *Union*, June 24, 1852; Philadelphia, PA, *Public Ledger*, Mar. 31, 1853; *Boston Post*, Mar. 24, 1853. In 1850 Marguerittes had published a derogatory sketch of Lola's brazen activities at a German spa (Sacramento *Transcript*, Aug. 8, 1850; *N.Y. Herald*, Apr. 13, 14, 1852).

[17]*N.Y. Herald*, May 1, 1852, also Apr. 19, May 3, *N.Y. Times*, May 1, 1852; Los Angeles *Star*, Mar. 27, 1852; S.F. *Golden Era*, May 22, 1853.

Kossuth, religion, Fourrierism, and other current interests. About midnight, however, matters began to get a bit out of hand. Intellectual subjects were put aside in favor of gossip about that juiciest of all scandals, the recently-concluded divorce case between Edwin Forrest and his wife. Forrest, having been found guilty of adultery, had just been saddled with a heavy burden of alimony, and his wife—no innocent herself— had recently begun a stage career in New York City, using her maiden name, Catherine Sinclair.

In Paris, Prince Como had been a *cavaliere-servente* of Lola, and he was rumored to have more recently provided a similar service to Mrs. Forrest. After Montez returned from Boston, she renewed her former acquaintance with Como but, after awhile, he directed his attentions back again to Mrs. Forrest. Then, after Mrs. Forrest left town on tour, Como once again resumed his allegiance to Lola, who received him and pardoned his repeated backsliding.

That evening at the Howard Hotel, Lola became exceedingly incensed at the mere mention of Mrs. Forrest's name, and began roundly denouncing her. Como, in turn, defended his dear Catherine, while at the same time reflecting adversely on the character of Lola, whom he said should be the last person in the world to make such an attack, particularly in the presence of one like himself, who had known her conduct in Paris and elsewhere.

Upon hearing Como's insult, Lola exploded. She wound up with such a firm grip on the prince's moustache that the pain made him forget himself and strike Montez in the face. Then, when he tried to leave her rooms, she placed her back to the door, locked it and summoned the landlord who came and tossed the abusive Italian out.

Como nursed his ego for a while downstairs at the bar, and then resolved to challenge Count Kazinski, who had taken

Lola's side in the abuse of Mrs. Forrest. The prince sent up his card to Kazinski, but Lola replied that she would neither allow the Pole to leave her apartment, nor Como to enter it. Nevertheless, Como and one of his countryman he had met in the bar came up by the back stairs and sneaked in to recommence the affray in earnest. The Italians were met by the Poles, Lola's Bostonian house guest, her poodle and serving woman. Even "Mr. Pick," Joe Scoville, arrived in time to join in the fray. A throng drawn by the terrible din of the struggle was treated to the sight of the two Italians being tumbled down the stairs. Not surprisingly, as a result of this melee, the Countess Landsfeld was asked to find other lodgings.

The free-wheeling Montez was popular with more than just fugitive European nobility and alcoholic journalists. She was also a special favorite of the denizens of that "great Wigwam," Tammany Hall. Captain Isaiah Rynders, the ruffian head of the Tammany Empire Club, and a one-time New Orleans gambler, wooed her particularly hard during her stops in New York. Another Tammany admirer was Robert H. Morris, a former New York mayor. So popular was she with the Tammany Society's Council of Sachems that one wag hinted they might initiate her into their midst as the "Royal Squaw, Lolychzchaw."[18]

At the end of April, Montez played two nights at the Broadway, and made plans to leave on May 3 for engagements in upstate New York. But, unexpectedly, just as she was about to depart, a "Jesuit, in the disguise of a bailiff" served her with a summons, requiring that she appear before a Justice of the Peace that day and pay $20.00 owed her most recent landlady for board and room. Lola was furious, but finally wrote a check on the Chemical Bank.

The following day, she was escorted out of the city with a

---

[18]*N.Y. Herald*, May 3, 1852; also July 6, 1852, Jan. 5, 1852; Gustavus Myers, *History of Tammany Hall*, 136-38.

great deal of pomp by Isaiah Rynders and a royal train of princes, counts, barons, mountebanks, agents, dancing men, and dancing women, *fille de chambre,* French poodle, and a whole host of camp followers. A writer for the *Herald* expressed regret that, with her departure, there would be no more of the "fun and drollery, and scandal and strifes," which had recently given such zest to life in New York.[19]

Not long after Montez began her tour of upstate New York, she evidently dismissed for a time her noisome following of long-haired vagabonds, and even hired an immense fellow in Albany to kick out any princes and such who might persist in annoying her. It was also said that, when not performing, she was behaving herself by attending theatricals, lectures, and prayer meetings. Despite the improved decorum, her dancing in rural towns like Rochester and Troy was considered by some to be much too reckless.

When Montez returned once again to Gotham she danced for a week at the Broadway, and then opened there on May 25 in a most unusual drama, entitled *Lola Montez in Bavaria.* This vehicle for her first known attempt at acting had been especially written for her by C. P. T. Ware, a young dramatist for the Broadway and Astor Place Theaters. The piece was a vainglorious interpretation of events during Lola's tumultuous two and one-half year adventure with King Ludwig. Its five parts portrayed her successively as danseuse, politician, countess, revolutionist and fugitive.

The plot begins with her appearance in Munich, where Ludwig is depicted as being attracted by her astute political instincts. The king—an old fogy, grown grey under the cares of government, and unaware that his ministers were deceiving him—becomes so charmed with the artless, but noble Lola that he asks her to take up residence with him and become his trusted counselor. She agrees, but, not wishing to overstep the

---

[19]*N.Y. Herald,* May 4, 5, 1852.

bounds of strict propriety, insists that the monarch fit up a palace especially for her, where he can visit her every day—but only under the watchful eyes of an old duenna with a great horror of scandal. Thus, Lola and Ludwig get acquainted, and soon she is calling him Louis, patting his cheeks while telling him that she isn't afraid of a king, and playfully tapping his forehead while saying she never will be able to beat any sense into it.

Despite its many distortions of the truth, the play did demonstrate the very real mutual hatred that existed between the Jesuit minister, Abel, and Lola. One scene had her hiding Ludwig behind a curtain so that he could overhear Abel's attempt to bribe her into leaving Bavaria. Thus the minister's treachery in deceiving his monarch and preventing the carrying out of Lola's reforms is exposed, and he is turned out of office. Our heroine's enemies, the Jesuits, subsequently subject her to a series of hair-raising perils: they try to poison her with arsenic; twice have her shot at; place a fanatic upon her stairs at midnight with a poniard in his coat, and they attempt to abduct her to an Austrian prison.

The denouement of the play's insipid plot was a scene depicting the revolution. It began with an imposing tableau showing the struggle between Lola's Alemannia and the Catholic students, the latter costumed so as to resemble mysterious-looking bandits or assassins. Then, to the accompaniment of a great ringing of bells and the continuous din of a gigantic noisemaker, women could be seen rushing breathlessly back and forth across a stage aglow with red-fire. Twenty footmen or soldiers (the audience was never sure which) struggled with twenty men in glazed blouses for the possession of twenty muskets. Lola was also seen scurrying around a great deal, frightened by the noise and confusion, finally fainting when ex-prime minister Abel fires a pistol near her head. The scene invariably left those who viewed it in a state of perplexity.

The lengthy play ended with Lola's "escape" from Bavaria in the disguise of a peasant, aided by a poor but honest student artist, Baron Ludwig von Schootenbottom.

The Broadway Theater had a ballet ready to replace *Lola in Bavaria* just in case it should bomb, but, oddly enough, Lola's apologia was widely viewed as a success. The consensus of the "oyster house critics" around town was that it was "very eloquent and effecting."[20] And, while Montez wasn't rated as much of an actress, she was credited with having a vivacious, offhand style which appeared perfectly natural.

After three more performances in New York, Lola took her play on the road for brief runs in Philadelphia and Washington, D. C. But, once again, she was unable to leave town without some sort of fuss. Just to catch a glimpse of her, a large crowd of people boarded her ferry across the Hudson and, as she, Joe Scoville and her agent debarked in Jersey City to catch their train, several emboldened fellows purposely crowded against her. But, as chance would have it, there was also a large party of Tammany men on the same ferry, bound for the Democratic National Convention in Baltimore. These fellows resented the insult to their "Royal Squaw," and promptly vanquished the offenders in a free-for-all fight. It was reported that Lola, whose nerves were supposedly not strong at times, fainted away and had to be carried to the railroad cars by Scoville and Mr. Dunlap of the Pewter Mug Saloon.

When Montez next returned to New York City she severed her business arrangement with E. A. Marshall, with whom she had been squabbling ever since arriving in the United States. Aside from the usual volatile displays of temper, Lola had several times broken the express provision of her contract which forbade her from becoming involved in political and religious subjects. She had also supposedly threatened to horsewhip or

[20] *Ibid.*, May 27, also May 6-16, 27, 1852; New Orleans *Picayune*, Jan. 4, 1853; Cannon, 84, from *Melbourne Age*, Sept. 14, 1855.

use her revolver against Marshall, and to sue him for some undisclosed breech of contract.

But the dancer didn't need Marshall any longer. Now having added acting to her skills, and with immense notoriety, she wasted little time in making new arrangements. Somehow Thomas S. Hamblin, the noted tragedian who had managed New York's Bowery Theater for many years, was convinced to come out of retirement and lease that place once again so that she might play there. While Lola waited for it to be remodeled, she performed again in Baltimore, where she got into a behind-the-scenes spat and boxed the ears of her latest dance partner and ballet master, George Smith. Sparked by comments Smith had made regarding Montez's character, the fight was serious enough to shut down the theater for several nights running.

The temperamental countess played the refurbished Bowery Theater for two weeks beginning June 28, doing *Lola Montez in Bavaria* and, usually, one of her dances. The Bowery had been a famous playhouse in earlier years, but was, by now, considered strictly second-rate, with a rowdy, peanut-chomping, cigar-smoking clientele. Lola was credited with packing in an improved class of audience, which included numerous ladies down slumming from the Broadway area. It was said that her genius had upped the nightly receipts some fourfold, even though all seats sold for 25 cents or less. As James Bennett noted, prosperity seemed to have blessed the "two repentant sinners"—Lola and Hamblin.[21]

But, like so many others, Hamblin was unable to deal for very long with Montez, and soon their arrangement was in a shambles. It is not likely that she and the fifty-two-year-old had anything more than a business relationship, but, still, Hamblin would die a mere six months later, raving mad of brain fever, and thus join that ever-increasing group of men

---

[21]*N.Y. Herald,* July 5, 1852; also Apr. 30, June 1, 5, 12, 23, 24, 30, July 8, 12; *N.Y. Times,* June 24, 1852.

who had had the misfortune to run afoul of Montez and her
apparent hex.

After quitting the Bowery, Lola signed a contract to perform under the management of Charles S. Thorne, beginning
in early autumn. Thorne, new lessee of the Astor Place Opera
House on 5th Avenue, was remodeling that place, and planned
to reopen it as the New York Theater.

By this time, summer's dog days had arrived, and Montez
laid plans to retreat to the Catskills for a brief rest. But, before
getting out of town, she was obliged to do battle with yet
another presumptuous scribbler. The controversy in this case
was over an article written in the New York *Times* by Ned
Buntline Jr. (Z. C. Judson). His insulting piece accused members of the city's common council of taking lessons from the
"brazen prostitute," Lola Montez, in denying allegations
against their integrity. Like her, they had asked their accusers
for the specific times and places when they had departed from
virtue. Buntline said this was a safe ploy, since there were certain crimes regarding which only the offenders knew the specific details.

Naturally, Lola couldn't allow such abuse. From her Warren
Street lodgings she wrote another indignant appeal for the
"real men" of America to defend her, a helpless, unprotected
female, a "homeless wanderer...in city after city, who was mod-
estly endeavoring to earn a livelihood." If she were the vile
character Buntline painted, Lola asked, need she have left "the
shores of abandoned and gay Europe"[22] to acquire money or
luxuries? In this latest of her biographical letters, Montez
claimed she had been forced by domestic troubles as a naive
girl of 14 (not 13) to marry Lieutenant James, and that his
death in India (not their divorce) had left her with no means of
support, requiring her to become a dancer.

Her plea was sufficiently eloquent to cause James Bennett to

---

[22]*N.Y. Times,* July 16, 1852.

drop his growing animosity toward the dancer long enough to say it was mean to slander her, whatever she might be. The *Times* people, Bennett said, should be "trotted through Broadway in the carts of dirt collectors, and sold for dog's meat out of town."[23] But such extreme measures wouldn't be necessary. Assisted by James T. Brady, a prominent Tammany Hall lawyer, Lola threatened Buntline with civil and criminal prosecution. This proved sufficient to cause the *Times* to print an apology of sorts, and the matter was dropped.

So, Montez left for her Catskill vacation under a cloud of controversy. Once arrived in the mountains, just who or what kept her amused can't be said. Ned Willis was long gone; Joseph Scoville had a newspaper to run; Prince Bobo had returned to Haiti, and all of Lola's counts and barons were reported to have gone to their respective watering places for the fashionable summer season.

In fact, there may have been nothing to distract her, since it was apparently during this period that she set about honing her acting skills and adding six new plays to her repertory. One was that old standard, Richard B. Sheridan's comedy, *The School For Scandal,* in which Lola portrayed Lady Teazle. Another was a new drama called *Charlotte Corday, or Jacobins and Girondists.* While there were other works extant on the same subject, including one by Victor Hugo, Lola said hers had been expressly written for her by H. J. Conway.

A third new play, *Maritana, or the Maid of Saragossa,* she said had been written by another American dramatist, whose name was not disclosed, but who was probably C. P. T. Ware, author of *Lola Montez in Bavaria.* Two other works, *Lola Montez in New York* and *Clarissa Harlowe,* would only be staged a few times before being dropped; the former of these was written by Ware, and the latter Lola professed to have authored herself. The sixth play, *Yelva; or The Orphan Girl of Russia,* was a three-act drama

---

[23]*N.Y. Herald,* July 17, 20; *N.Y. Times,* July 19, 1852.

which Montez claimed she had translated from the French. She would advertise it several times as "her most admired role"—one she had played "with ultra success, in Europe, after her banishment from Bavaria."[24] She never had, of course.

Lola made a huge splash upon returning to New York in late August. Taking a page from Barnum's book, she and Joe Scoville held a monster picnic for over 800 guests, including Isaiah Rynders, Edwin Forrest, Barnum, Horace Greeley and other celebrities and theater critics. The group traveled by steamboat to Yonkers for a huge feast at which Lola, the featured attraction, made a speech and presented the standard of the "Pick Club of Brooklyn and New York," no doubt a recent invention of Scoville's. The publicity stunt was obviously calculated to boost Lola's notoriety and the circulation of Scoville's two-cent weekly, *The Pick*. An account of the affair, complete with illustrations of a spicy character soon appeared in that paper.[25]

But Lola Montez might have spared herself the effort, since she was not destined to perform again anytime soon in New York City. Before her scheduled engagement at the renovated New York Theater could begin, manager Charles Thorne took deathly sick of the "Chagres Fever," which forced the theater to close in mid-September, and eventually to fail financially.

Though thwarted in New York, Lola went on to test her new repertoire and improved acting skills in Boston and Philadelphia during September and October. Then, in late November, with a new traveling agent named John Jones accompanying her, she sailed from New York in the mail steamship *Marion* to Charleston, South Carolina, to begin a tour of the South.

Unluckily for Lola, in the same ship was Master Benson A.

---

[24]Cincinnati (OH) *Courier*, Mar. 13, 1853.
[25]*N.Y. Herald*, Sept. 2, 1852; also July 11, Sept. 3, 1852.

Lola Montez as she appeared at New Orleans.
Portrait by an unknown artist. It was said to have been buried beneath
a theater during the Civil War occupation of the city.
Courtesy, Nevada County, California, Historical Society.

English of Macon, Georgia, age 3 ½, also known as "the Infant Drummer." This world-renowned little boy completely capti-vated Charleston audiences for a nearly a week, playing two jam-packed concerts on his traps each day at Hibernian Hall. The students at The Citadel loved the tiny fellow so much they presented him with a miniature version of their military uni-form to wear while he performed. Montez had to sit on the sidelines for a week before commencing her engagement at the Charleston Theater, and even then she was not well received. When she left town after only a few performances, young Master English was still thrilling his audiences.

After Charleston, however, Lola completed a highly-suc-cessful week in Mobile at a theater under the management of Joseph N. Field. There, she told packed houses that this was the first city in the south she had visited. It was not, of course.

Next came a successful engagement of nearly a month at Placide's Varieties in New Orleans, much to the pleasure of that theater's stockholders. It was here that Lola fainted upon hearing of the supposed drowning of former husband George Heald off Lisbon, Portugal, by the foundering of his yacht, the *Sparrow Hawk*. Within a few days, the drowning story was con-tradicted, and then reaffirmed once again, the last report adding that Heald had left a will in which he bequeathed Lola 30,000 pounds. But, still later in 1856, there would be another report that the Englishman had died in his bed. His true fate remains a mystery.[26]

After finishing at the Varieties Lola became embroiled in another highly-publicized fuss. When her maid, Ellen,

---

[26]Montomery (AL) *Daily Alabama Journal*, Apr. 2, 1853; Philadelphia *Public Ledger*, Sept. 15, Oct. 13-24, 1852; Boston *Daily Evening Transcript*, Sept. 20-Oct. 2, 1852; *N.Y. Herald*, Aug. 15, 1852, Jan. 22, 1853; S.F. *Daily Evening Journal*, Mar. 12, 1853; *N.Y. Times*, Jan. 14, 22, 1861; New Orleans *Picayune*, Sept. 22, 27, Oct. 7, Dec. 17-29, 1852, Jan. 3-31, 1853; Charleston (SC) *Daily Courier*, Nov. 30, Dec. 2-10, 1852; Cincinnati *Daily Enquirer*, Feb. 4, 1853; *London Times*, Jan. 1, 4, 1853; Louisville (KY) *Daily Courier*, Feb. 4, 1853.

expressed the desire to leave her service, Montez refused to pay the woman the wages she was owed and so, on Ellen's complaint, the New Orleans recorder issued a warrant for Lola's arrest.

Captain Forno and another police officer went to Lola's rooms to make the arrest, arriving at the peak of her daily levee. The countess, of course, refused to go with the captain, asking imperiously if he really wanted "to stick his nose in the private affairs of a peeress of the realm?" In the ensuing argument, she drew a dagger, and before Forno and his assistant could manage to disarm her, their hands were bitten and Forno was kicked in the "bread basket." The countess' admirers interceded to persuade the officers to unhand her, all the while attempting to calm her by "My ladying" her in soothing tones. The seemingly-distraught Montez took a hanky from one votary, blew her nose and threw it back to him.

As Lola brought more of her new acting skills into play, the scene grew even more ludicrous. She stepped to a sideboard, seized a small vial labeled "Poison," quickly swallowed its contents, and then in a triumphant voice exclaimed, "Now I shall be free from all further indignity!" The much-offended woman then collapsed. Although the police didn't for a moment believe the poison was real, Lola's frantically-concerned courtiers did.

What followed next was recorded for us by a cynical observer who managed to remain above the fluster. A stomach pump was called for while a handsome and gallant bachelor druggist hurried to and fro supplying antidotes. Stretched out on a couch across from where Lola lay was another devoted admirer—the picture of despair—a scientist "who, though familiar with magnets and the properties of the electric field, was completely overcome by this last flash from the battery of the divine Lola." In the center of the room stood a distinguished city official, with arms folded and head on chest, posed in an attitude resembling that of "Napoleon's favorite, Mameluke, standing at the bedside of his dying Emperor." This man was heard to ask, "Can this country be aught but barbarian, when the wrist of a Countess is subject to the rude grasp of an ungloved police?" Also hovering nearby was a well-known dramatic poet of New Orleans, "taking notes to weave into his forthcoming poem of 'Early Stricken Flowers.'"[27]

But Lola still lived. She revived, smoked two cigarillos, then swooned briefly once again. Of course, by now the police knew better than to pursue the matter further, so they left with a promise from her friends that she would appear before the recorder. This she did, and a compromise was reached with the maid.

Soon afterward, a large crowd of the troublemaker's southern friends saw her off on the steamer *Eclipse* for a trip up river to Cincinnati. Here, she shone resplendent during the first half of March 1853, playing to large, appreciative audiences at the National Theater.

Unfortunately, Lola also showed Cincinnatians her eccentric side. Just as she was preparing to leave town, John Jones decided it was time for him to follow the maid Ellen's lead, and seek employment elsewhere. Hearing of his plans, Montez confronted her 'traveling agent' and the two began debating about whose character and conduct was worse. Finally, with a curse, Lola sprang on Jones and, before bystanders could restrain her, gave him a fist to the jaw. Her fury soon subsided, but not before she had destroyed some $200 in checks just to show that "filthy lucre" was no object to her.

But Montez showed the locals that she could do more than merely hurl thunderbolts. When the editor of the Cincinnati *Sun* criticized her actions in his paper the next day, she astonished the printers in the Cincinnati *Nonpareil* office by going

---

[27] New Orleans, *True Delta*, Feb. 9, 13, 1853.

there with a letter of rebuttal she had written, and taking up the stick and rule to personally set it up in type, a skill she had perhaps learned earlier from Joe Scoville.[28]

Later that month, the audacious performer took St. Louis by storm, playing at a theater managed by the same Joseph N. Field for whom she had worked at Mobile. By now, however, Field had become disenchanted. Midway in the engagement, he took out an advertisement to explain an increase in ticket prices, in which he said they had been raised upon "the imperative demand" of Montez. Although the details are somewhat obscure, his action was the apparent cause of an imbroglio in which Lola gave the citizens of St. Louis "a taste of her quality by trying to whip...[Field], and by breaking the nose of her agent with a heavy brass candlestick."[29] But agents were easy for Lola Montez to find. With a new one, J. H. Henning, she left St. Louis and traveled once again to New Orleans. By this time she had finalized plans to sail from that port for an artistic tour of California.

Lola's second sojourn in the Crescent City was judged by newsmen to have been immeasurably more scandalous than the first. Duey Barre, a dancer whom Lola had encouraged in her career, was performing on the night of April 8 at the Varieties Theatre, where Lola herself had played on her first visit to the city. Wishing to offer encouragement to Barre, Montez came to the theater, entered by the alley door, and went to observe from that area of the wings normally occupied by actor-prompter George T. Rowe. Rowe, who was preparing to ring up the curtain, pointed out that she was violating house rules, and he asked her to leave the theater. With her usual cool insouciance Lola at first ignored the prompter, but, when he

---

[28]In Montgomery *Alabama Journal*, Apr. 2, 30, 1853; also see S.F. *Golden Era*, May 22, 1853; Cincinnati *Enquirer*, Mar. 2-16, 1853; New Orleans *Delta*, Feb. 18, Apr. 15, 1853; Louisville (KY) *Courier*, Feb. 25, 26, Mar. 13, 1853.

[29]George R. McMinn, *The Theater of the Golden Era in California*, 361; New Orleans *True Delta*, Apr. 15, 1853; St. Louis *Missouri Republican*, Jan. 8, Mar, 13, 17, 20-24, 1853; Louisville *Courier*, Mar. 17, 1853.

persisted, Montez launched a furious "wild-cat attack" with fist and fingers, calling the hapless man names and kicking him at the same time.[30]

As the noise from the scuffle in the wings increased, the audience became so excited that Duey Barre's dance had to be stopped. Lola called agent Henning for help, and he obliged by viciously grabbing Rowe by the cravat and choking him, while Lola retreated to the green room. Theater manager Thomas Placide found her there mumbling to herself: "Lola Montez! Lola Montez! to be turned out of a theatre by a common actor!" Placide asked her to leave but she again refused, calling him "a damned scoundrel, a damned liar, and a damned thief." Nonetheless, Lola and Henning finally left the theater by the alley entrance, and witnesses said they heard her swearing like a trooper as she stormed off.[31]

On charges of disturbing the peace lodged by Placide, Lola and Henning were examined before the New Orleans recorder on April 14 before a huge crowd of curiosity seekers. After unsuccessfully feigning illness in an attempt to evade the hearing, Montez, smoking two perfumed Havanas enroute, had to be brought in by officers of the court.

Lola's quarrel with Tom Placide had not begun with the incident backstage. Earlier, he had refused to let her dance at a benefit performance for Duey Barre, and he owed her money for some liquor she had bought. He was also guilty of wandering around the theater dressing rooms "in negligee."[32] Now, in court, Lola titillated onlookers by asking Placide: "Didn't you come behind the scenes in your shirt tails one night, when I was playing in your theatre, in a very immodest manner? and

---

[30]New Orleans *True Delta*, Apr. 10, 1853, also Apr. 8; Louisville *Courier*, Mar. 30-Apr. 2, 1853.

[31]Panama City *Daily Panama Star*, May 6, 1853. Thomas Placide was the brother of noted actor Henry Placide. Both men did mostly low comedy.

[32]San Francisco *Bulletin*, Nov. 9, 1895.

you know, Mr. Placide, that you're far from being a handsome man!"[33] Lola also accused prompter Rowe of having made improper advances toward her during her engagement there.

The press made great sport of this latest escapade of "Lady Marie," as Lola was said to be known to her intimate circle. One satirical article spoke of her new dance—the "Rowe Kick Step." Another rhymed:

> That you should raise your pretty foot to kick the old man Rowe,
> Is more than e'en I thought you would attempt to do, I vow.
> That foot was made to dance a jig—to draw the vulgar eye—
> And that's the reason why, methinks, you lift it up so high.[34]

The story of that first day's examination before the recorder sold so fast that the *True Delta's* steam press couldn't keep up with the demand. The editor said that he, for one, was willing to forget the "brevity of Placide's linen," and to pardon the charming Lola for trying to vindicate her honor, provided the recorder would also "forgive and forget, admonish all parties for their silly behaviour, destroy 'them papers,' and speed the sweet, fitful, delicious, but irascible Lola...on her way rejoicing to the auriferous placers of El Dorado, and to the more ardent welcome of the less fastidious...gallants of California."[35]

And that, in fact, is what happened. All parties agreed to drop the matter, and Lola turned her attention to preparations for her California voyage. Those she chose to accompany her included C. Ritchter, the female private secretary who had come to America with her; a new maid, Hyacinth Fhlerey—known also as Periwinkle; Charles Eigenschenck, the leader of her orchestra, said to be formerly of the Royal Conservatoire in Paris, and, of course, agent Henning. Lola's intention was to stay in California only until fall, and then return to the Eastern states via Mexico City and Havana. Before embarking in the

---

[33]New Orleans *True Delta*, Apr. 15, 1853.
[34]*Ibid.*, Apr. 16, 1853   [35]*Ibid.*

steamer *Philadelphia* for Aspinwall, Panama on April 22, Montez visited New Orleans's Second District jail to provide a demented young girl with some much-needed clothing.[36]

After an uneventful voyage, *Philadelphia* docked at Aspinwall May 2, and its passengers began the arduous 30-hour journey across the Isthmus of Panama to the Pacific—first by railroad to Gatun, then in canoes up the Chagres river to Gorgona and, finally, atop mules for the last 25 miles to Panama City.

In her lifetime, Montez was accused by newspapermen of horse-whipping men everywhere she went, and Panama proved to be no exception. Years after the fact, William H. Russell of the London *Times* described Lola as a big, impudent-looking woman, who crossed the Isthmus dressed in man's attire and carrying a riding whip, which she used to beat a man across the face for presuming to touch her coat. While, indeed, Lola may have donned a mannish costume for the rugged trip, such as the one made notorious by Amelia Bloomer, Russell's story seems to be sheer fabrication, since Lola didn't travel to California until two years after the time he claimed she did.[37]

Panama City was bustling with some 500 passengers, obliged to wait a few days for the next steamer to San Francisco. Many were prominent Californians and political appointees of the new Franklin Pierce administration who had just arrived from New York City. Among them were Thomas O. Larkin, Senators William M. Gwin and John Weller, as well as former Mormon leader and prominent businessman Samuel Brannan. Also awaiting passage were the editor-owners of three prominent California newspapers, and Alvin Adams, the senior partner of Adam's Express Company.

Given its squalor and inequable climate, cholera and other diseases were always a concern in Panama. At the behest of local businessmen, Montez joined some of the other well-

---

[36]*Ibid.*, Apr. 21, 22, 1853.
[37]San Francisco *Wide West*, May 30, 1858; Montez, *Lectures*, 78-81.

known personages in publishing a statement in the local paper, certifying that in crossing the Isthmus and during their stay in Panama they had enjoyed good health and had seen no sickness. She took rooms at the Cocoa Grove Hotel on the outskirts of town, which was advertised as being a healthy and popular stopping place.

In her fashion, Lola held court at her hotel on the evening of her arrival, and there managed to conquer the hearts of a number of men who had come eagerly to meet her. One of them, editor Lewis Middleton of the *Panama Star*, had expected the dancer to be the huge, masculine sort of woman portrayed by the likes of William Russell, and he was thus pleasantly surprised to see that she was of ordinary size and of a "delicate frame, possessing the most regular and handsome features, a pair of brilliant and expressive eyes and an exceedingly winning address." Middleton also appraised her as being well educated, self-possessed and without the "simpering mock-modesty which makes many people look so ridiculous."[38] He and the others were about to be treated to a bit of the fabled Montez daring.

As darkness fell, Middleton and the other men sat talking with Lola around the front door of the hotel, with only the lamp in the hall to light the porch and yard. One of the men, David B. Milne of Sacramento, got up to take a stroll around the premises, and inadvertently wandered a short distance outside the gate, into the intense darkness. His absence went unnoticed until his companions plainly heard two rapid clicks of a revolver being fired, without discharging. Milne called out that a man was trying to shoot him; then, immediately afterward, those on the porch heard three or four more clicks of the revolver. But once again, fortunately for Milne, the gun misfired, its caps apparently damp from the humidity.

At Milne's outcry, Lola neither fainted nor had palpitations

---

[38] *Panama Star*, May 5, 1853.

of the heart. She arose from her chair—cool and collected—
and, telling one of the men near her to get a light, rushed into
the darkness toward the sounds, the men close on her heels.
The assailant was seen for a moment as he made his escape into
the woods, and one of Lola's companions snapped a double-
barreled pistol twice at the fleeing man, but it also failed to fire.

Lola found Milne and led him to the lamp, then set about
cross-examining him regarding his activities since arriving in
Panama, trying to determine if he had offended anyone who
might now be seeking revenge. Finding this not to be the case,
she adjudged the incident a hoax gotten up by the Panama City
hotel keepers to frighten Cocoa Grove residents into taking
rooms in the city. Lola also scolded poor Milne for simply having stood an easy target for his attacker, instead of grabbing
him by the hair and shouting for help, as she would have done.
Editor Middleton didn't know if the mysterious affair had
been a hoax, but he came away from it immensely impressed
with Lola, expressing regret that she couldn't stay on awhile
and perform at Panama City's theater in her "native language,"
Spanish.[39]

But the Golden State with its promise of excitement and
riches awaited the adventurous Montez. Two days after the
Cocoa Grove incident, she and the throng of transient Americans boarded the Pacific Mail Steamship Company's sidewheel
steamer *Northerner,* bound for San Francisco.

---

[39] *Ibid.,* May 3, 1853, also May 6.

CHAPTER THREE

San Francisco Conquered

Oh Yankee Doodle beats the world for music, fun and frolic,
And when he gets his tarnal gripe he hangs on like the colic.
Yankee Doodle strayed from home to hunt up some new notion,
He found a slice of Mexico near the Pacific Ocean!

When Yankee found the slice was rich, to grab it was no sin, sir,—
He told the Greasers they were out, and Jonathan was in sir;
So Yankee built a little town and San Francisco called it,
Then went to digging tons of gold and straight to hum he hauled it!
...David G. "Yankee" Robinson, "The City Council."[1]

One can be sure Lola Montez bedazzled many of the male passengers aboard the steamer *Northerner* on its fifteen-day voyage from Panama to San Francisco. But, judging from subsequent events, she gave most of her attention to a San Francisco newspaperman named Patrick Purdy Hull. True to both her fondness for unwashed journalists and shipboard liaisons, sometime during the passage to San Francisco Lola apparently took Hull as her latest lover.

Twenty-nine year old Pat Hull, who was returning from a visit in the East, had originally come to California as Zachary Taylor's appointee to supervise the 1850 census. He had stayed on in the new state to start up the San Francisco *Pacific Courier* and, when it failed after five months, he joined B. G. Matthewson in establishing the San Francisco *Whig and Com-*

---

[1] David. G. Robinson, *Comic Songs: or Hits at San Francisco*, 32.

mercial Advertiser, with Frank M. Pixley and Louis R. Lull as its
editors. In the single year of its existence, the paper had prospered, thanks largely to a lucrative city printing contract.

Like Lola, Hull was Irish and an entertaining conversation-
alist. Sloppy in dress, dissipated, and not at all good-looking, it
must have been his wit that attracted Montez. A fellow journalist, James Ayers, once characterized him as a good writer
and one of the best-natured fellows ever to straddle a tripod
while composing type.

After stops in Acapulco, San Diego and Monterey, *Northerner* passed through the Golden Gate at first light on May 21,
1853. Because the passage of time in those early years of San
Francisco was marked by the arrival and departure of the
steamers, the signal station which then sat atop Telegraph Hill
no doubt displayed, for all to see, the symbol announcing the
arrival of a sidewheeler—two long black boards, extended like
outstretched arms on either side of a black pole.

By 6:30 A.M., the ship was safely moored alongside Long
Wharf, also known as Commercial Street, which extended
some 2,000 feet out into the bay. At the time, a good portion
of the city was built on such piers or streets, that branched out
over 3,266 new "water lots." This extension of the city—centered around Commercial, Pacific, Jackson, Clay and California streets—was still being filled in over the remains of some
of the ships abandoned by their crews in the first giddy days of
the Gold Rush. The waters of the bay, which originally lapped
at the edge of Montgomery Street, had successively been made
to recede to Sansome, Battery and Front streets. As the
wharves were covered by fill dirt and sand, streets were extended, graded, and then planked or cobbled, and many of the
existing wooden buildings were raised by means of screws to
the level of the new grade.

This newly-wrought "Bagdad By The Bay" was a precarious
place in which to live. It had already been razed by six huge fires

between December 24, 1849 and June 22, 1851. Moreover, although there had yet been no damaging earthquakes, the sure knowledge existed, even then, that an upheaval of devastating proportions would ultimately strike the city. Just before Lola's arrival, Mariano Vallejo had told a newspaper about the shock that had occurred in 1810 at the site of the future city. Vallejo said it had been strong enough to have laid all the fancy new structures which were then going up "as low as Solomon's temple." The editor therefore warned the sinful people of San Francisco not to pile the stories upon their buildings too high, since one of these days an earthquake would fetch them down. He cautioned those who slept in the fourth stories "to put their boots where they can get at them easily."[2]

California in those early days was largely a male society, and San Francisco's population of some 50,000, floating and permanent, was no exception. One fellow who came there was struck by its many "spiritualists, jugglers, modern Don Quixotes, pickpockets, public speakers, hucksters, Brazilian monkeys, virtuosos and trained parrots," all striving to fill their pockets by quick and adventuresome speculations. "Hustle!" this man said, "is the word which is here symbolical of all earthly wisdom."[3]

Mostly young, far from their homes in the East, and without female companionship, California's men lived the hairy-chested life. To celebrate their masculinity, a good many gave up shaving. To save money, they washed their own clothes; white shirts were usually discarded in favor of those made of more practical red flannel or calico. Often a man's dressiest

---

[2]Sacramento *Union*, Oct. 8, 1853, Dec. 26, 1858; James J. Ayers, *Gold and Sunshine*, 98; Peter W. Van der Pas, "The Lola Montez Homes," 18; Leman, 239; San Jose (CA) *The Pioneer*, Aug. 15, 1900; *Nevada* (City) *Journal*, Jan. 21, 1853; Los Angeles *Star*, June 19, 1852, July 16, 1853; New Orleans *True Delta*, Aug. 9, 1853; S.F. *Alta*, May 25, 1858; S.F. *Daily Evening News*, Aug. 31, 1854.

[3]Miska Hauser, "Adventures of Miska Hauser," *Musical Courier*, 59:4, p. 5; also S.F. *Daily Placer Times and Transcript*, June 28, 1952, May 26, May 10, 1853; Sacramento *Union*, May 23, 1853.

outfit would consist of a pair of fringed buckskin pants, red silk sash, fancy shirt and a coat of buckskin trimmed with bell buttons. Broad-brimmed felt hats were common headgear, and often a revolver, Bowie knife or a pair of foot-long skins could be seen slung from the hips of these two-fisted fellows come West to seek their fortune.

There was but little choice for them in entertainments, so most chose to drink and gamble. In San Francisco, there were well over five hundred places where liquor was sold, many of which were also gaming halls. In the heart of the city, around Portsmouth Plaza alone, stood the El Dorado, Bella Union, Rendezvous, Empire, Parker House and the Verandah. These lavishly-decorated emporiums were usually fitted-up in Oriental splendor with huge nude figures, elegant mirrors from floor to ceiling, and elaborate glass chandeliers to illuminate patrons in dazzling brilliance. Long rows of leather-covered mahogany tables were piled with tempting heaps of glittering silver and gold coins, nuggets, slugs, and bags of dust. At one end of the hall could usually be found a handsome bar where sumptuous free lunches were served. There also, at two-bits a glass, a visiting miner might build up his courage before losing the earnings of months of hard toil and privation.

A popular myth holds that for days there had been little else talked of in the gambling halls than the coming of this most fascinating of women, Lola Montez. A throng of over 7,000 sex-starved, cheering men is supposed to have been at the wharf to greet her, and tradition has hundreds of them running excitedly alongside her open carriage on the route to her hotel. But, sad to say, Lola's coming was much more prosaic. While there were reports as much as a year earlier that she might visit California, in actual fact, her arrival, without prior theater bookings, came as a complete surprise, drew no crowds, and was noted by only a few lines in the papers.

The fictitious story of her advent, as well as much of the other imaginative history concerning Montez's California years can be traced to a trio of articles published in San Francisco papers toward the end of the last century. These Sunday-supplement features were purportedly based on the reminiscences of a certain Dora Knapp, recounted a short time before she died at Pomona. Each successive article seems to have fed upon and embellished the previous one. Whoever made the stories up—whether Knapp or, more likely, inventive writers—obviously did so with only the vaguest knowledge of the real Montez history, since they contain gross errors of time, place and fact. As an example, Knapp and her husband are supposed to have traveled as fellow cabin passengers with Lola to California, but one can search in vain for their names on the list of arrivals.

Although the coming of Montez was a surprise, once she had arrived there was indeed great excitement and curiosity to see this person so much talked about throughout Europe and America for the past several years. Especially, said one wag, among the "quid nuncs" who frequented the Bella Union Saloon.[4] The interest of Bella Union tipplers was no doubt heightened in succeeding days by publication of the details of her most recent problems: the ludicrous donnybrook at New Orleans's Varieties Theater; the pitched battle in Cincinnati with her agent and traveling companion, John Jones, and news of the death of that other former "agent" Edward Willis.

The earliest of San Francisco's newspapers were often as careless with the truth as were those later, in Dora Knapp's era. During Lola's time there, the city had ten or more dailies, almost equalling the number being published in New York

[4]Sacramento *Union*, May 23, 1853; S.F. *Golden Era*, May 22, 1853. The Dora Knapp stories are in the San Francisco *Daily Chronicle*, Jan. 17, 1897; San Francisco *Bulletin*, Aug. 14, 1897; S.F. *Morning Call*, June 17, 1900.

City with its half a million inhabitants. To survive, each paper tried to outdo its rival in the profuseness with which it catered to the appetites of its readers. There was no shortage of hyperbole, nonsense and vicious comment.

But, perhaps because of her well-known habit of assailing overly-clever editors, Lola's presence was generally treated with great courtesy by San Francisco's fourth estate. Pat Hull's *Whig*, as might be expected, predicted that she would doubtless succeed in California, since she had come in a quiet, unobtrusive manner. The *Herald* noted that everyone was in a fever to catch a glimpse of this "lioness" and "world-bewildering puzzle", who had "savaged hearts and potentates, and editors, and public opinion, and ill-natured criticism, and what not!" The sedate and respectable *Daily Alta California* wondered who among its readers had not heard of Lola's "gallant spirit" and "independent and Republican nature," and of how she had been exiled because of her "troublesome Democracy." Calling her "the favorite of monarchs, of Patrician and Plebian...the fearless, the eccentric Lola," as "ready with the pen as with the steel, and dangerous with both," the editor urged a just and generous reception. "Gallantry," he said, "should not forget that she is a woman, and among strangers"[5]

No doubt basking in such a warm greeting, the countess put agent Henning to work negotiating with theater managers, and within a few days it was announced that she would open at the American Theater on Thursday, May 26, doing Lady Teazle in *The School For Scandal.*

It had only been a bit over three years earlier, in January 1850, that San Franciscans had seen the city's first theatrical performance. A company down from the Eagle Theater (a tent) in Sacramento had played at a place called Washington

---

[5] *San Francisco Herald,* May 22, 1853; *Alta,* May 22, 23, 1853; S.F. *Daily Whig* and *Commercial Advertiser,* May 23, 1853.

Dr. David Gorman
"Yankee" Robinson.
Courtesy, California State Library.

Hall, on the second floor of a building across from Portsmouth Plaza. In succeeding weeks, there were occasional productions held in such transitory places as the Olympic Circus Amphitheater, Theater Nationale, the New Phoenix and the Phoenix Exchange. After these tenuous beginnings, larger theaters had been erected by two dauntless entrepreneurs, Thomas Maguire and Dr. David G. "Yankee" Robinson.

Maguire, a former bar owner from New York City, opened his Parker House Hotel and saloon on the east side of Portsmouth Plaza in October 1850, fitting up the second floor as a 500-seat theater he called the Jenny Lind. It was consumed in the great fire of May 3-4, 1851, so Maguire started building a second playhouse bearing the same name on a nearby lot. This one burned down the following month before it could even open, but Maguire, undaunted, cleared the rubble and erected a third Jenny Lind, this one of brick, on the site of his old Parker House. The imposing three-story structure was used for theatricals from October 1851 until being sold to the city for use as a city hall in July 1852, in what many thought was a swindle. Subsequently, Maguire had built and was still operating his San Francisco Theater—or Hall, as it was sometimes called—on Washington Street between Kearny and Montgomery.

But it was "Yankee" Robinson who would figure most prominently in Lola Montez's California adventure. This forty-eight-year-old native of Maine had graduated from Yale as a physician, but was really more inclined toward a theatrical career. After touring the East doing his temperance play, *The Reformed Drunkard*, he came to San Francisco, where he set up in medical practice and opened a drugstore on Portsmouth Square. In May 1850 he built a small "Dramatic Museum" on Montgomery Street only to see it destroyed by fire in less than a month. Unbowed, he and James Evrard, formerly of Mitchell's Olympic Theater in New York City, built the "Little Dramatic" on California Street and opened it that July 15 after the city had been without a theater of any sort for several months.

Robinson used his small theaters for vaudeville and topical satires, writing the skits, stories and songs, and acting many of the parts himself. Both he and Evrard were of a class known as "Yankee" comedians, but the tall, angular Robinson had a particularly quiet style of humor which was more natural than most of the others. He was immensely popular, despite his habit of delivering temperance lectures between acts, and his somewhat bawdy language. He even managed to get elected alderman in 1850 after a campaign of biting satire delivered from his stage against incumbent city officials.

In February 1851, Robinson tore down his Little Dramatic and built a larger version, but it operated for only nineteen days before it too was—destroyed along with the original Jenny Lind and Adelphi theaters—in the huge May fire. Thus floored again, but not beaten, the doctor journeyed with a troupe to Marysville for a few weeks, and thence to Nevada

City where, on June 20, he produced the first play ever witnessed in the state's gold-bearing mountains. Returning to San Francisco, he and a partner borrowed $65,000 and began building themselves a new brick theater. This would be the American, in which Lola Montez was engaged to perform.

Located between California and Sacramento Streets, a bit back from the east side of Sansome, the American had been opened in late October 1851, a mere 35 days after ground was broken, with James Stark as its first manager. The grandiloquent opening ceremonies had included a "Grand National Overture," followed by the salutary address customary at such premieres, written by Robinson and delivered by Mrs. Stark. As she spoke, the hurriedly-erected house, built on landfill over what had recently been the bay, settled several inches, carrying a surprised audience with it.

Unhappily, within a few months, Robinson was forced to give up the American in bankruptcy. He stayed on for a time as lessee, but was at odds with the new owners over their policy requiring performances every night. On one memorable February, 1852 evening, he showed his dissatisfaction by treating patrons to an impromptu production quite typical of his humorous insouciance: a man called "Charley" was enticed onto the stage to dance a hoedown; the property man was dragged out of the wings to sing a song; another amateur from the audience impersonated a backwoods actor, and so forth. Several months after this incident an embittered Robinson put aside the stage for a time to engage in other enterprises.[6]

[6]San Francisco *Alta*, Jan. 18, 24, Feb. 2, Mar. 6, 23, July 4, 15, 1850; *Alta* steamer edn., Aug. 1, Oct. 31, 1850; *S.F. Herald*, May 31, June 11, Aug. 16, Sept. 10, 22, Oct. 5-21, Nov. 10, 1851, Jan. 22, Feb. 20, Mar. 28, Nov. 5, 1852, Nov. 20, 1853; Sacramento *Union*, Nov. 9, 1854; Sacramento *Placer Times and Transcript*, June 4, 1853; *N.Y. Herald*, Dec. 2, 1851; Marysville (CA) *Daily Evening Herald*, May 22, 1851; Edmond M. Gagey, *The San Francisco Stage*, 5-10; Leman, 233-34; David Dempsey with R.P. Baldwin, *The Triumphs and Trials of Lotta Crabtree*, 99-102; Bordman, 454, 583. One source indicates there may have been a theater in San Francisco as early as Oct. 31, 1849 (Franklin A. Buck, *A Yankee Trader in the Gold Rush*, 53).

At the time of Lola Montez's arrival, the American was the largest and most elegant of San Francisco's playhouses. Sixty feet of its 160 by 54 foot interior was taken up by private dressing rooms, the green room and a stage which was considered to be as big as any in the United States. Each side had fourteen entrances and it was well-equipped with "traps" in the boards and extensive machinery for its magnificent drop curtain and scenes. For sound effects, there were somewhat primitive rain and thunder machines and other devices.

The American's interior boasted grand Corinthian columns, drapes to cover the walls, and thick, soft carpets. The ceiling arched equally from the building's dome in every direction, and, at its center, was placed a revolving sun, covered with burnished gold. Machinery turned the ornament slowly on its axis and, by candle light gave the impression of its rays shooting out in all directions, to be lost in an encircling wealth of brilliant clouds. On either side of this elaborate gadget were two spread eagles, from whose beaks descended two chandeliers.

Although plans were well underway for lighting the city with gas from a plant then abuilding at First and Howard, lighting effects at the American were still dependent upon candles or whale oil lamps. The footlights, shielded by rows of metal scallops, always posed the threat of catching props and long costumes afire. Because of the ever-present fire hazard, the building had been designed to allow the audience to evacuate within three minutes and, out back, sat a capacious reservoir from which water could be pumped throughout the entire house, as well as to flood the iron roof.

The theater had just reopened a few weeks earlier, after an extensive rework to improve ventilation, acoustics and seating. A handsome new dress circle had been installed on the ground floor, along with the parquet; a new "family circle" was now built into the second tier and, with the third floor gallery above this, over 2,000 patrons could now be accommodated.

Since the theater was one the few alternatives to gambling and carousing in the bordellos, California's men were enthusiastic and frequent patrons. San Francisco audiences were generally a hodge-podge of merchants, mechanics, clerks, sailors of all nations, and miners down from the diggings to see the town. Most men of that era, while rugged and individualistic on the one hand, were also exceedingly sentimental and chivalrous, and, at least outwardly, preferred their women, including those on the stage, to be modest and chaste. Their tastes in drama ran the gamut from the darkest of tragedy to the lowest of farce—and, usually, both could be found on the same program. A Shakespearean tragedy might be followed by a preposterous afterpiece such as John Morton's *Box and Cox*, or perhaps that California favorite, *Did You Ever Send Your Wife to San Jose?*

The knowledge that the performing arts could prove very profitable had drawn some surprisingly good talent to California. The day Lola arrived, her old rival for the attentions of Prince Como, the queenly Catherine Sinclair, was just finishing an engagement in San Francisco. Mezzo-soprano Catherine Hayes, the "Swan of Erin," had also been performing that month at the American, and had just left California, nearly $30,000 richer for her 40-odd concerts.

Even the stock companies in California were generally of a high caliber. These troupes, whose rosters changed frequently, provided the framework for visiting artists, and each actor was usually hired to play some special type of character or characters: the Old Man, the Heavy Father or Heavy Lead, the Heavy Woman, the Juvenile Lead, to name but a few. The stock companies operated on true repertory basis, sometimes with a nightly change of bill.

The managers of the American, John Lewis Baker and J. W. Thoman, had put together a competent and versatile group to support Lola. As was often then the custom, Baker and Thoman were themselves working actors who had leased the theater from the owners for a specific period of time. One of the best performers in the company was Baker's talented and popular wife, Alexina Fisher Baker. She and Baker had arrived in California in February 1852, both well known in the East, and had been lessees at the Jenny Lind and Adelphi theaters before coming to manage the renovated American. Mrs. Marietta Judah, the small, stocky, square-faced grand old woman of the Western stage was another noted stock player in the American's company. A widow who had come to California at the behest of Thomas Maguire, her considerable skills ranged from comedy to Lady Macbeth.

Another of Baker's talented group was young Henry Coad, formerly of the New Orleans stage. A real-life drama in which he played a major role tells us a good deal about the occasional goings-on backstage, even in those days of copper-plated convention. In January 1851, Coad was involved in an affair with Mrs. Hambleton, an actress whose husband abused her physically. One night at the Jenny Lind, the play *Pizarro* had just commenced when Hambleton's husband confronted the lovers and made Coad promise to quit the country instantly. Coad left the theater, and Mrs. Hambleton, believing that she had been abandoned, took her life by swallowing a large dose of corrosive poison. A few hours later, when he learned of her death, Coad himself took poison, but the timely administration of an emetic by friends saved him. Needless to say, that evening's entertainment was cancelled.[7]

---

[7]Sacramento *Union*, May 19, 1853; Gagey, 11-14, 28-29; *N.Y. Herald*, Nov. 18, 1851; *S.F. Journal*, May 12, 1853; Sacramento *Times and Transcript*, May 10-25, 1853; *S.F. Alta*, May 13, 16, 1853; *S.F. Herald*, Nov. 16, 1851, Feb. 7, 1852; Sacramento *Transcript*, Jan. 16-18, 1851; Stockton (CA) *Weekly Times*, Jan 18, 1851.

In the Eastern states Lola Montez had usually been on the "star system," which paid her eighty percent of a theater's gross—some $200 to $600 per night. There were reports that her share at the American would be two-thirds. Whatever her cut might actually have been, seat prices were hiked substantially for Lola's debut and, following the pattern she had set in the East, she would insist on the higher prices until such time as audiences began to dwindle.

It was sometimes the custom in those days to hold an auction of the choicest seats in the house when some special celebrity was scheduled to open. Six months earlier the sum of $1,150—the highest ever in California—had been paid for a seat at Catherine Hayes' first concert. And, just before our delightfully-racy dancer had first opened in New York City, such an auction had obtained steep ticket prices from an unusual number of that city's "Smiths" and "Joneses." But, much to Lola's displeasure, the auction held by manager John Baker on the day before her debut in San Francisco yielded no such handsome return. A certain Captain Bowman bought the first seat for a mere $65, and the few others sold commanded very little more than box office prices.[8]

For a relative novice at acting to open with *The School For Scandal*, so well-known to theatergoers of the day, took a certain bravado. But no one had ever accused Montez of timidity, and audiences in the East had seemed to enjoy her portrayal of Lady Teazle. However, this first San Francisco performance by Lola proved to be, at best, merely adequate. When the curtain rose that evening at a quarter of eight, the American was by no means full. Perhaps upset at the disappointing turnout, Montez muffed some of her lines, and took time to warm to the

---

[8]San Francisco *Alta*, May 25-26, 1853; Sacramento *Union*, May 27, 1853; Stockton (CA) *San Joaquin Daily Republican*, June 1, 1853; Gagey, 33; *N.Y. Herald*, Dec. 28, 1851, May 25, 1852; *Panama Star*, May 6, 1853; Sacramento *Times and Transcript*, June 28, 1852, May 24, 1853.

part, but she was nonetheless heartily applauded at the end and called out before the curtain, where she made a flattering speech to the audience.

The newspaper drama critics the following day were quick to recognize her lack of acting training, but they found other qualities to praise: grace, vitality, her "eclat," the exquisite and tasteful toilette, her buoyant and beautiful walk, and the carriage of her head.[9]

While Lola's Lady Teazle had been merely nice, the program for her second and third performances was totally to the liking of San Francisco's men. Despite the price of private boxes having been raised to $25, on both nights every seat in the house was occupied by the time the stock company began with its usual farce. Lola followed with *Yelva* in which, ably supported by Judah and Coad, she portrayed in pantomime a dumb and suffering orphan girl. After *Yelva*, as was her custom, Montez shrewdly kept the audience fretting impatiently while the stock company did another farce, then, finally, it was time for what everyone had really come to see—the notorious "Spider Dance." As always, there was an anxious flutter in the crowd as the moment approached and, when the dancer appeared on stage, she was greeted with a storm of applause.

In America, this dance had been billed variously as "*La Tarantula,*" the "Spanish *Tarantula,*" "*El Zapateado,*" and the "Neapolitan." Whatever it might have been called on a particular night, the routine was Lola's unique treatment of the *Tarantella,* whose origins were in the south of Italy. Such dances with a Latin flavor had been the rage for several years and were performed by anyone who could shake a leg. And nobody could shake one quite like Lola.

Her lubricious interpretation of the Italian dance depicted the shocking discovery of imaginary spiders in the folds of her

[9]Sacramento *Times and Transcript,* May 26-28, June 13, 1853; S.F. *Alta,* May 26-30, 1853; *S.F. Herald,* May 27-30, 1853; Sacramento *Union,* June 4, 1853.

dress, and the subsequent series of maneuvers required to shake them off. She usually danced it in flesh-colored tights and tiers of multicolored petticoats, with her hair at shoulder length. Her presentation varied widely from performance to performance, according to her mood and the enthusiasm of the audience. Sometimes she would spread out on her feet and hands, herself a tarantula, and bounce grotesquely from one side of the stage to the other.

So exaggerated were her movements that often the stage floor was watered down to prevent a bad fall such as she had once taken in New Orleans. Lola usually ended the dance and demolished the last spider by stomping on a bouquet or another object thrown on stage by admirers. The eroticism—such as was by today's standards—never failed to generate immense enthusiasm.

Although one San Franciscan found the dance "indescribable," most who saw it had no such trouble. "Fresh," "thoroughly Spanish," "eccentric," "novel"—these were just a few of the many adjectives used to explain it. One fellow thought it was "most graceful." Another agreed that "while there may have been grace enough, and poetry of motion, and all that, a pretty foot and ankle did surely never before cut up such antics." One man, who had come up to the Bay City from Stockton, told the folks back home that the frenetic Lola had jumped around the stage, stamping and kicking "in a very exciting manner," and when shaking her petticoats to rid herself of the spider, her action was "so extremely natural that one almost imagines he sees the 'varmint' itself." Still another admirer concurred that the dance was "as natural as if the whole scene were real."[10]

When Lola had performed the dance at Hartford, Connecticut, a year earlier, one sniffing Puritan had said that "she

----

[10]San Francisco *Alta*, June 15, 1853; Sacramento *Times and Transcript*, May 28, 1853; Stockton *San Joaquin Republican*, June 1, 1853; New Orleans *Picayune*, Jan. 25, 1853; S.F. *Bulletin*, Sept. 23, 1916.

flounces about like a stuck pig, and clenches her short clothes, raising them nearly to her waist, while with a thin, scrawny leg she keeps up a constant thumping upon the stage, as if she was in a slight spasm."[11]

But the best description to have survived comes from Pat Hull's newspaper—perhaps written by himself:

> Up went the curtain, and on came Lola, fermenting the pit, agitating the gallery, and sensationising the dress circle. And the Spider Dance! has not every son of Columbia witnessed the Spider Dance? No? Well then...Lola comes in—sails in—flies in—arrayed in a costume to which Joseph's coat could never think of comparing. She stands an instant full of fire, action and abandon. One is reminded at first glance of a full-blooded Arabian—eloquent with force and freedom. Lola apparently represents a country girl in some flowery mead. She unwittingly gets into one of those huge nests of spiders found during the Spring time in the meadows, with a long radius of leading spires and fibres stretching away into an infinity of space. She commences to dance and the cobwebs intangle her ankles. The myriads of spiders...begin to 'colonize.'
>
> The music, a slow measured, but a fascinating amalgamation of polka, waltz, march, mazurka and jig, conforms admirably to the step. The spiders accumulate, and the danseuse stamps. They appear in myriads—hairy monsters with five clawed feelers and nimble shanks—they 'crawl and sprattle' about the stage, invading the fringe of Milady's pettycoats, and taking such unwarranted liberties, that the spectator imagines an inextricable mass of cobwebs and enraged spiders, and would sympathize with the demoiselle, but she seems to take it so easily herself, that one quickly jumps to the conclusion that she is enough for them. It is Lola versus the spiders. After a series of examinations and shaking of dresses, she succeeds in getting the imaginary intruders away—apparently stamps daylight out of the last of the ten thousand, and does it with so much naivete, that we feel a sort of satisfaction at the triumph. The picture winds up with Lola's victory, and she glides from the stage overwhelmed with applause, and smashed spiders, and radiant with parti-colored skirts, smiles, graces, cobwebs and glory.[12]

---

[11]*Nevada* (City) *Journal,* July 17, 1852.
[12]San Francisco *Whig,* June 3, 1853.

Another vivid description of the finale comes to us from former lover Ned Willis. In his widely-published letter of 1852, previously alluded to, the embittered man asked facetiously that Lola obtain for him a commission from the Congress to sculpt her statue, to be placed atop the Capitol building. "I would suggest the pose in your Tarentella," Willis said, "when after having crushed the scorpion, you rise suddenly on the points of your toes, with the triumphant air of a lion over his prey, to say, with a look once seen never forgotten, now then, I have done it!"[13]

A day of rest on May 29, allowed Lola to bask in the glow of her many favorable reviews. While some conceded that she had portrayed Yelva with truthfulness, it was not her acting that got raves. Said the *Golden Era:* "Lola Montez the artiste, the politician...and the fair 'shoulder-striker' is among us, and...her name has attracted...the most brilliant and overflowing audiences ever witnessed in this city and who have given her talents a most unequivocal endorsement...We can't say that we admire Lola's acting, but we do think her dancing is heavenly." The *Alta* critic agreed that "As an actress, Lola pleases, but in the dance she excites!"[14]

Even some of San Francisco's few women were anxious to see Lola's dancing, regardless of its blatantly sexual character. Here are the thoughts of young Mary Jane Megquier, who led a drab life cooking and cleaning in a boarding house:

> Lola Montes is making quite a stir here now but many say that her playing is...not proper for respectable ladies to attend but I do want to see her very much. Mr. Clark said in dancing the spider dance...where she performs the antics of one with a tarantula upon their person...some thought she was obliged to look rather higher than was proper in so public a place.[15]

While enjoying the favorable press, Lola also took time to

---

[13]*New York Herald,* Jan. 13, 1852.
[14]San Francisco *Golden Era,* May 29, and *Alta,* May 31, 1853.
[15]Mary Jane Megguier, *Apron Full of Gold,* 80, letter of May 31, 1853.

revel in the attentions lavished on her by San Francisco's panting men. She was frequently seen at the Pioneer Track spring
races surrounded by an adoring cluster, paying court. Her
famous name had been given to yachts and horses everywhere
she went. Likewise now, at San Francisco, a gray mare was
dubbed "Lola Montez," and on the second racing day it won
the feature event. When this same nag triumphed again on the
fourth and final day, Lola won $500 betting on her namesake.
Afterward, she was escorted to the stables where, with a pretty
speech, she generously presented the horse's owner with a magnificent horse blanket. Within a few days the value of "Lola
Montez" had jumped to an estimated $3,500, enabling her
owner to raffle the mare off at $10 per ticket.[16]

But not everyone in the city was captivated by the Montez
glitz. The company at Thomas Maguire's rival San Francisco
Theater, perhaps, saw her merely as an interloper, drawing all
the big crowds and headlines. The lessee there, Junius Brutus
Booth Jr., was, after all, the son and namesake of America's
foremost tragedian, who had died recently while returning to
the East after an acting tour of California. The younger Booth
and his wife had managed the third Jenny Lind for Maguire
until it was sold in 1852, and then had assumed their present
post.

Two others in Booth's company also most likely resented the
upstart actress Lola Montez. No tyros themselves, Caroline
and William B. Chapman were a brother and sister who came
from a family which had been on the stage for generations.

---

[16]Stockton *Republican*, June 1, 4, 1853; Sacramento *Times and Transcript*, May 28, June 13,
1853; S.F. *Herald*, May 30, 1853; S.F. *Alta*, May 28-30, 1853. Located on the ground now
bordered by Mission, Folsom, 24th and 26th streets, the Pioneer Racetrack was reached
via a plank road, boasting a four-horse omnibus line, which wound from California and
Kearny streets in the heart of the city, through the sparsely-populated sandhills to the Mission Dolores. This fine toll road was San Francisco's grand boulevard and promenade, and
every pleasant day brought forth throngs of people to take the air. (John S. Hittell, *History
of the City of San Francisco*, 152.)

Samuel Chapman, their father, had been for 30 years the actor-manager of the Theater Royal, Covent Garden, London, where his entire brood had performed. In 1827, he had emigrated with his wife and three of his children to New York City where they continued acting.

About 1830, the Chapmans had begun operating one of America's earliest river showboats. After testing the concept with a flatboat, Sam took his family to Pittsburgh and embarked them in a side-wheel steamer which had been fitted out as a combination theater and floating home. As "Chapman's Floating Palace" he took the boat up and down the Mississippi and its tributaries, putting in at any wharf where it seemed likely an audience could be gathered. The family offered a mixed bag of tragedy, high-toned comedy, farces and even the occasional song and dance between acts.

When Sam died, the family scattered. Son George Chapman and his actress wife Mary were among the first performers to come to California, arriving in 1849. They worked the earliest theaters in every city and town of the state, and were now members of Lewis Baker's company supporting Lola at the American. Caroline and William, known popularly as "Uncle Billy," had arrived in San Francisco in March 1852, along with Billy's wife Phoebe (a fine organist) and sister Sarah and her actor husband William B. Hamilton. The entire family group used San Francisco as their home base. Billy bought a few lots on Telegraph Hill, and built cottages on them, in one of which he, his wife and Caroline lived.

Caroline was the Chapman best-loved by theater patrons, and she probably had performed more often in California than any other woman. She was not only a fine dancer, but an actress of great ability, who had been prominent in Burton's *corps dramatique* during her New York City days. Her versatility encompassed Shakespearean tragedy, comedy, and even the lowest of burlesque. She played the hand organ, and often so charmed the audience that it stood in the aisles and sang along with her. Although small and plain-looking, with a somewhat weak voice, she nonetheless had a certain dash and graceful offhand-edness that endeared her to audiences. As fellow actor Walter Leman said of her: although she lacked "feminine beauty," she was "beautiful in soul and brilliant in talent."[17]

In his childhood at Covent Garden, "Uncle Billy" Chapman had honed his skills under the tutelage of the famed Sarah Siddons and her brother, John Philip Kemble. Later, he had sung comic songs at the English Opera House. With his wonderful sense of the impromptu, he was best known as a low comedian. At New York's Bowery Theatre he made his American debut in 1827 as Billy Lackaday in *Smiles and Tears.* Later, before coming to California, he had helped manage the Walnut Street The-atre in Philadelphia. This eccentric little old man of 66 years had been on the American stage a quarter-century by the time Lola Montez arrived in California and began upstaging Junius Booth's troupe at the San Francisco Theater.

After seeing the brash interloper's initial success, "June" Booth and the theater's owners decided to close and refurbish it so as to be more competitive. Booth also thought it was time to begin capitalizing on the bothersome Lola's advent in Cali-fornia. And who better to help than that master of parody, "Yankee" Robinson?

The doctor was again available after his brief but busy sab-batical from the theater. Right after leaving the stage he had tried his hand at auctioneering in San Francisco, but failed when fellow businessmen found his country bumpkin antics irritating and ineffectual.

Then, for awhile, he had engaged in the manufacture of a patent medicine called "Mountain Extract For the Cure of Fever and Ague." The fanciful advertisements for this snake oil

---

[17]Leman, 258; also S.F. *Herald,* Mar. 15, 24, 1852, June 12, 1853; Sacramento *Daily Democratic State Journal,* Nov. 13, 1857; *Times and Transcript,* Feb. 14-18, 1853; Gagey, 29.

portrayed an angel descending from heaven to present a bottle
of it to a poor miner bent nearly to the ground by disease.
Although "Yankee" assured his friends he had orders for the
tonic "from Oregon to Cape Horn," the project failed miserably within a short time. The restless Robinson was soon back
composing and singing songs for fifteen dollars a night, joking
to his audiences that he'd "been improving his voice by putting
it in soak."[18] His wife, a former actress, was constantly con-
cerned about her husband's heavy drinking and his incessant
cursing, but the doctor evidently had the power to assuage her
easily with his wit.

Junius Booth was quick to take advantage of Robinson's
return to the theatrical arena. On the evening of May 29, just
before he closed the San Francisco Theater for remodeling,
Booth had his younger brother, Edwin, and Harriet Carpenter
sing a new Robinson song spoofing the imperious Lola, her
theater manager, Baker, and the events surrounding her first
few days in California. The ditty went like this:

> Oh, have you heard the news of late
> Of what has happened in our State?—
> There has arrived a monarch mate,
> Imported from Bavaria!
>
> If you would like to see the sight,
> And ain't afraid the crittur'll bite,
> Just pay five dollars any night,
> And Baker'll get the show up right!
>
> She'll glance at you with those sparkling eyes,
> And other means she will devise
> To make you puff her to the skies,
> While she the spiders will surprise!
>
> And all the Bakers in the town
> Will find the Countess does it Brown,

---

[18]Megguier, 62, 73; Dempsey, 101; McMinn, 148, 153; Gagey, 26, 27; S.F. *Journal*,
Sept. 3, 1853; Bordman, 133, 166; Helen Throop Pratt, "Souvenirs of an Interesting
Family," 282-85; *Nevada* (City) *Journal*, Nov. 8, 20, 27, 1851.

When with the dust they must come down—
To the Countess of Bavaria!

A Baker once, as I am told,
Became so fond of shining gold
That he at public auction sold
The Countess of Bavaria!

Altho' he got but small advance,
Yet he went in and stood his chance,
Relying on that Spider Dance
To put the public in a trance;

But when to see her they did go,
The ladies thought, but didn't know,
The Countess lacked some calico,
Which would improve the classic show!

Altho' some men were fairly sold,
Yet Lola thanks them for their gold;
Her dancing knocks all dancing cold—
She learned it in Bavaria!

That classic play-house down below,
To which all moral people go,
Requires no trump of fame to blow—
The Countess of Bavaria!

Altho' her fame was often told,
The morning that her tickets sold
She did poor Baker curse and scold
Because they brought so little gold!

While frightened Lewis did protest
That with them he had done his best,
For all his supes [supernumeraries] he had well dress'd,
And they had each out-bid the rest!

But all his efforts were in vain,
And as his nose, to him 'twas plain,
That gold would not be showered like rain—
On the Countess of Bavaria![19]

---

[19]Robinson, 24-26; also S.F. *News*, Dec. 15, 1853; S.F. *Daily Evening Picayune*, Mar. 15, 1852; Sacramento *Times and Transcript*, July 28, 1852; Cincinnati *Enquirer*, Mar. 24, 1853. Another of the elder Booth's sons was John Wilkes Booth, assassin of President Lincoln.

This jabbing little morceau would prove to be only a fore-taste of the satire yet to come.

At her fourth appearance, Lola introduced Californians to her apologia, *Lola Montez in Bavaria*, which, it will be recalled, had been the vehicle for her first attempt at acting almost a year earlier in New York City. Lewis Baker encountered serious problems in staging the play, and he had to hire some fifty supernumeraries off the street to fill the cast roster of 34, and flesh out the crowd scenes. The stock company, given little time to rehearse, performed miserably on opening night. But, all this not withstanding, Lola carried it off, aided by a strong performance from Henry Coad playing the foppish Count Papen, private secretary and adjutant to Ludwig.

A well-filled house received the production with great applause, but it was largely for Lola, not the play. Quite a num-ber of critics who saw the lengthy production, as had been the case in the East, thought it had no dramatic merit and was dull, pointless and poorly-constructed. Even a reviewer for Pat Hull's *Whig* dubbed it "rather prosy," and admitted that he might have taken a pleasant nap, except for "the close proximi-ty of a Goth who amused himself...making experiments in marksmanship with tobacco juice"[20] at his patent leather shoes.

Another who saw it was just as cynical in summing up the play's threadbare significance. The "principal 'teachings of his-tory'...which Americans are to learn and profit by," he said, "are that kings are not such bad old gentlemen after all, and...a great deal better than our Presidents...[and, that] the best form of government would be an old king with a plebeian ministry, and a foreign dancing girl for counsellor of state."[21]

Montez would always insist that the play's characters and events had been sketched true to history, but, as one San Fran-cisco reviewer pointed out, only a fool would present herself in

---

[20]San Francisco *Whig*, June 3, 1853.
[21]San Francisco *Bulletin*, Aug. 12, 1856.

a bad light. Another wag could only agree that the piece was "strictly histrionic."[22]

Still, as with *Yelva*, the Bavarian drama generally appealed to American audiences. Many persons truly believed Lola to be a great politician and devoted republican, and credited her with infusing the first germ of democracy among the Bavarian masses, despite that "nincompoop" and "royal blockhead," Ludwig.[23] Thus, there were those who thought a stage production simply couldn't do justice to her career in Bavaria as a wily diplomat and able leader. Capitalizing on these notions, Lola always gave a rousing curtain speech after each performance, cleverly conceived to appeal the republican spirit which beat so strongly in nineteenth-century American hearts.

Lola's drama, of course, gave her most of the clever repartee, and some thought it was impossible to criticize her acting, for who could say that anybody could portray her better than herself? But, as had been the case in the East, she was generally praised for her spirited, unstudied and original style, and even more so for her independent spirit. The stricken *Alta* critic waxed poetic:

> With her there is no impossibility...She has a...disregard for foolish formality which is a merit, not to the soulless sensuality only, but likewise to the independent thinker, who recognizes something holy in man's nature. Yes, Lola...has swallowed formulas. She thinks that her own spirit teaches as correct a rule of conduct as traditions and old customs, which for her have no authority. Lola is singular, but it is her right.[24]

The Bavarian play was repeated four more times. On its final night, Montez also danced for the first time in California her

---

[22]San Francisco *Herald,* May 30, 1853.

[23]San Francisco *Herald,* Nov. 8, 1851.

[24]San Francisco *Alta,* May 31, 1853, also May 30, June 1, 5, 1853; Sacramento *Times and Transcript,* May 31, 1853; Stockton *Republican,* June 11, 1853; *New York Herald,* Feb. 22, Apr. 6, May 25-30, July 11, 1852; S.F. *Golden Era,* June 5, 1853; S.F. *Herald,* May 31, June 1, 1853; S.F. *Bulletin,* Aug. 9, 21, 1856.

"Sailor's Hornpipe," which was sometimes also billed as the "American Sailor's Dance." This production was staged using devices which San Franciscans were not at all used to seeing in a terpsichorean exhibition—elaborate, changing backdrops; nautical properties, and sound effects which imitated the ocean's angry roar and the howling of a storm. Dressed in a boy's costume which set off her radiant beauty, Lola pantomimed, in turn, a young seaman climbing an imaginary vessel's rigging, being shipwrecked, struggling in the ocean and, finally, arriving safely on shore.

Some of her admirers noticed that her dancing that evening lacked its usual spirit and vivacity. For several days, in fact, Lola had been showing signs of illness and a flagging of her energies such as had been observed with some regularity since her coming to America. But, always the trouper, Montez carried it off. She completely captivated the audience at the dance's finish by waving a miniature American flag over her head, and then pressing it fervently to her lips. Responding to the thunderous applause that followed, in her curtain speech she called San Francisco, "the greatest place in the world."[25]

The next of Lola's plays to be introduced was one which had been a rousing success in the East. Performed June 6 and 7, *Maritana, or the Maid of Saragossa* was a drama about a well-known episode in the Spanish Peninsular War of 1804-1814, wherein a young woman of Saragossa fought heroically at the ramparts of the city against Napoleon's army to avenge her fallen lover. As well as the title role, Lola assumed two others: Gita, a Granadan gypsy, and Alphonso, a young guerrilla. As the latter, she was thought to be particularly fetching in the short jacket, loose trousers and broad sash of a Spanish mountaineer.

Since June 7 was billed as the last night of her original engagement, Montez "took a benefit"—her first in California.

[25]San Francisco *Alta*, June 4, 1853; S.F. *Herald*, June 5, 1853.

Much like today, the proceeds of such performances in 1853 were often given to charities. They might also be held in behalf of persons in distress, such as arriving overland immigrants, for departing performers or, as in Lola's case on that particular night, one who was simply popular.

Artists often gave more than one "last" performance, so nobody was surprised to see June 8 billed as another final night and benefit for the star. A crowded house watched her dance "El Olle" for the first time, along with "Spider Dance" and the second act of *Yelva*. It may be recalled that it was "El Olle" Lola chose for her first public appearance, back in 1844. Andalusian in character, the dance was a lively affair, punctuated frequently with pauses for graceful poses, each one of which "might prove a study for a sculptor," said one observer.[26]

By this time, Montez was still as popular as ever, her houses well-filled each night despite enormous ticket prices. We can get some insight into that feverish adoration, which caused young men to pack her performances wherever she went, from a newspaper article written by San Francisco humorist George Horatio Derby, who used the pen names "John Phoenix" and "Squibob."

Tongue-in-cheek, Squibob related how, after being assigned the important position of literary critic for the *Herald*, he had placed a cigar box in one corner of Parry's saloon, into which poetical contributions could be dropped—knowing that Parry's was "the favorite resort of the wits, literati and savants of the city."

He checked the box daily, after imbibing his morning glass of "bimbo" which he described as being a temperance drink of three parts root beer and two of water-gruel, "thickened with a little soft squash, and strained through a cane-bottomed

[26]San Francisco *Herald*, June 9, 1853, also June 4, 7; S.F. *Alta*, June 3-9, 1853, Aug. 10, 1856; Sacramento *Times and Transcript*, June 6-7, 1853; Stockton *Republican*, June 11, 1853; New Orleans *Picayune*, Jan. 23, 1853; S.F. *Sun*, June 2-3, 1853; S.F. *Golden Era*, June 5, 1853; Sacramento *Union*, July 11, 1853; *N.Y. Herald*, Feb. 12, 1852.

chair." For a time, the only contributions to the cigar box, Squibob said, were two or three "old soldiers" and a half-dollar deposited by an inebriated member of the previous legislature, whose friends had told him the box had been placed there "for the relief of distressed Chinese women."

Then there began to appear a number of "amatory and pathetic verses" inscribed to Lola. Squibob published the best of these, which he surmised had been contributed by some "impulsive young fellow," who, having gotten his hands on five dollars, had used it to buy a ticket to see Lola, "where he incontinently fell in love...and...hastily 'threw off' the poem," written doubtless on the back of a playbill, immediately after the conclusion of the Spider Dance, when he probably found himself in a sweet state, compounded of love, excitement and perspiration, caused by a great physical exertion, in producing the encore. The verse (which the satirical Squibob had probably written himself) read as follows:

> Fair Lola!
> I cannot believe, as I gaze on thy face,
> And into thy soul-speaking eye,
> There rests in thy bosom one lingering trace
> Of a spirit the world should decry.
> No, Lola, No!
>
> I read in those eyes, and on that clear brow,
> A Spirit—a Will—it is true;
> I trace there a Soul kind, loving, e'en now;
> But it is not a wanton I view;
> No, Lola, No!
>
> I will not believe thee cold, heartless and vain!
> Man's victim thou ever has been!
> With thee rests the sorrow, on thee hangs the chain!
> Then on thee should the world cast the sin?
> No, Lola, No![27]

[27]George Horatio Derby [John Phoenix, pseud.], *Phoenixiana, or Sketches and Burlesques*, 172-75.

Well, Lola may not have been free of sin, but the poet was certainly correct in believing her not to be cold and heartless. Everywhere she had traveled in America she had been acknowledged as a generous woman of great goodness of heart, even by those who disapproved of her morals. Her services had been freely given in performances for local charities and for those in her profession who were in need. Even at her best, though, Lola couldn't help stretching the truth a bit: when given a bouquet in a silver vase after a benefit in York City, she remarked that she valued it more than the $25,000 diamond necklace the Emperor of Russia had placed on her neck.

San Francisco would also come to know Lola's generosity. On June 9 she performed with a number of other volunteers in a gala for San Francisco's First Hebrew Benevolent Society. The artists involved were proclaimed to be the finest assemblage of talent ever collected on a San Francisco stage, a group who could "fill Drury Lane at an hour's notice."[28] True or not, the show did net some $5,000 from a standing-room-only audience that was called the largest yet seen in San Francisco.

Caroline Chapman, "San Francisco's pet," opened the evening with a little burletta called *Actress of All Work* in which she sustained four different characters—a country girl, a high-spirited actress, a crack-voiced and garrulous old woman, and a French danseuse. The piece was one of Caroline's favorites, and she had done it many times, expanding the number of characters portrayed to five, and even six. Perhaps its inclusion on this particular night was a deliberate jab at Lola for her recent interpretation of the multiple characters in *Maritana.*

The Lewis Bakers also appeared on the program, as did Billy Chapman, who sang several comic songs. Lola offered the second act of her *Yelva* and, to conclude the program, "El Olle." During the dance Squibob of the *Herald* noted the gallery, "that

---

[28]San Francisco *Herald,* June 9, 1853; S.F. *Golden Era,* June 12, 1853; *N.Y. Herald,* Jan. 17, 29 Feb. I, 1852.

paradise of miners and minors, rang as from a dragoon stable the never-ceasing cry of hay!"

Miska Hauser, a thirty-one year old Hungarian violinist, was another who performed that evening. Listening to Hauser play the "Carneval of Venice," Squibob observed that the virtuoso "went up higher, and came down lower" on his instrument, and fiddled variations to the extent you couldn't distinguish the original tune. He "made it to squeal, and to bray, and to groan and to whistle, and to grunt, and looked fiercer at the audience while he was doing it, than any concentrated number of musicians ever collected." Although Hauser was greeted with roars of applause, Squibob confessed that he himself was not perhaps as ecstatically delighted as he should have been. But, all in all, the writer said, he doubted that ever an audience departed a theater more satisfied.[29]

This was quite likely the occasion on which Montez first met Hauser, who would soon figure prominently in her California adventure. The violinist had toured Europe for ten years before drawing the attention of impresario P.T. Barnum. Barnum signed him, changed his Christian name from Michael to the more foreign and exotic "Miska," and brought him to the United States in 1850. After playing in the East with some success for two years, the Hungarian cut his ties with Barnum and came to California a few months before Lola's arrival.

In the Golden State, the violinist began to record his adventures in letters to his brother Sigmund, in Vienna, who gave them to the Ostdeutsche Post in that city. The letters, along with information from Miska's diary, were published in a two-volume book, Aus dem Wanderbuche Eines Oesterreichischen Virtuosen, at Leipzig in 1858-59.

Unfortunately, Hauser's observations must be taken with a rather large handful of salt. Many of the dates he gives for

---

[29]Derby, 166-69; S.F. Herald, June 7, 11, 15, 1853; Sacramento Union, June 13, 1853; Times and Transcript, June 10, 1853; S.F. Alta, June 10, 1853.

events are skewed a month or two from actual, and he obviously fabricated a good number of incidents to show himself in a
better light. Some of his biographers have labeled him a bit of a
charlatan and cheap trickster, who catered excessively to popular tastes in his desire to make a fortune. It is easy to agree with
such an assessment.

The pap Hauser wrote is replete with references to the
excessive court paid him by ardent admirers, who treated him
"like a spoiled child."[30] He bragged incessantly of his successful concerts and of the many banquets given in his honor. He
would even claim that it was he, not Lola, who was the chief
attraction at the concert for the Hebrew Benevolent Society,
and would conjure up a program for the event which showed
the singer Catherine Hayes, a supposed great friend of his, also
performing when, in fact, Hayes had long since left California.

Some compared him favorably to a more famous violinist of
the day, Ole Bull, but Hauser had, nevertheless, been miserably
received in California, playing many of his concerts to near-
empty benches in churches or saloons. After meeting with
indifferent success in San Francisco, he had made two tours of
the interior in company with other equally unappreciated
musicians. Only recently, after returning to San Francisco, had
a small group of music-loving businessmen taken Hauser
under their wing.

Following the Jewish benefit, Montez was re-engaged at the
American for four nights. On June 10 and 11, she played the
title role in *Charlotte Corday; or, Jacobins and Girondists,* a tragedy
which dealt with the assassination of the French revolutionary,
Jean-Paul Marat, at the hands of Marie-Anne-Charlotte Corday D'Armont. When she had performed this play in
Philadelphia soon after acquiring it, her early dramatic short-

---

[30]Hauser, "Adventures," 4: 5. Hauser's California activities can be traced in Sacramento *Times and Transcript,* Feb. 9, 10, 21, 22, Mar. 16, Apr. 26, May 12, 1853; S.F. *Alta,* Apr. 2,
3, May 24, 30, 1853; Sacramento *Union,* Mar. 10, 1853; S.F. *Journal,* Feb. 2, 16, Mar. 12,
1853; Stockton *Republican,* Mar. 9, May 4, 7, 1853; Miska Hauser, *Letters.*

comings in portraying the fiery Charlotte had earned her only ridicule. One critic in the City of Brotherly Love thought that instead of depicting the "Martyrdom of Charlotte Corday," the work should have shown the "decollation [beheading] of the Countess of Landsfelt."[31] But, by the time she had reached New Orleans a few months later, she was being praised for her ease and grace in sustaining the rapt and abstract air demanded by the play.

Now, in San Francisco, her acting skills seem to have improved even more. Squibob perhaps accurately assessed her progress:

> Although [Lola] makes no pretensions to equality with the celebrat-
> ed tragediennes of the day, and confines her efforts within a sphere
> somewhat contracted, she has nevertheless a peculiar earnestness of
> manner and utterance, a depth of feeling and a power to display the
> passions of an ardent and high-souled woman.[32]

Another San Franciscan who saw it, George E. Barnes, would remember Lola's portrayal of Charlotte as the best thing she ever did. Her eyes—the only striking feature in her pale and thin face—he said, made the assassination scene come alive. They absolutely flamed when she killed Marat, whom she held to be the enemy of her king and country.

Pilsbury Hodgkins of the Sacramento *Union*, who used the pseudonym "Chips," also saw the play and the "Spider Dance" which followed. He, like Barnes, was impressed by Lola's eyes, but perhaps more so with other parts of her anatomy. He told his readers:

> Lola Montes is in the zenith of her glory here...On Saturday
> night...she exhibited "a beautiful leg" and "brought the house
> down" in thunders of applause. The "Spider Dance" is consider-
> ably after the style yclept model artists...with all her singularities,
> you will find [her] a woman of rare wit. Although not strictly hand-
> some according to the physiognomical standard, she has an eye-lash

---

[31]McMinn, 326; S.F. *Herald*, June 9, 1853.
[32]San Francisco *Herald*, June 12, 1853.

whose outline is distinctly defined from the remotest parts of the theater, and which when it falls…reminds one of the patches of summer shade coursing over a field of ripened corn.[33]

The Model Artists, referred to by "Chips," were a troupe which had performed in March and April, 1850 at San Francisco's Phoenix Exchange. The same troupe, or one much like it, had also performed later under John St. Luke in New York City at the "Temple of the Graces," on Broadway, under various descriptions such as "living models," "tableaux vivants," and "ancient and modern statuary." The female "models" were normally clad only in flesh-colored body stockings and skirts just a few inches in length, and the men were dressed just as scantily. During one shocking performance entitled *Midnight Intruders*, in which the performers undressed and went to bed, the New York police had stormed on stage to arrest St. Luke and six of his male and female players. Found backstage were two pornographic wax figures that St. Luke had allowed patrons to view, for an additional fee.[34]

Sunday, June 12, was a day off for Lola. She spent it unwinding from the exigencies of doing *Charlotte Corday* by attending a "matinee musicale" given by Frederick A. Woodworth at his warehouse at 130 Clay Street. Woodworth was an importer of pianos and prominent patron of the arts, who had also been a former member of San Francisco's notorious 1851 vigilance committee. The featured artists at his little recital included Miska Hauser, and Catherine Hayes' former pianist, Rudolph Herold.

Being the only woman among some forty guests, Lola was, as usual, the center of attention. While the musicians played, she could be seen nodding the tempo with her head, "beating it with her fan, and puffing it gracefully with her cigaretta."

---

[33]Sacramento *Union*, June 15, 1853; S.F. *Herald*, June 6, 13, 1853; Sacramento *Times and Transcript*, June 13, 1853; Julia C. Altrocchi, "Paradox Town," 28.

[34]San Francisco *Herald*, June 24, 1852; S.F. *Alta*, Mar. 25, 1850; Megguier, 40.

Between pieces she conversed animatedly with the men around her "in whatever language she happened to be addressed."[35]

Lola's stock company, the George Chapmans, took advantage of her absence on that Sunday to engage in a bit of harmless lampooning of their star. As an afterpiece they offered American Theater patrons a little burletta entitled *Lola Montez, or Catching a Governor*. The origin of this satire can be traced back to a one-act farce called *Pas de Fascination; or, Catching a Governor!* which had been written for the London stage by J. Stirling Coyne in 1848, soon after Lola was forced out of Bavaria. Later in that same year, the Coyne piece, or an adaptation of it, found its way to New York City, where it was done periodically, including the period when Lola was performing there.

Sometimes also called *Lola Montes; or, A Countess for an Hour*, the burletta was a spoof based somewhat loosely on Lola's European experiences. The character Zephirine Jollijambe (Lola) is depicted as a pistol-packing, horsewhipping dancer who is wanted by the Russian chief of police, Grippenhoff, for failing to fulfill a commitment to appear on the St. Petersburg stage. When Zephirine appeals for assistance to Katherine Klopper, an innocent laundress, Katherine assumes Zepharine's identity, and is subsequently arrested and brought before Count Muffenuff, the Russian governor of Neveraskwehr. For him alone Katherine does a comic-mock dance—the *Pas de Fascination*—which so enchants the governor that he lavishes gifts on her and makes her a countess. But, the pure and simple Katherine eventually resumes her true identity and is happily reunited with her true love, the state barber, Michael Browsky.

Introduction of the Coyne burletta by the George Chapmans may have inspired the troupe at San Francisco Hall to further satirize Lola. After being remodeled, that theater was once again opened and, after several days of the usual fare, on June 13, Booth's company began doing their own version of

---

[35]Sacramento *Union*, June 15, 1853; S.F. *Bulletin*, Nov. 9, 1895.

Coyne's work, which they called *Lola Montez, or Pas de Fascination.* Caroline Chapman portrayed the heroine, Katherine; Mrs. Loder, wife of the musical director, did Zephirine, and Billy Chapman played Michael Browsky.

It seems likely that it was Billy and Caroline who had brought the burletta with them to California in March of 1852, since they, the Hamiltons and others of their company had been doing it periodically ever since. Caroline had most often been cast as Katherine Klopper, although the role was sometimes assumed by a young dancer, Miss Celeste.

The satire of Montez was repeated several times at San Francisco Hall over the next week, as an afterpiece to other works. In one instance, it followed a program comprising a dance by Miss Celeste, an original song by Dr. Robinson on the subject of duelling, and *Hamlet.* Playing the melancholy Dane that evening was June Booth's nineteen- year old brother, Edwin Thomas Booth. This serious and pensive young man had come to California in 1852 with his father, whose favorite he had been, and had stayed on when the elder Booth, ailing, returned to the Atlantic states. Like his famous father, Edwin Booth was destined to become one of America's greatest trage-dians. He had rendered his first interpretation of *Hamlet* only a few months earlier.[36]

On the same night that Junius Booth's people began satiriz-ing her, Montez was the feature attraction of a second benefit concert, this one in behalf of the charitable fund of San Fran-cisco's fire department. The volunteer fire fighters were always

---

[36]The history of the Coyne burletta can be traced in S.F. *Picayune* and S.F. *Herald* of Mar. 17-19, 1852; Sacramento *Times and Transcript,* June 9-14, 1853; *N.Y. Herald,* 4, 23, 1852; S.F. *Golden Era,* June 12, 1853; and McMinn, 329-31. The term burletta, meaning a play in verse set to music, was devised in 18th-century England to avoid licensing laws. Legally it meant any piece in three acts with at least five songs. This allowed the adaptation and presentation of plays by Shakespeare and other legitimate dramatists. Miss Celeste is not to be confused with Madame Celine Celeste (1814-82), a noted dancer, dramatic actress and pantomimist who performed in America.

a popular object of charity, since nearly every California town of that era had been devastated by flames at sometime during its existence. San Francisco's first great fire in December 1849 had led to the organization of an initial three volunteer companies and, by the time of Lola's coming, there were some fifteen. A few of these were the hook and ladder companies responsible for demolishing buildings to prevent the spread of a fire, but most were engine companies, who fought a conflagration head on.

Each engine company had its own pumping machine, equipped with up to 1,000 feet of leather hose, well-preserved with neat's-foot oil. Fire-fighting water was pumped from wooden, brick or cement cisterns buried at strategic locations throughout the city, each capable of holding up to 40,000 gallons. In the earliest days, these tanks were filled by calling out the companies after business hours to pump from ponds and streams but, in later years, they were replenished from a huge reservoir at Clay and Dupont, which itself was filled by pumping from the bay.

Some of the best-educated and most prominent young men in the city joined in this worthwhile service, which was as much a social diversion as a civic obligation. The companies held frequent outings, at which fierce intramural contests were held to test fire fighting skills. One such competition consisted of dragging a hose cart as fast as possible over a given distance with 500 feet of hose attached.

Montez organized the benefit for the firemen, recruiting Miska Hauser, flutist Christian Koppitz and singer-actress Emily Coad to appear on the program with her. And, in a move calculated to lend them a helping hand, she also invited the city's long-languid French and German theater groups to participate.

The French had been trying to establish a regular theater of their own ever since March 1850, when several men opened the short-lived Theater Nationale on Washington Street, doing light drama, pantomime and vaudeville. The second Adelphi—a small, unattractive three-story theater on Dupont—had also originally opened as a French theater in August 1851 under Misses Adelbert, Racine and Courtois and, in recent months, another French troupe under Paul Sasportas had occasionally used it. Construction of a new three-story brick French playhouse, the Union, had been started by a certain Mr. Munie in October 1852 on Commercial Street, but it was still uncompleted for lack of funds.

The Germans had appeared on the San Francisco scene more recently. A company of ten men and two ladies had been giving Sunday evening performances sporadically since the previous January, with E. Wehler as director, using the Olympic Theater at Sansome and Washington streets, and the second Adelphi.

Lola's highly-successful benefit not only raised some $4,000 for the firemen, it also revitalized interest in the French theater project to the extent that $10,000 was subsequently subscribed to complete the building. After the notable performance, Fred Woodworth honored all the artists with a supper at his house, where they were serenaded by the German Male Singer's Association, as throngs of San Franciscans stayed up on the streets to listen to their songs.[37]

After this second benefit, Montez played only two more nights in San Francisco. For her final evening, June 15, it was announced that she would take a personal benefit. Several

[37]San Francisco *Alta,* June 14, 1853; *Golden Era,* June 19, 1853; S.F. *Journal,* June 13, 1853; *Panama Star,* July 1, 1853; Sacramento *Times and Transcript,* June 11, 13, 1853; S.F. *Herald,* July 8, 30, 1851, Sept. 28, 1852, June 11, 12, 1853; S.F. *Picayune,* Mar. 16, 1852; Sacramento *Union,* May 17, 1853; Hauser, *Letters,* 47; S.F. *News,* Dec. 2, 1853. Christian Koppitz (1829-1861) lived in San Francisco for six years beginning in April 1853, and hardly a concert was given during this period without his services either as soloist or accompanist.

papers, praising her tact, skill and many graces, made an appeal for an overflowing house, and reminded their readers of her generous aid to the local charities.

The firemen rose to the occasion. On the morning of that last performance, Engine Company Number 3 celebrated its third anniversary with an excursion. These "Howards" were truly the elite of San Francisco's volunteer firemen. "Faithful and Fearless," just as their motto proclaimed, they had distinguished themselves, first in the May 1851 blaze, and then again in June, despite their engine house on Long Wharf having been destroyed in that latter fire. They wore with pride their handsome uniform—glazed black cap with an ornamental front; rich scarlet cloth shirt with blue collar and lapel, and black cloth pants and patent leather belt.

The "Howards" and their guests—many from other fire companies—met that morning at the new engine house on California Street, whence they proceeded, band playing and colors flying, down to the wharf and on board the steamer *Kate Hayes* to cross the bay to the more rural Contra Costa County. The day was spent playing cricket and other "manly sports,"[38] and in partaking a sumptuous dinner, all the while making toasts and speechifying.

Upon their return to San Francisco that evening the "Howards" were met at the wharf by the "Empires" of company number 1—also heroes of the May 1851 fire—and were escorted to the Union Hotel and Saloon. Here the celebration continued until the two companies, in full uniform, marched together to the theater to see the divine Lola strut the boards.

With firemen packed into every vacant space, Montez was assured an enthusiastic reception. She appeared first in *Yelva*, followed by a rendition of the final act of Victor Hugo's *Ruy*

[38]San Francisco *Alta*, June 16, 1853; S.F. *Herald*, June 15, 18, 1853; S.F. *Journal*, June 15, 1853.

Blas by her friends in the French troupe. Next came the old standby "El Olle," then an instrumental solo by Charles Chenal, and the farce *Family Jars* by Mr. Vinson and Mrs. Judah. And finally, just to make sure her audience got its money's worth, she offered the "Spider Dance."

This is what the virile, young firemen had come to see, and an extremely high-spirited Lola rose to the occasion. She had scarcely appeared when several of the firemen threw their hats upon the stage. She ignored them at first, dancing gracefully while keeping time with the castanets, now slowly flitting across the stage, then rapidly whirling away and shaking out the spiders from her skirts. But as the climax to the dance drew near, Montez transformed one of the caps into a spidery sex object. After pirouetting around and over it petticoats, spread to their utmost, she poised herself with a foot on either side, and dipped her body down till there was almost contact. She then sprang angrily to her feet, stamped upon and crushed it to the floor, ending the dance amid such "thunders of applause and laughter as caused the building to tremble in every joint."[39]

A shower of bouquets having fallen around her, she took deliberate hold of the edge of her short outer skirts, gathered the bouquets into her lap, picked up the caps and kissed them, shook her head archly at the audience, and strutted out. She returned for a curtain speech, holding one of the fireman's caps filled with bouquets. Her voice tinged with its bogus foreign accent, she handsomely complimented the firemen, saying San Francisco could only become the great city it was destined to become by having the firemen to safeguard it; they had thrown their hats, but she believed she also held their hearts. She then withdrew to a rousing three cheers.

Thus Lola's contract in San Francisco was fulfilled. Although it was said that she could have been a winning card

---

[39]San Francisco *Alta*, June 16, 18, and *Journal*, June 16, 1853.

for a month to come, she had apparently decided to take a brief rest and then make a tour to see the gold-bearing regions of the state. Or perhaps she knew better than to sate her audience. In any case, by mid-June she had acquired Catherine Hayes' cast-off agent, H. D. Adams, and he had been dispatched to negotiate the details of a tour of the interior, starting in Sacramento. Word had it that she wouldn't return to perform in San Francisco for some months to come.

The dancer continued to quietly enjoy San Francisco, apparently radiating most of her sunshine on Patrick Hull, since there were strong hints that the two might soon marry. She created quite a stir one afternoon when seen rolling ten pins in the Commercial Saloon, and she was the target of some good-natured ribbing when her "bleary-eyed" little spaniel named Flora mysteriously disappeared from her boarding house on Bush Street. Although the grieving Lola offered a reward, the animal was never found, causing one newspaper to report that the dog's skin had been discovered in a sausage factory, and to wonder just how many people had eaten of those sausages.[40]

But, with Lola no longer performing, the stage was now set for some really serious teasing by professionals. The J. B. Booth company at San Francisco Hall had been exceedingly busy for days preparing a full-blown "burlesque and extravaganza"[41] which would capitalize on the Montez foibles and, on June 20, a mere five days after Lola had finished at the American, it was offered for the first time. The product of "Yankee" Robinson's ruthless and prolific pen, and called *Who's Got the Countess, or The Rival Houses*, it was an outrageous spoof of the tempestuous interloper's doings since breaking into San Francisco's close-knit little theatrical circle.

[40]Stockton *Republican*, June 28, 1853; S.F. *Wide West*, Mar. 28, 1853; S.F. *Golden Era*, June 12, 15, 1853, June 3, 10, 1855; S.F. *Herald*, June 16, 1853; Sacramento *Union*, June 21, 1853; F.C. Ewer, ed., *The Pioneer, or California Monthly Magazine*, 4: 54.

[41]San Francisco *Alta*, June 25, 1853.

However crass, the piece was one of the first successful original stage productions written in California. Its heroine was "Mula, Countess of Bohemia," portrayed by Caroline Chapman. The plot, such as it was, revolved around the rivalry between theater managers to sign Mula when she first arrives in San Francisco, and her ensuing stormy relationship with actor-manager Lewis Baker at the American. Baker became "Louis Buggins," played by Billy Chapman; supporting characters included Buggin's right hand man, Mula's servant Gosling, and the King of Bohemia, among others. "Yankee" Robinson himself played the part of a prompter.

Caroline Chapman's depiction of Mula-Lola, was an outlandish caricature of a fiery, but coquettish, actress who always seem to have trouble with her lines. Yet, while Caroline's performance was well-received, it was "Uncle Billy" who brought down the house each night with a ridiculous "Spy-Dear" dance. After seeing him bounce and leap to shake off the spiders, one wag proposed that an additional hundred feet be added to the stage so that Billy "could do it up brown." But another critic thought perhaps he was already laying it on a "leetle too thick." Pat Hull's *Whig* suggested the dance be done with a bit more regard for "propriety and with a more decided view of the careful arrangement of drapery."[42] Each of Billy's dances ended in roars of laughter and showers of vegetables thrown by an adoring audience, themselves burlesquing the manner in which bouquets were tossed at Lola's feet. A few nights after the show opened, a woman—perhaps one of the stock players—rushed on stage from the side scenes, just as Billy finished, and gave him a severe switching, much to the delight of the audience.

Robinson's creation was presented to overflowing crowds for nearly two weeks, as an afterpiece to more serious works.

---

[42]Sacramento *Times and Transcript*, June 20, 21, 24, 27, 1853; S.F. *Golden Era*, June 26, 1853; S.F. *Whig*, June 27, 1853; S.F. *Alta*, June 20, 1853; S.F. *Herald*, June 20, 1853.

On one evening, Caroline Chapman cavorted in the parody immediately after playing opposite Edwin Booth in *Romeo and Juliet*. Most San Franciscans who saw *Who's Got The Countess* agreed that it was all great fun. But the *Alta* critic, who was fast becoming Lola's constant defender, thought the play's plot to be "miserably arranged," and the dialogue to lack "wit, point, appropriateness and even common sense." And, to crown it all, it was "bunglingly arranged in bad rhyme."[43] But even he grudgingly agreed that its ludicrous surprises and Billy's dancing were indeed funny.

One fellow, who identified himself only as "S" in his letter to the *Herald*, enjoyed the production when he first saw it, but changed his mind after a second viewing. Except for Caroline's comic bravura and Billy's grotesque dance, he labeled the whole affair a "vulgar misrepresentation" of Lola's behavior and peculiarities. Despite her faults, this man pointed out, Lola had proven herself a noble-hearted and generous woman, who didn't deserve ridicule and scurrility. He reminded readers of the many dollars she had raised for local charities, and he appealed to all gentlemen to remember that she was an unprotected lady.[44]

Others were just as convinced that even Lola wouldn't be offended by the satire, and, indeed, if she was, she gave no outward indication. She became close enough friends to the Chapmans to give Caroline's little niece a sampler she had made. Moreover, on June 23, when she volunteered to dance at the Adelphi Theatre as part of a benefit for actor C. E. Bingham, "Yankee" Robinson was on the same bill, singing the opening song from *Who's Got The Countess*.

Today, that opening song is all that remains of Robinson's preposterous spoof of Lola Montez. Although there is good evidence the doctor changed its lyrics almost nightly to include

---

[43]San Francisco *Alta*, June 25, 1853; Sacramento *Times and Transcript*, June 24, 1853.
[44]San Francisco *Herald*, June 26, 1853.

his latest jab, this is the version of the little ditty that has survived:

> Some weeks ago the Countess came to fill us with delight,
> And drew admiring throngs to see her spider dance each night;
> The nice young men in tender strains impressions tried to make,
> And tho they sighed and threw bouquets, she didn't seem to take;
> But these gallants determined each that he not quit his hold,
> And tho she could not take them all, she kindly took their gold.
>
> She took herself out to the race and there she took the purse;
> She took poor Buggins by the nose, which made poor Buggins curse;
> She to an alley took some gents to see her bowl a pin,
> They took her challenge there to roll and then she took them in;
> She took poor snob ["S"] so by surprise he to the *Herald* wrote,
> And tho he thought that she d take him, she wouldn't take a shoat.
>
> Now after all these takes, I'd say that some were taken in,
> Who think that she won't take a joke whenever she can win,
> And while she s in this taking way, she s causing great distress
> In some young men who fear she'll take some member of our press.
> Tho' Democrat she long has been, tis thought by some she'll dig
> And leave the party in the lurch and fasten to the *Whig*...
>
> But since you've come out in such crowds to see poor Buggins dance,
> I ll throw bad rhyming to the dogs and give the star a chance;
> For in our burlesque every night his graceful winning ways
> Have loaded him with cabbages, more valued than bouquets,
> For he s a man of family, and though the bouquets sweet,
> The flowers are only fit to smell, the cabbages to eat.[45]

---

[45]Robinson, *Comic Songs*, 50-53; also S.F. *Herald*, June 23, 29, July 2, Sept. 5, 1853; S.F.
Journal, July 11, 1853; S.F. *Alta*, June 27-28, 1853; Marysville *Herald*, Oct. 18-19, 1853.

CHAPTER FOUR

Who's Got The Countess?

Novelty is a great gloss of love—a varnish that soon wears off. If some
Yankee boy could discover a means of preserving love, as we preserve
pork, what an excellent thing it would be! But alas! no salt could cure
the great bane of love—too much of each other's company.
                    ...Lola Montez, "Comic Aspects of Love."[1]

Somewhat remarkably, the Countess of Landsfeld had managed to get through her entire stay in San Francisco without
once having to justify her morality in the newspapers, and
without ever having done battle with a creditor or lover. This *pax
Montez*, however, would prove but a temporary aberration.

For her forthcoming interior tour, Lola planned to avoid
the bother of staging plays in a variety of small theaters by presenting only what were described as "soirees dansante and
musical." She would supply the dansante, of course, and, for
the music, she hired violinist Miska Hauser and the multi-tal-
ented Charles Chenal, who played clarinet, flute, flageolet and
the piano. Her faithful Charles Eigenschenck would double as
a violinist and conductor of the other two, comprising a small
orchestra. Lola undoubtedly was inspired to add this musical
refinement to her tour while attending Fred Woodworth's
matinee concert.[2]

---

[1]As reported in *N.Y. Times,* Mar. 19, 1858.
[2]Sacramento *Times and Transcript,* June 22, 1853; also S.F. *Alta,* May 4, June 19, 21,
1853; S.F. *Herald,* June 21, 1853; Sacramento *Union,* June 20, 1853.

Miska Hauser was fascinated with Montez, and delighted to have been asked to tour with her, despite her having conned him shamelessly in order to secure his services. According to Hauser, Lola invited him to her hotel, where she profusely complimented his talents at composition and gave him a beautifully-made silver ink stand, with a pen of pure gold and California gold dust as blotting sand. Overwhelmed by Lola's beauty and all this flummery, the Hungarian readily accepted her proposal for the tour. He somewhat dazedly left the interview believing "the beautiful Andalusian" had only been speaking English for a year.

Hauser wondered if perhaps his new artistic companion had drunk from the fountain of youth, since he saw in her no sign of age. Her face he likened to an eternal midsummer where two suns, her eyes, shine on the horizon. But, the violinist hadn't been totally blinded. He was also aware of the dangerous side of the free-spirited woman. "She is very naughty," he wrote in his diary, "like a small child—and speaks about fire as if she had not yet been burned." "Woe to him who falls into her disfavor," he warned, "She has a very excitable nature and for the slightest reason her whole body will tremble and her eyes flash lightning."[3]

Hauser himself was the victim of Lola's naughtiness on at least one occasion. Fred Woodworth and others arranged a benefit concert for the violinist on June 18, 1853, and, as a practical joke that evening, Lola sent Hauser masses of flowers, much like an agent would have done to puff up an artist. Afterward—also just as an agent would have done—she presented him with a huge bill for the floral tribute. Hauser, who had cleared $1,822 on the benefit, said he paid the bill good-naturedly, but couldn't bring himself to inform her that, if flowers in San Francisco were so enormously expensive, it could only be because Lola Montez was in town.

---

[3]Hauser, *Letters*, 32, 49-50.

As the day approached for Lola to leave on tour, still more rumors surfaced to the effect that she planned to marry a San Franciscan. Late on the night of July 1, Fred Woodworth and a few other prominent city businessmen dropped into H. J. Clayton's restaurant on Commercial street to reveal to its owner that, indeed, their mutual friend, Patrick Purdy Hull, would wed the dancer at matin bells the next day at the Mission Dolores. Clayton was asked to keep the secret, since Woodworth and the others weren't really sure it would come off, and they were afraid they might all have been hoodwinked.

Clayton returned home to bed and, keeping the news from his wife, arose early and walked the several miles to the Mission outside the city. When he arrived at sunrise he found some twenty of his friends pacing listlessly around the outside of the old church. Most were men of some importance: Beverley C. Sanders, a former Collector of the Port of San Francisco; Alexander Wells, an associate justice of the California supreme court, and Alexander G. Abell, former consul to the Sandwich Islands. James E. Wainwright, the county clerk—whose wife was with him, and apparently the only woman present—asked Clayton why he was there. Laughingly, Clayton said he was just out for a walk. Wainwright replied that he knew better, and told Clayton that everyone present was in on the secret, but that he also thought they were all victims of a practical joke.

All doubts vanished when a carriage containing Lola, Hull, Alderman A. Bartol and Louis R. Lull, of the *Whig*, came into sight, having been driven from the Adams House on Bush street where Lola was staying. The wedding party alit at the church door and entered with a few of the close friends who had been waiting but, before Lola could turn and indicate that the door was to be closed, some forty other people, including some from the mission, had already gotten inside. The bride brought in two vases of artificial white flowers, which she presented, with appropriate demonstrations of devotion, to

Father Flavel Fontaine at the altar. The priest placed them at the feet of the Virgin, and then conducted a brief, but nonetheless strictly Catholic ceremony.

Why the Jesuit-hating Montez once again married in a Catholic church is an enigma. Perhaps it was to please Hull, who was Catholic; or possibly she wanted to reinforce the pretense of her having Spanish origins. Equally unclear is the status of her two previous marriages. Certainly, Captain James was still living—he would not die until 1871 at age 74—and, as best can be determined, so was George Heald. Furthermore, there is no evidence that she had been divorced from either of them. But, no matter—having dealt before with bigamy, Lola would know how to cope with trigamy.

After the ceremony, Father Fontaine entertained the wedding party in his apartments with a spread of cake, wine, cigars and cigarettes. The bride was reported to have been in good spirits during the festivities, with a pleasant word for everyone. James Wainwright, emboldened perchance by the wine, gave Clayton a sly wink, and, despite the presence of his wife, approached Lola and kissed her. Clayton followed suit, "just to make the occasion memorable," he said. But, although Lola remarked, "such is the custom of my country," none of the other men were brave enough to kiss her.[4]

Some indication of the course the marriage would take was given at the party's conclusion, when Lola asked where a good breakfast might be had. Hull suggested the Bull's Head right there at the Mission, but, no, Lola insisted, she preferred the Tivoli in the city. And, that was that.

Later in the day, the newlyweds hosted a reception at Mrs. Hannah Gates' fashionable boarding house on Bush Street, where Hull lived. Still more prominent California men came there to pay their respects, among them Senator John B.

---

[4]San Francisco *Alta,* Jan. 24, 1874; S.F. *Herald,* July 2, 3, 1853; Sacramento *Times and Transcript,* June 25, 1853; S.F. *Call-Bulletin,* Oct. 4, 1933.

Weller. The news that a fellow Californian had won the hand of the famed dancer—the embodiment of every lonesome miner's secret dreams—created a vicarious stir of excitement throughout the state. Said one San Francisco newspaper of Hull's accomplishment, with no small degree of pride: "The question of 'Who's Got the Countess?' we presume, is thus forever put at rest."[5]

The Hulls, accompanied by a number of friends, sailed from Long Wharf on the afternoon of the wedding day by the steamer, *New World*, for the seven hour trip to Sacramento. It has been said that Lola and Hull made the trip in the new steamer *Arrow* on its maiden voyage, and tells of a fight they had while dining that evening with the ship's captain, A. D. Averill. Hull is supposed to have questioned Lola about a topaz necklace she was wearing, to which she replied that it had belonged to the family of her former husband, George Heald. When Hull asked her why she hadn't returned it, an irate Lola replied, "What for? So that old maid aunt, Susanna Heald, could wear it around her scrawny neck?"[6]

This makes a good story and Hull, no doubt, often had jealous anxieties about his none-too-virginal bride. But it was reported specifically that the pair had sailed in the *New World*. Then too, while Averill was indeed the *Arrow's* captain, that steamer didn't begin running to Sacramento until July 11, well after Lola and Hull made their trip. If true, the incident probably occurred on a round trip to San Francisco Montez and Hull made on July 12.

The town of Sacramento, as Lola Montez first laid eyes on it, was a booming place. It had sprung up just a few years earlier near the little settlement of New Helvetia, which had been established by the Swiss emigrant, Johann A. Sutter, on his

[5]San Francisco *Golden Era*, July 3, 1853.
[6]Helen Holdredge, *The Woman in Black*, 188; S.F. *Herald*, July 12, 1853.

sprawling Spanish land grant. Some of the streets of the soon-to-be state capital were still adorned with the fine white oaks that had originally lined the banks of the Sacramento River.

Upon arrival, Lola and her entourage took rooms at the Orleans Hotel on Second Street. Like most California towns, Sacramento had been ravaged a number of times by fire, most recently the previous November. The luxurious Orleans, with its splendid, brilliantly-lighted saloon, was one of the many new brick buildings to have been built since that time. The city had also been badly flooded the previous winter when runoff from a heavy snowpack coincided with day after day of torrential rain. But levees had since been built along the river banks, and the city now seemed secure enough to warrant the grading and planking of more streets.

Having arrived just in time for Independence Day festivities in the young town, Lola was invited to attend a shooting match being held by the Swiss Rifle Club at its grounds on Jacob Rippstein's farm along the American River. Always the theatrician, she, of course, timed her arrival on the scene to coincide perfectly with the peak of activity, and was rewarded by an enthusiastic chorus of cheers and the firing of cannons.

Since it was to Switzerland that Montez had fled for sanctuary after being driven from Bavaria, she had always claimed a deep fondness for that tiny nation. The toast she offered during the festivities that afternoon, which reveals her affection, must have deeply stirred the hearts of her hosts. "The Land of Tell—brave, beautiful Switzerland," Lola proposed, charmingly, "May it long continue to produce telling men." Somewhat less charmingly, she added, "I hope you will one day use your skill with the rifle against Austria."[7]

This perfectly glorious Fourth of July ended that evening with the city's fire companies parading in front the Orleans

[7]San Francisco *Alta*, steamer edn., July 15, 1853; also *Alta*, July 3, Sacramento *Union* and *Democratic State Journal*, July 4, 1853; Buck, 51.

The Levee, Sacramento City, California, ca. 1852

Courtesy, Eleanor McClatchy Collection, City of Sacramento, History and Science Division, Sacramento Archives and Museum Collection Center.

Hotel, where they shouted three hearty cheers as the much-adored dancer appeared at the window, bowing gracefully and blowing kisses.

In what was billed as a "grand musical and terpsichorean festival," the Montez troupe opened the following day at the Sacramento Theater. This small playhouse, of frame construction, seated 800, and had just been erected that spring on Third Street, between I and J. Charles A. King, the actor-manager, had a financial interest in it, along with James Evrard and several others.

Sacramento had recently acquired a reputation as being a tough town to play. J.B. Booth the elder, famous as he was, had received a somewhat cool reception in 1852 and, a mere three months before Lola's arrival, Catherine Hayes had left town in a huff, after a misunderstanding with the city's firemen over a benefit she gave for them. But there was certainly no friction on Lola's first evening. A huge success, she played to what was called the largest number of ladies and gentlemen ever to attend a theatrical event.

At the conclusion of her first dance, "El Olle," she was wildly cheered, and then called out a second time. Violinist Miska Hauser, backed by the orchestra, fiddled a lively "Yankee Doodle," and Chenal vigorously attacked the piano keyboard in his warm-blooded *piano russe* style, both men receiving warm approbation. Lola's "Spider Dance" at the program's close, of course, carried the house by storm. She found, amidst the many bouquets thrown on stage by enthusiastic admirers, the leather belt of one of Sacramento's firemen. It was tenderly gathered up and kissed to thundering applause, and when she said "It bears the inscription 'Excelsior,' a company to which I really believe I belong," the uproar redoubled.[8] But, ah, me! All

---

[8]Sacramento *Demo. State Journal,* July 6, 1853; Sacramento *Union,* Apr. 21-25, June 18, July 6, 1853; S.F. *Alta,* May 25, 1853; Leman, 243; Sacramento *Times and Transcript,* Feb. 14, 1853.

of this sweetness and light would vanish at the following night's performance.

As Miska Hauser was to recall the scene, the curtain for the "Spider Dance" went up in front of another packed house, to reveal Lola standing poised "in fairylike costume." Advancing to the center of the stage, she let her challenging, dazzling eyes stray for a moment over the crowd, and then she began. But, suddenly, someone near the footlights started to laugh so loudly as to be heard throughout the house, and this perceived affront to her dignity sparked another typical Montez donnybrook.

Something similar had happened to Lola while playing the National Theater in Washington, D.C., a year earlier. There, a man thumbed his nose at her while she was taking a curtain call, but she had stared and talked the rude fellow down, and the audience rose to her support. She wouldn't be so lucky this time.

The dancer signaled with her hand, and the music stopped. She stood, erect and proud, and cast a withering glance into the audience, causing an uncomfortable titter and stir. At this, incensed and perhaps slightly disrespectful, she stepped forward to the foot lights, bowed and made a short speech, in which she informed those who were dissatisfied that, if her dancing didn't suit them, she would retire.

Miska Hauser's embellished account of the speech and subsequent events is highly suspect, since it gives him so much credit as an artist. Perhaps the little Hungarian was more than a bit jealous, having to play second fiddle to such an unaccomplished dancer. In any case, according to him, Lola began her skirmish with the audience by explaining that she had too much respect for the people of California to attach any importance to stupid laughter coming from a "few silly puppies." But, when, at this, the laughter renewed, she demanded that she be allowed to speak, and shouted "Come up here...give me your men's trousers and take in their place my woman's skirts; you are not worthy to be called men," and so forth in the same vein.

However the battle may have been joined, Lola then left the stage in high dudgeon to the accompaniment of hearty hisses, and perhaps, as Hauser claimed, bombarded by rotten eggs and apples. After this, the audience was uncertain how to react. Some laughed, some applauded, others hissed; a few even left the theater. Some, who had tried unsuccessfully to get their money back, returned to add to the general dissatisfaction in the auditorium.

Miska Hauser related that he had been watching the impending storm from a seat in the loge, thanking God it was Lola in the eye of it, not him. Then, to his horror, manager Charles King rushed up, breathlessly wringing his hands, and begged Hauser to go out and improvise something to calm the audience—even offering $600 if he would do so. Hauser having acquiesced, King went on stage to calm the audience, explaining that Lola had taken offense at something said concerning her by some person in the house, but that, if they approved, she would return to finish her dance as soon as Hauser played.

The Hungarian was apprehensive but, in less than five minutes, he stood armed with his fiddle and bow before the hostile audience. Expecting to have to shield himself with his violin from a renewed onslaught, he was pleasantly surprised, he said, to be received by a storm of applause.

Besides "Yankee Doodle," Hauser's usual repertoire included his original compositions, "Souvenir of Niagara" and "Grand Fantasia on Othello," as well as the many old standbys played by nearly every hack instrumentalist of the day. But he took his greatest pride in something he had written called *"Der Vogel auf dem Baum,"* or "The Bird on the Tree," a gaudy virtuoso piece replete with harmonic trills imitating a canary bird.

Although he called it his "musical joke," and a "fable for children," he nonetheless played it at nearly every performance, thinking it to be well-suited to the banal musical tastes of Californians.

Thus, the violinist chose "Bird on the Tree" to calm the rowdy Sacramentans. He claimed he played it twice, after which, he said, the crowd shouted again for Charles King and told him they didn't want to see the unworthy Montez again. Instead, they wanted to hear more of "the much esteemed Miska Hauser and his magic bow.[9]" Hearing these words while listening in the wings, he said, Lola rushed on stage and began to dance, which only incited another upsurge in the crowd's fury—everyone pressing toward the stage, overturning benches and chairs, breaking windows and demanding of the scoundrel King their money back. Hauser said he then had to play "Carneval," "Yankee Doodle," and even "Bird in the Tree" once more before order could be restored.

Newspaper accounts say only that Hauser played once, after which calm returned, allowing Lola to complete her dance, and that the remainder of the performance proceeded without incident.

But a certain number of the audience were still dissatisfied when they left the theater. Some two hours later, after Lola had returned to her rooms at the Orleans Hotel, she was treated to a noisy mock shivaree—a regular "Pike county serenade"— from a few of her erstwhile fans, who used drums, bells, tin horns, old kettles, and penny whistles to discordantly poke fun at the arrogant woman from below on the street.

Shades of Bavaria! In just a few minutes, the noise drew a huge crowd, and an excited but fearless Montez appeared at her window—some said with a pistol in hand—to greet those who dared ridicule her. She tried to speak above the noise, but to no avail. In his version of the incident, Miska Hauser would say that

---

[9]Hauser, "Adventures," 6: 5, 59; 4: 5-6; also *N.Y. Herald,* Feb. 18, 1852.

she used words like "cowards," "low blackguards," and "cringing dogs," and that a man climbed onto her balcony to blow out her lamp. Finally, after giving her three groans, the "band" marched off to the sound of their instruments. Montez then told those few who remained below that she didn't think "such proceedings were countenanced by the citizens of Sacramento, and that no man would be guilty of such conduct."[10]

Her little speech, whatever its content, caused a renewal of the booing and yelling, and a return of the band, which saluted her with another serenade. Lola stood firm, however, and finally found an opportunity to invite all her detractors to come with their money to the performance she had offered to give for the benefit of Sacramento's volunteer fire department two days hence. But the following morning, July 7, shocked by the ruckus at the theater and hotel, the governing board of the fire department met and voted to decline the benefit. Local papers skewered the temperamental dancer, saying they had never seen such a general indignation against anyone, and that it was well deserved in light of her cavalier treatment of the audience.

Thus chastised, but undaunted, Lola set about to captivate and retake the city. That night a throng filled the theater, most of them hoping and expecting to witness another wrangle. Marshal White was present with the entire Sacramento police force, determined to arrest the first man to show the slightest symptom of being unruly. Curiosity to see what would happen next with the fiery Lola had even brought Sacramento's most venerable citizen, Johann Sutter, to the theater. The "noble old hero"—as the Sacramento *Union* fondly called him—on whose property gold had first been discovered in California, entered the house to the accompaniment of great applause, after which everyone else took their seats in eager anticipation of the battle to come.

At the conclusion of the overture by the orchestra, manager

---

[10]Sacramento *Demo. State Journal*, July 7, 1853; Hauser, "Adventures," 6: 5.

Charles King appeared to tell the audience that Lola wished to speak to them. The idea was applauded, so King brought the seemingly-repentant, and now thoroughly-genial dancer out by the hand, to allow her to offer a *mea culpa.* She said:

> Last evening there was an occurrence in this theatre which I regret. It is a small theatre...I am almost alongside of you and the sound is not always distinctly understood. I am subject to a palpitation of the heart and since I have been in Sacramento I have suffered with it very much, which makes me at times feel very bad. While I was dancing I stamped my foot several times upon the stage and someone laughed, as I supposed to insult me. I have many enemies who have followed me from Europe and offered me insults and I supposed that it might be some of those who followed me with that intention.
>
> I knew it was no American for I have been moved and cherished by the Americans wherever I went...I can't always find the spider when I hunt for it—it can't always be seen—I can't always put it to the ground; and when I stamped it was only in a joke. It is sometimes customary for my friends to throw a bouquet of flowers on the stage and for me to trample on it to represent a spider, as it is not always convenient to find a real spider...I will wipe out from my memory what occurred. It was unworthy of me and I shall speak of it no more. Ladies and gentlemen, if you wish me to go with my dance, you have only to say the word.

Real spiders? Hardly, but this tender plea met with thunders of applause as Montez smiled sweetly, curtsied and gracefully left the footlights. After Miska Hauser and Charles Chenal had performed, she returned for her first number, a Swiss dance, set to music from the opera *William Tell.* Although she averred that she had danced it in the Rossini work at the Paris Opera, this was the first time she had ever offered it in California. And what could have been more appropriate with Johann Sutter sitting in the theater? At its conclusion, the applause was so loud and long that Lola came forward with another pretty speech, flattering the Sacramentans who had "twice built up a city; once from ruin by a flood, and once from fire." Now, she said, these marvelous people had also "redeemed the character of Lola Montez."[11]

After Hauser had played again, Lola capped her triumph with the "Spider Dance." It prompted so many curtain calls that she made a third speech, asking fetchingly if she might be permitted to dance in Sacramento one or two evenings more. And who could object?

But perhaps Montez wasn't truly as repentant as she should have been. According to Hauser, she had laughingly skipped up to him on the day following her altercation with the audience and said: "Believe me, dear Hauser, last evening was worth more to me than $1,000. I was delightfully amused to have added another to my list of adventures."[12]

On the day following her apology, July 8, two of Sacramento's three newspapers gushed with a new-found amity, while at the same time expressing amazement at the racy happenings of the previous two evenings. One sheet frankly admitted that the townsfolk had been unable to resist Lola's eloquence, and that this singular woman had entirely "retrieved herself by the force of...[her] genius." Of this sudden reversal in attitude, the San Francisco *Alta* could only conclude: "Lola is a great woman and the Sacramento people an unstable people. One night she is chivareed, hissed, hooted and insulted, and the next she is applauded, clapped and glorified by the same people."[13]

The editor of the Sacramento *Daily Californian* stood in sole disagreement that Lola had redeemed herself. He claimed, instead, that the enthusiasm on the previous evening had been the response of a hired audience—claqueurs impelled by mere curiosity and the use of free tickets. This comment, in turn, led to a revival in the Sacramento *Union* of another of those recurring

---

[11]Sacramento *Union*, July 8, 1853; also July 6, 7; S.F. *Golden Era*, July 10, 1853; Sacramento *Times and Transcript*, July 9, 1853; Stockton *Republican*, July 9, 1853.

[12]Hauser, "Adventures," 6: 5.

[13]Sacramento *Union*, July 8, 1853; S.F. *Alta*, steamer edn., July 15, 1853.

legends about Lola—the "Pistols or Pizen" story. It was reported that she had sent the Californian editor a petticoat and a pair
of pistols, asking him to choose which of them he pleased.

The *Alta* then picked up the story and modified it somewhat. It published the supposed text of a letter from Lola to
the *Californian* editor, berating him for his lies and ungallant
conduct, and ending with this challenge:

> I do not advocate women's rights, but at the same time I can right
> myself by inflicting summary justice upon all jack-an-apes!!! After
> such a gross insult, you must don the petticoats [which]...I can lend
> you for the occasion—You must fight with me. I leave the choice of
> two kinds of weapons to yourself, for I am very magnanimous. You
> may chose between my duelling pistols or take your choice of a pill
> out of a pill-box. One shall be poison and the other not, and the
> chances are even. I request that this affair may be arranged by your
> seconds as soon as possible...[14]

The letter, signed with a signature uncharacteristic of Lola,
was most likely totally bogus, patterned by some hard-pressed
editor after a similar one which Californians had seen before,
in October 1851. At that time, irritated by the publication of
several disparaging articles, Lola had purportedly written a
scathing epistle to the editor of the Lyon *Constitutionnel* which
had included this threat:

> As for the poniards or pistols, I do not know their use; but you, in
> your paper, have some powerful weapons...falsehood, ridicule and
> perfidy...If you continue, sir, I will be obliged to send you my card,
> and my seconds, to put an end to your ridiculous animosity; but it
> will not be with pistols...I will offer you two pills, in a box; one of
> them will be poisoned, and you will not be able to refuse a duel with
> arms which are so familiar to you. I have the honor of saluting you![15]

Despite the grumbling by the editor of the *Californian*, the
remainder of Montez's Sacramento engagement went swim-

---

[14]In San Francisco *Alta,* July 10, 1853
[15]In Sacramento *Union,* Dec. 18, 1851.

mingly before full houses, which now contained a greater proportion of women curious to see her. And, once again in the
good graces of the city's firemen, she gave them their benefit on
July 8, as originally planned. More speeches were made each
night to audiences she now familiarly called her "old friends."[16]

The only complaints heard anywhere in town had to do
with Hauser and Chenal. While both were praised for their
musical ability, Hauser was taken to task for the lack of variety
shown by his too-frequent playing of the "Carneval of Venice"
and "Bird in the Tree;" Chenal was criticized for the bad taste
displayed when he stood on stage on a chair and played his flageolet—a small fipple flute resembling the treble recorder—
with one nostril, while at the same time smoking a cigar.

The sixth and final night of Lola's engagement, July 11, was
a benefit for her. And, what a success it was for the now-cher-
ished dancer. Three fire companies—the Protection, Alert
and Tehama—arrived at the theater in full regalia, preceded by
a band. At the end of Lola's first dance they arose and gave her
three cheers, and she responded with a speech. During the
"Spider Dance," the enthused firemen emptied a champagne
basket full of bouquets, and cast them at her feet to trample on.
After three more cheers at the dance's conclusion, Lola laid her
hand sentimentally over her heart, spoke of her overwhelming
emotions, and bade her patrons farewell.

But, the adoring fire fighters weren't yet through with their
newly-redeemed goddess. They formed into ranks and
marched with a band to the Orleans Hotel to await her arrival
under the same window where, a few nights earlier, the rowdy
mob had hooted. But now, when Lola appeared, the hoots were
replaced by cheers; instead of hurling curses at those below her,
she threw them as a token of her affection a small American
flag, which she said she had carried with her all through the

---

[16]Ibid., July 11, 1853; also July 7, 9.

United States. Theater manager Charles King and husband Pat Hull both responded to calls from the crowd for a few remarks, after which the amiable Hull invited the firemen to step into the hotel's barroom for a drink at his expense.

The newlyweds left the scene of Lola's victory to return by steamer to San Francisco for a day, probably for Hull to finalize the selling of his interest in the *Whig* to W. B. Farwell and Company. They were back in Sacramento in time for her and her musicians to appear in a July 14 benefit for Charles King, who was financially overextended after building his theater.[17]

Lola and her troupe journeyed next up the Sacramento, Feather and Yuba rivers on the small steamer *Comanche* to Marysville, which was then the center for supplying the needs of the northern end of the Mother Lode. The dancer's first performance in the little town, on July 16, ended, a-la-Sacramento, in a general muss, after she somehow fell out of grace with her audience. This, in turn, led to a melee with Miska Hauser—during which his violin was said to have been "broken all to smash." Apparently in a truly foul mood that evening, Lola next vented her wrath on husband Pat Hull, which resulted in his decamping from their hotel in a hurried manner for another place to sleep. At its peak, this conjugal warfare waxed so fierce "that it was with difficulty that police officers were restrained from taking the contestants to the station house."[18]

The Dora Knapp stories in the San Francisco tabloids of the 1890s would come to greatly distort the Marysville fight with Pat Hull, as they did so many other incidents in Lola's

[17]Sacramento *Demo. State Journal*, July 11, 1853; *Union*, July 11-16, 1853; S.F. *Herald*, July 15, 1853; *Alta*, steamer edn., Aug. 1, 1853.

[18]Sacramento *Union*, July 18, 1853; S.F. *Herald*, July 19, 1853; Sacramento *Demo. State Journal*, July 18, 1853; Auburn (CA) *Weekly Placer Herald*, July 23, 1853; Stockton *Republican*, July 19, 1853.

life. They laid the cause of the argument to money matters and to her continuing correspondence with several men in Europe. She is credited with summarily pushing poor Hull out of their room and down the stairs of the non-existent "old Exchange Hotel," after which she threw his gripsack and other personal belongings out of the second-story window. A few years after the Knapp articles, another person who claimed to have been a friend of the Hulls, Lemuel Snow, parroted the same general story, except that he placed the Exchange Hotel in Grass Valley.

Pat Hull was able to temporarily reconcile his differences with Lola, but Miska Hauser had gotten his fill. He left his once-adored "Andalusian" to carry on without him, and returned to Sacramento where he gave the newspapers all the juicy details of the blowup. Oddly enough, for Lola's second and final night, the townspeople of Marysville turned out in large numbers, just as if nothing had happened, for what proved to be an uneventful and pleasant performance. The only bit of tension occurred during Lola's curtain speech when she berated the defector, Hauser, for departing despite having been engaged for the entire trip through the mines.[19]

The Hungarian violinist would go on to make other tours of the interior and play at small musical gatherings in San Francisco for a few more months, meeting with little financial success. His problem was, most likely, just as one unsympathetic observer guessed, "Sentimental 'cat-gut scraping'"[20] didn't pay in rough-and-tumble California. At his farewell concert in November, Hauser favored a San Francisco audience with "The Bird on the Tree" one final time, and then departed for South America and Australia.

---

[19]*San Francisco Examiner*, Feb. 19, 1899; *Call*, June 17, 1900; *Chronicle*, Jan. 17, 1897; *Bulletin*, Aug. 14, 1897; San Jose *Pioneer*, Aug. 15, 1900; Stockton *Republican*, July 23, 1853; Sacramento *Union* and *Times and Transcript*, July 19, 1853.

[20]San Francisco *Golden Era*, July 31, 1853; Sacramento *Union*, July 25-Aug. 1, 11, 15, Sept. 2, 1853; S.F. *News*, Nov. 12, 1853.

The tumult of Sacramento and Marysville behind her, Lola took her diminished little troupe, and what must have been a much-ruffled Pat Hull, still farther into the back country to the little village of Grass Valley. When Montez first laid eyes on the region surrounding this town, it was still a most beautiful place—though not nearly so pristine as it had been before the discovery of placer deposits there in August 1849. At that time, Wolf Creek ran clear as crystal, and the encircling Sierra Nevada foothills were thickly covered with huge first-growth pines, towering two to three hundred feet into perfectly clear skies. In the upper part of the valley, where it broadened out, the waist-high grass grew which gave the place its name.

Then, in October 1850, rich, gold-bearing quartz deposits were discovered on what would come to be called Gold Hill. There, a certain George Knight—so the story goes—stubbed his toe on some jutting quartz, which he picked up to discover flecks of gold. Little attention was paid to the quartz ledges at first because the placers were paying so well but, within a few months, deep quartz mining had begun and would soon spread to other California gold regions.

Grass Valley's first houses had been erected at the Boston Ravine end of town and, from these few shanties, the village grew rapidly at the expense of the ancient forests. By the time Lola alit there from her Concord coach on a hot July 1853 day, the hamlet had become a very busy place. The celebrated "Lola Montez" placer diggings northwest of town near Slate Creek were still paying well, and there were at least fifteen quartz mills in operation within a six-mile radius, crushing and processing the output of numerous mines. Lumber mills in and about town were supplying needs as far away as Marysville and Sacramento, and new houses and businesses were going up on every street. The valley resounded day and night with the din of hammer and hatchet, the puffing of steam engines and

Grass Valley in 1852
Courtesy, California State Library.

windlasses, and the whipping of sawmills. And, behind all, one could hear the crushing mills with their incessant rattling, banging and thumping.

Ditches, shafts, and piles of dirt and ore were everywhere. The grading and macadamizing of streets had begun, but residents were still advised to walk them with care at night so as to avoid the many foraging pigs. Then too, there were occasional complaints about miners digging holes and undermining the foundations of houses in their relentless quest for gold.

Efforts were being made to establish a decent cemetery, and to get a brick kiln operating so that fire-proof buildings could be erected. Pipes were being run to bring water to more houses from nearby Cold Spring Valley. There had even been talk of laying a sixteen-foot wide plank road over the forty miles to Marysville. And—wonder of wonders—within just a few weeks, a connection would be made to join the village to the telegraph line recently strung between Marysville, Sacramento, San Francisco, San Jose and Stockton.

With its population well over 3,000, Grass Valley was then the sixth-largest town in California. Residents liked to boast of it being different from other mining camps, in that its people were interested in making it a permanent home. The families that had settled there, many of them from New England, had thus far established three churches, two flourishing schools, a Bible society, two Sunday schools and even a sewing circle.

Of course, the town had its share of rough inhabitants. There were five prosperous gambling houses staffed with compliant female companions, and, as one old timer would remember, the usual number of dance halls "full of Spanish women in full blast."[21] In all, there were at least fifty places

[21]Edwin Franklin Morse, "The Story of a Gold Miner," 226; *Nevada* (City) *Journal*, Apr. 19, 1851, Apr. 15, 1853; Grass Valley (CA) *Telegraph*, Sept. 22, Oct. 27, 1853, Feb. 2, Mar. 30, 1854; Sacramento *Union*, Apr. 16, Sept. 29, Dec. 31, 1853; S.F. *Alta*, Dec. 19, 1851; S.F. *Journal*, July 25, 1853; S.F. *Picayune*, Aug. 7, 1854; Alonzo Delano, *California Correspondence*, xxv, 115; Stockton *Record*, Nov. 11, 1933; Edwin F. Bean, *Bean's History and Directory of Nevada County, Calif.*, 48, 186, 200.

where a person could get a drink. And there were other diversions. Shortly after Lola arrived, Charley Foy added a large pen at the rear of his saloon, lighted by a chandelier, where, of an evening, he held dog fights, rat killings and other sports to amuse his customers. But, while there were also frequent fist fights between the men of Boston Ravine and the Irish colony, Grass Valley, on the whole, was more peaceful and free of lynch law, knifings and gunplay than other camps, perhaps because of its higher proportion of educated men.

One of those wonderful, enlightened men who made it a special place was forty-seven-year-old Alonzo Delano. Equally as famous for his large nose as for his humorous writing, Delano had settled in Grass Valley in 1850 after having tried his hand at mining, trading with the Indians and speculating in land. For awhile he had owned his own mining company on Massachusetts Hill, but it had not prospered, and he had sold out in September 1851 to return East for a brief visit with his wife. Since his return, he had done better as proprietor of his own bank and as the local agent for Wells, Fargo Express Company, which was owned by three men from his native region of New York.

As "Old Block," Delano wrote widely for newspapers and magazines as far away as New York. Just prior to Lola's coming, the Sacramento *Union* had collected some of his better pieces and published them as *Pen Knife Sketches*, the first of several books he would write.

Delano had as a close friend Simon Pena Storms, the sub-agent for regional Indian affairs. The two had planned a short vacation trip to the summit of the Sierra Nevada on July 20, in company with old chief Weimar, Storm's father-in-law and head of the local tribe. But Delano and Storms became so enthused when they heard that Montez had arrived in town, they delayed their departure in order to catch her opening that evening, and then afterward rode five miles in the darkness to commence their vacation.

Lola's performance was held in Alta Hall, the upper floor of a gambling saloon which had recently been altered for theatricals by its two owners. "Old Block" described it as having been "neatly fitted up, the drop curtain and scenery from the hands of a true artist, with foot lights, orchestra, and...[an] audience to fill, which is more than can be said of all theaters."[22]

Despite having to pay substantially higher prices to see her at their small theater, most Grass Valley residents were quite taken with Lola and her dancing. A prominent businessman and pioneer California publisher, General Jonas Winchester, noted that her coming had "stirred the inmost soul of Grass Valley, waking from lethargy those on whom Gabriel's horn would fail to evolve a sign of life." The echo of the cheers on opening night, he said, could be heard "through the bounds of our lovely berg," drowning even the clatter of the eternal quartz stampers.[23] At least one villager who saw Lola, however, grumbled that she had also relieved the townspeople of a "considerable amount of oro, through curiousity to witness her performance."[24]

Lola played once more in Grass Valley, and then took her act a few miles away to Nevada City, where she performed July 25 through 30 at Dramatic Hall on the second floor of Hamlet Davis' store at Broad and Pine Street. Here again, despite admission prices having been doubled, houses were crowded and enthusiastic. The dancer's good behavior and flattering, piquant speeches, with their many "pregnant hits," were said to have reversed former prejudices about her. Indeed, her gracious

---

[22]Alonzo Delano, *Pen Knife Sketches*, 70-71; S.F. *Picayune*, Apr. 6, 1852; Sacramento *Union*, July 23, 1853; *Nevada* (City) *Journal*, June 17, July 22, 1853; Sacramento *Times and Transcript*, Jan. 27, 1853.

[23]*Nevada* (City) *Journal*, July 29, 1853; Sacramento *Union*, July 22, 1853.

[24]Sacramento *Union*, July 30, 1853.

mood proved to the satisfaction of one Nevadan that "where the Jesuit's annoyances intrude not like spiders on her arrangements, she can be as sunny as any of her sex."[25]

Although Alonzo Delano had mentioned that Lola intended going to Downieville next, more for the mountain air than to make money, she apparently instead returned directly to Grass Valley. By August 3, three days after closing at Nevada, she was reported to have been for some days the guest of a young bachelor named Gilmor Meredith at his cottage on Mill Street. Captivated by the charm of the "valley of engines and quartz," she could be seen, in the cool of the evenings, gracefully swinging in the hammock on Meredith's porch, surrounded by the "gallant host and a select circle of worshipers at the shrine of Beauty and Genius." The widely-popular Meredith was the envy of the whole town, a "lucky dog...to have a live Countess at his bachelor box."[26]

Montez had attempted another performance at Alta Hall, but attendance had been too thin to justify it, and the money was returned to ticket holders. But, afterward, a private performance of the "Spider Dance" was given to about a dozen "favorite hombres." The panting fellow who reported this event said that the lovely Lola had taken the "rag off 'the bush' ...with extra touches, to the infinite delight of the few admiring friends," and that "all that was seen on the occasion" was not divulged.[27]

With such goings-on, it hardly seems likely that, by then, Lola and Pat Hull were still living together. The last mention of Hull came from Alonzo Delano when the couple first arrived in Grass Valley. Delano noted then that, despite all the

[25]*Nevada* (City) *Journal*, July 29, 1853; also July 22.

[26]Ibid., Aug. 5, 1853, and Auburn (CA) *Placer Herald*, Aug. 6, 1853. The Downieville Theater was operating in July, but the Sacramento *Union* of August 3 and 10, quoting the Downieville *Mountain Echo* of July 30, Aug., 6, 13, 27, makes no mention of Lola being there. See *Union*, July 22, 1853.

[27]*Nevada* (City) *Journal*, Aug. 5, 1853.

Gilmor Meredith, about age 40
Courtesy, Nevada County, California,
Historical Society.

ugly stories in the papers about a Marysville fight, the "smiles of the honeymoon were still on Hull's face," and that the couple appeared happy. But thereafter, news reports dealt with Lola as though she were alone.[28]

Several years earlier Gil Meredith had lived in San Francisco where both he and Hull were active in Whig politics and in the earliest volunteer fire companies. The two almost certainly knew one another and, since Meredith checked into the Orleans Hotel in Sacramento during the Hulls' stay there, it seems probable that they had been invited by him to be his guests in Grass Valley. In any case, by August 12, after a mere month of connubial bliss, Lola had initiated divorce proceedings against Hull. She had also by then decided to quit the stage and take up residence in Grass Valley.

Why she and Hull broke up within such a short time is not

---

[28]Sacramento *Union,* July 22, 1853; also July 25.

clear, but is completely understandable in light of Montez's past stormy relationships. James J. Ayers, who knew Hull, said Lola alleged that her husband was incompatible because of "a distressingly constitutional affliction he suffered from." Some have implied that this mysterious affliction was body odor, or flatulence, but more likely, judging from the manner in which he was soon to die, Hull had syphilis.

Corroboration of this theory, however tenuous, was provided by a report in the Philadelphia *Press*, eight years after the fact, which noted that Hull had fallen sick and Lola had nursed him back to health just prior to their marriage—about the time Hull would have been expected to exhibit the primary signs of the disease. Whether or not Hull had syphilis, and may have acquired it from Lola can't be said, but it is certainly possible that her infectious period hadn't run its course by the time the two first met.

But whether Hull got it from her, or whether, in fact, neither of them had the venereal disease, poor Pat Hull had nonetheless received the Montez kiss of death. After separating from her, he associated himself in the spring of 1854 with the San Francisco *Daily Town Talk*, first as its editor, then as publisher. Then, in the fall of 1857, he suffered a stroke, was paralyzed, and for months lay in pain, completely helpless, nursed by a family in Marysville. Here he died on May 21, 1858, in the prime of life, at age 34. His mother arrived too late from Ohio to see him laid to rest.[29]

Having separated from Hull, sometime in August Lola purchased Gil Meredith's little cottage. Her two remaining musicians had been dismissed and were playing in Sacramento for Mademoiselle Dimier, a dancer somewhat younger and—they no doubt hoped—less volatile than Montez.

---

[29] Ayers, 99; also Sacramento *Daily Record-Union*, Jan. 1, 1884; *Nevada* (City) *Journal*, Apr. 6, 1855; S.F. *Fireman's Journal*, Apr. 25, 1857; S.F. *Alta*, May 25, 1858; Sacramento *Union*, May 25, 1858, Feb. 18, 1861; S.F. *Bulletin*, Nov. 9, 1895.

Lola's new home in Grass Valley had been built two sum-
mers earlier to serve as a combined office and living quarters
for the Gold Hill Mining Company. Meredith, a stockholder
and company secretary, owned the house and had lived there
along with the vice-president, James Walsh, and another officer. But, recently, a group of English capitalists calling themselves the Aqua Fria Company had bought a majority of the
Gold Hill stock, including that of Meredith and his father,
who lived in Baltimore. New engines and boilers had arrived,
and Aqua Fria was erecting a 40-stamp mill at the enormous
cost of $200,000. When Lola bought his house, Meredith was
merely awaiting his share of the Gold Hill stock proceeds.[30]

The much-traveled and worldly dancer was delighted with
her rustic mountain home. The small house contained only a
parlor, dining room, bedroom, kitchen and a servant's room,
but it was, as depicted about a year earlier by Alonzo Delano, a
neat, pretty little place, painted white, with a "piazza lemonad-
ing all around it."[31] Its grounds were adorned with bright green
manzanitas, jasmines and beautiful rose beds, and the branches
of a tall oak tree hung gracefully overhead.

There is no evidence that Lola made any major changes to
the house. Eventually a second story would be added by another owner but, as late as 1868, it was still described as being a
one-story building. Montez did, however, furnish the interior

---

[30]Marysville *Herald,* Aug. 17, 1853; S.F. *Fireman's Journal,* May 3, 1856; *Nevada* (City)
Journal, Apr. 15, June 24, 1853; Sacramento *Union,* Sept. 12-14, 1851, Apr. 26, May 26,
Nov. 2, 1853, Feb. 18, 1861; S.F. *Herald,* Aug. 28, 1851; Van der Pas, 15-20; Bean, 186-
87; S.F. *Journal,* Aug. 23, 1853; Sacramento *State Journal,* Sept. 28, 1853. Twenty-nine-
year-old Meredith had originally come to San Francisco from Baltimore as the first agent
for William H. Aspinwall's Pacific Mail Steamship Co. In January 1851 he joined Walsh,
George W. Bissel, S. Sanborn and others at Grass Valley in forming the Gold Hill Mining
Co. Grass Valley's first school had been on the same lot as the Gold Hill cottage; it may
have been in the same building (S.F. *Daily Pacific News,* Jan. 13, 1851; Sacramento *Times and
Transcript,* Sept. 23, 1852; Gilmor Meredith letter to his father Aug. 3, 1853, Meredith
Papers, Vol. 29).

[31]Delano, *Pen Knife Sketches,* 73; other descriptions of the house are in S.F. *Alta,* July 11,
1868; Grass Valley *Union,* Dec. 22, 1856; *N.Y. Times,* Apr. 26, 1856

in good style and had a large and costly greenhouse built, which she filled with exotic plants.

There was general agreement that the tempestuous dancer had set about to live in quiet and peaceful retirement. Alonzo Delano noted that she was living very unostentatiously and making friends by her good nature and amiability. He found that her varied experiences and quick intellect made her a most interesting and agreeable companion. From the beginning, Lola could often be seen hard at work, plainly dressed, digging and planting to further beautify the cottage grounds.

Edwin Morse, a tall and lanky twenty-year-old, would claim in his later years to have lived in the Robinson boarding house across the street from Lola's cottage, and to have become well acquainted with her. The young miner thought Montez still retained a graceful figure, beautiful black hair, and the most brilliant, flashing eyes he had ever seen, but he also noted that her charms had begun to fade. He conceded that she was still very handsome when carefully dressed, but, ordinarily, she appeared to him to be a disgusting slattern. When seen in her usual low-necked gown, even the liberal use of powder, Morse said, failed to conceal the fact that Lola stood much in need of a good application of soap and water.[32]

Montez told one interviewer, early in her Grass Valley days, that she was in fine health and spirits and was greatly enjoying her mountain home by hunting, riding, exploring the mines, entertaining her many visitors, reading, and writing up the notes of her eventful life. Another observer noted that she could occasionally be seen riding out on horseback, "puffing her cigar with as much gusto as a Broadway dandy."[33]

But, whether she was in fine health is arguable. One senses that the thirty-five year old was totally clapped out and fed up

---

[32]Morse, 339.

[33]San Francisco *Golden Era*, Sept. 4, 1853; also Marysville *Herald*, Aug. 17, Nov. 7, 1853; Grass Valley *Telegraph*, Dec. 15, 1853; Sacramento *Union*, Oct. 11, 1853.

with fast living. Periodic reports of fatigue and illness had increased in frequency since her coming to America, and it is likely that syphilis was beginning to affect both her health and stamina. There seems to be no other plausible explanation for her choosing to quit the stage at this particular time.

She may have made the decision to retire even before commencing her tour of the interior. Earlier, in June, there had been rumors that she had become quite enamored of California and, after a professional tour of several towns, would buy an extensive ranch in one of the state's fertile valleys and there devote the rest of her days to agricultural pursuits. Well, her Grass Valley cottage was no ranch, but there she would find, for a time at least, a bit of peace and contentment in her otherwise tempestuous life.

And why Grass Valley? Both Dora Knapp and Lemuel Snow took credit for influencing that decision, but their accounts are totally unreliable. The most probable explanation is that Lola simply was taken with the beauty and climate of the place and, with her marriage gone on the rocks, that is where she remained, in hopes of recruiting her physical and emotional strength. What more appropriate place for this woman who called herself "Montez"—a "dweller in the mountains?"[34]

---

[34]*New York Herald,* Apr. 1, 1852.

Steamboats *Antelope* and *Bragdon*
at San Francisco's Jackson Street wharf.
From *Hutchings' Magazine*, July 1859,
Courtesy, California State Library

CHAPTER FIVE

A Dweller in the Mountains

There's not a virtuous woman in Madrid, in this whole city! And would you persuade me that a mere dancing-girl, who shows herself, nightly, half naked, on the stage, for money, and with voluptuous motions fires the blood of inconsiderate youth, is to be held a model for her virtue?

—"Spanish Student" Henry W. Longfellow

In early autumn, Lola Montez waited quietly in Grass Valley for her divorce suit to be heard. Even in her newfound sanctuary, however, she was unable to completely avoid the public eye, as several bothersome newspaper editors made great sport of the ruined marriage. The nearby *Nevada Journal* quipped that she had applied "to be divorced from the bonds of Hully wedlock." San Francisco's *Golden Era*, in a cryptic reference to an unnamed new romantic interest, revealed that Lola had begun to show "a decided distaste for the Hull, believing that the Colonel (kernel) is somewhat more digestible."[1]

Just which colonel had attracted Montez is a mystery. There were several in the region who might have attracted her, but the most likely was Colonel Robert H. Taylor. A 31-year old widower and newspaperman, Taylor was just the sort of fellow Lola might find interesting. Although he had founded the

---

[1] *Nevada* (City) *Journal*, Oct. 7, and S.F. *Golden Era*, Sept. 4, 1853; also Stockton *Republican*, Sept. 13, 1853; Sacramento *Union*, Sept. 13, 1853; Marysville *Herald*, Sept. 28, 1853.

Marysville *Herald* in August 1850, the witty and sophisticated Mexican War veteran was an actor at heart. He sang well, wrote poetry, was an excellent comedian and a stirring speaker. Two of his best friends were the celebrated journalist-performer, Stephen Massett, and the indefatigable "Yankee Robinson."

Earlier that very year, Taylor had sold his interest in the Marysville newspaper so that he might try his hand at acting. About the time Montez arrived in Grass Valley, he had just finished playing an engagement in nearby Downieville, where, in December, having satisfied his curiosity about acting, he would begin practicing law. It is entirely possible that before taking up residence in Downieville he came down to Grass Valley to meet Lola and stayed on for a brief dalliance.

At all events, Lola was intent on divorce. On October 10 she traveled via Concord coach to Sacramento, where she boarded the side wheel steamer *Antelope* for San Francisco, probably intending to settle the details with Hull. Enroute, near Benicia, on what was a perfectly clear night, another steamer, the *Confidence*, sheared toward and collided with *Antelope*, tearing a large hole in the latter's hull near the waterline. The *Confidence* steamed heedlessly on after the impact, its captain mistakenly believing that *Antelope* required no assistance.

But Captain William Bushnell of *Antelope* was obliged to use his passengers to heel the ship to starboard while he and his men tried to plug the serious leak with bedding. At the same time, he steered slowly toward shore, where he eventually ran her aground. Another steamer arrived to take off Lola and the other 300 passengers, all unharmed, and the next day they arrived safely in San Francisco. Bushnell later complemented his lady passengers for their cool behavior, and Lola, in turn, spoke in flattering terms of the polite attentions of the steamer's officers.

Montez was back in Grass Valley within twelve days.

Although Nevada County court records were destroyed by fire, we know that her divorce suit was to have been heard beginning about November 20 in Grass Valley. It seems almost certain that her petition was granted on or about that date.[2]

Despite the appearance of prosperity in Grass Valley, the period of Lola's residence there coincided with the difficult beginnings of quartz mining. By 1857, the industry would be in a flourishing condition and, eventually, millions of dollars would be taken from the mines but, in 1853, it was still a very tenuous business. Most companies had proven to be disastrous failures: expensive mills had been built, based on faulty assumptions regarding the amount of gold the quartz would yield; there were few miners in California who knew how to properly open and work a quartz ledge; crushers were inadequate, and—most important of all—the amalgamation process was still very primitive.

Nevertheless, there were frequent and unabashedly-optimistic reports regarding yields. Quartz samples were sent to San Francisco and the Eastern states to lure investors; some from Grass Valley were even exhibited that year in the huge, new Crystal Palace on Madison Square in New York City. Every new visit by prospective investors, former politicians or "scientific men" helped build the illusion that all of Grass Valley's operating quartz mills were making money. Although most of these promotions were honest attempts to attract new capital, there were said to be a few quartz operators, eager to dump their holdings, who were busy mining "on a large scale in the pockets of Eastern investors."[3]

One group promoting their operation particularly hard was

---

[2]Grass Valley *Telegraph*, Jan. 9, 1854; S.F. *Herald*, July 13, 22, 1853; Earl Ramey, *The Beginnings of Marysville*, 45-46, 88; Marysville *Appeal*, Feb. 24, 1863; Marysville *Herald*, Apr. 24, 1854; S.F. *Journal*, Oct. 11, 1853; Stockton *Republican*, Oct. 13, 1853; *Nevada Journal*, Oct. 14, 1853; Sacramento *Union*, Jan. 19, 1852, Jan. 22, July 21, Sept. 23, Oct. 11-22, 1853; S.F. *Picayune*, Feb. 19, 1852; S.F. *News*, Nov. 8, 1853.

[3]Delano, *California Correspondence*, 137.

the Empire Quartz Mining Company, which, since the previous year, had been working a ledge less than a mile southeast of Grass Valley's Main Street. The Empire would eventually become one of the richest, longest-producing hard rock mining operations in California. But in 1853, it, like most others, was struggling.

The Empire's steam-powered, 16-stamp crushing and amalgamating works, with an attached sawmill, was situated at the foot of Ophir Hill, on the east bank of Little Wolf Creek. The principal owners, C.K. Hotalling, John Eddy Southwick, and William Wright, all shared a nearby cottage. Alonzo Delano once described these men as all being either crusty old bachelors or, like himself, "miserable grass widows, who eat, and sleep, and smoke, and chew with a single damnableness, far from the pleasing sound of prattling babes and the cheering smiles of happy wives." Yet, he said, they all had souls, and would make glorious husbands for a few lucky girls, since they were "taking out gold in a way that would have made Solomon roll his eyes with wonder."[4]

One of these Empire bachelors, Massachusetts-born John Southwick, would figure very prominently in Lola's life in Grass Valley—but not as her husband. The twenty-six-year-old Southwick supervised the amalgamation and retorting processes for the company and was, at the time Lola arrived, tinkering with a cylinder amalgamating device recently invented by Captain Smith Cram of Grass Valley, which was supposed to save at least 25% more gold than previous processes. There were at least a half-dozen such gadgets being experimented with, and none were very effective.

Lola's young neighbor, Edwin Morse, said the well-educated and handsome Southwick became deeply infatuated with Montez, and that he purchased Gilmor Merideth's cottage and established her in it as his mistress. Lola was no fool, Morse

---

[4]Sacramento *Union,* Sept. 13, 1853; S.F. *Herald,* July 12, 1852, June 27, 1853.

declared, "and she knew a good thing when she saw it and that good thing was Johnny Southwick, while his money lasted."[5] Morse was most likely correct in assuming that the pair were lovers, but all the evidence points to Montez having purchased the house herself.

Yet, the finances of Montez and Southwick did eventually become thoroughly entwined. The only question is, which one supported the other? To judge from subsequent events, it was probably Lola who was the provider. She arrived in Grass Valley with a full purse and is known to have invested in a Grass Valley quartz operation. Doubtless, it was Johnny Southwick's Empire Mining Company.

Lola Montez had always surrounded herself with animals, and now, in her new country home, she wasted little time in acquiring a menagerie that eventually would include sundry dogs and cats, pet birds, goats, sheep, chickens, turkeys, pigs, and a pony. In previous times—perhaps to draw attention to herself—she had shown a proclivity for some exceedingly fierce creatures. There was, of course, her bulldog in Munich. It was also while living there, if one can believe Auguste Papon, that she had tried to purchase a rhinoceros and a lion. Thus, those who knew her background were not surprised to learn in November 1853 that she had added a young male grizzly bear cub to her collection. Tongue-in-cheek, a San Francisco newspaper said she was also "negotiating for a pair of rattlesnakes."[6]

Bears—particularly the enormous, ill-tempered grizzlies which were then so plentiful—held a great fascination for early Westerners. Hardly a week went by in California without a

[5]Morse, 339; Sacramento *Times and Transcript*, Apr. 22, 1853; Grass Valley *Telegraph*, Oct. 20, 27, Nov. 24, 1853; S.F. *Golden Era*, Sept. 4, 1853; S.F. *Alta*, steamer edn., Sept. 16, 1853; Sacramento *Union*, Sept. 29, Nov. 2, 1853; S.F. *Journal*, Aug. 23, 1853; Marysville *Herald*, Nov. 7, 1853; L.A. *Star*, Feb. 28, 1852, Jan. 11, 1853; S.F. *Herald*, Nov. 26, 1853.

[6]San Francisco *Golden Era*, Nov. 6, 1853; Stephen C. Massett, *Drifting About*, 247; N.Y. *Daily Tribune*, Jan. 16, 1855; Richardson, 20, 28.

Lola Montez' Cottage in Grass Valley
From San Francisco, *The Wide West*, July 1, 1854. The caption said: "The representation of the bear...is a correct likeness of the beast that recently treated so ungratefully the hand that fed him."
From the author's collection.

report of some huge creature being encountered and killed. Cubs were frequently captured, reared, and then used in cruel fights with other animals and other entertainments. At the American Theater shortly after Montez left San Francisco, manager Lewis Baker placed on the playbill, along with the other acts, a "Grand Polka" by two grizzlies. And Lola's new ursine friend, perhaps, was the same young animal, captured near Downieville, that had appeared on stage there August 11 at Mrs. Emma Waller's benefit—inadvertently performing an act "more funny than savory."[7]

Edwin Morse thought Lola had acquired her cub merely to

[7]Marysville *Herald*, Aug. 17, 1853.

maintain her image as a lover of ferocious pets, but, in reality, he said, she was mortally afraid of the creature. The animal was kept chained to a stump in front of the cottage, and Morse noticed that Lola always stood at a safe distance while tossing it food.

Well, not always. One day in February 1854, while being fed some sugar, the grizzly seized his mistress' hand in his mouth and then attempted to strike her with his paw, but was not quite able to reach her. Only when a man standing nearby grabbed a club and stroked the bear across its head, did it let go of the badly wounded hand of the startled countess. Seemingly unsympathetic to the injured Lola, newspaper writers had a field day with the incident. From Frank Soule, editor of the San Francisco *Chronicle*, came the poem, "Lola and Her Pet:"

> One day when the season was drizzly,
> And outside amusements were wet,
> Fair Lola paid court to her grizzly,
> And undertook patting her pet.
>
> But ah, it was not the Bavarian,
> Who softened so under her hand,
> No ermined king octogenarian,
> But Bruin, coarse cub of the land.
>
> So all her caresses combatting,
> He crushed her white, slender hand flat,
> Refusing his love to her patting,
> As she refused hers to Pat.
>
> Oh, had her bear been him whose glory
> And title were won on the field,
> Less bloodless hap ended this story,
> More easy her hand had been Heald!
>
> But since she was bitten by Bruin,
> The question is anxiously plied;
> Not if tis the Countess's ruin,
> But whether poor bear has died?[8]

---

[8] Stockton *Republican*, Feb. 15, 1854; Marysville *Herald*, Feb. 11, 1854.

The gallant "Old Block" wrote a letter of apology on behalf of the bear, for biting fair Lola's hand, but said it was nothing against the beast's character, because:

> When Lola came to feed her bear,
> With comfits sweets and sugar rare,
> Bruin ran out in haste to meet her
> Seized her hand because twas sweeter.[9]

Apology or not, Lola soon disposed of the bear. By early March, with her wound mostly healed, she showed that she too could find a bit of humor in the incident. She advertised that the animal was for sale for either "public or family uses" and that "like his present mistress," Mr. Grizzly "was amiably inclined, and was never known to interfere with the rights of others unprovoked."[10]

Simon P. Storms found a use for the ill-behaved grizzly. In addition to being an Indian agent, this enterprising man also ran an amusement center on his property near Grass Valley. The day after Lola advertised, Storms came to town, bought the bear, and laid plans to use it for the entertainment of his guests at the upcoming July 4 celebration. Six of the best dogs, two at a time, he said, would fight the bear until either it or the dogs were vanquished. Other attractions Storms planned to offer in that Independence Day's "jorum of fun" were a big dinner, some good music, cock fights, horse racing, a foot race between an Englishman and an Indian for $200 a side, and "the jangling" of dog against dog.[11] Lola's former pet apparently whipped the dogs set against him. By that fall—then fully grown and ferocious—the bear was in the hands of a new owner, who featured him in a fight with a cougar as a Sunday amusement at Iowa Hill.

---

[9]San Francisco *Golden Era*, Mar. 19, 1854.

[10]Grass Valley *Telegraph*, Mar. 9, 1854; S.F. *Golden Era*, Mar. 5, 1854.

[11]Grass Valley *Telegraph*, July 6, 1854; also June 15, 22, Oct. 11, 1854; Morse, 235; S.F. *Herald*, Oct. 9, 1853; *Nevada Journal*, Oct. 6, 1854; S.F. *Alta*, May 26, 1855.

Far-fetched anecdotes abound regarding the Montez bear. One has an itinerant violinist (Miska Hauser perhaps?) asking for a lock of Lola's hair, and being told by her that he could have enough to make a bow for his fiddle if he would but wrestle the grizzly for three minutes. The love-stricken violinist accepted—so goes this tale—but stipulated that the bear should be muzzled. He somehow managed to endure the required three minutes and, mauled but happy, carried off his promised souvenir.

Another story portrays Lola acquiring not one, but two bears while still in San Francisco, and taking them with her everywhere. One of the Dora Knapp articles also mentions two grizzlies, one of which was so tame that Montez—with help from a manservant—could attach a chain about its neck and proudly walk it along Mill Street.

Most far-fetched of all the two-bear stories is the tall tale invented by newspaperman James Ayers, years after Pat Hull's death. Ayers, who had known Hull when the latter was assistant editor of the San Francisco *Courier,* said that Hull had lost the better part of two pairs of trousers, during his courtship of Lola, in getting past "those grizzly guardians of her palace gates." After finally succeeding in his marriage proposal, Ayers said, Hull had to "hug the pets before he was allowed to embrace the mistress of his heart."[12] Ayers also tells us that Lola asked for her divorce as the result of Hull killing one of the bears, which had playfully fastened his mouth on his leg.

One of Lola's visitors at Grass Valley noted that her favorite pet seemed to be the pony she rode on her mountain rambles. It was during one these frequent outings that she was nearly killed, while trying to jump the horse across a ditch to get at a cluster of attractive flowers. The steepness of the other side caused the animal to fall backward and, had Lola not landed under some timbers, she would have been crushed beneath it.

---

[12]Ayers, 98-99, and Sacramento *Record-Union,* Jan. I, 1884.

Alonzo Delano
Courtesy, Nevada County, California
Historical Society

But, as we have seen, Lola was no shrinking violet. A few weeks after the riding accident, dressed in Bloomer fashion, she was in the saddle again for an extended excursion up and over the summit of the Sierra Nevada. Joining her to escape the July 1854 heat were John Southwick, Alonzo Delano, Simon Storms, the brothers James C. and Lewis T. Delevan, and Miss C. Ritchter, Lola's private secretary who had come with her from Europe. A pack horse carried provisions sufficient for the two or three weeks the group intended to be gone.

The first few days of the trip were eventless, save for the several times the pack horse stumbled and rolled downhill. James Delevan soon turned back to attend to the press of his business affairs, but Lola and the rest continued on to Truckee Meadows and camped near the Donner cabins, where, a mere seven and one-half years earlier, entrapping snows had brought tragedy to that ill-fated immigrant party. Characteristically, the unorthodox Lola collected as souvenirs a few of the human bones that still lay scattered about.

It was also at Truckee Meadows that her petulance spoiled the trip for her secretary and Alonzo Delano, causing the pair to turn back to Grass Valley. The ruckus was described thus by one newspaper:

"Old Block" at the Summit. We have taken the liberty of withdraw-ing the injunction of secrecy from the transactions of "Old Block" and party, while making their tour to the "Downer Cabins." He informs us that he enjoyed himself hugely, notwithstanding the eccentricities of "the divine Lola" who was one of the party and who contributed not a little to its interest. After reaching the sum-mit...Lola found vent for an exuberance of feeling or indignation at a supposed want of consideration for her rank, manifested by some party, by quarrelling with her "private secretary," during the entire of one long cold night, and the next morning...[Delano] might have been seen descending the western slope of the Sierra in the direction of Grass Valley...He was prepared to face the tumult of a howling wilderness—nothing more.[13]

Lola and her remaining men—Southwick, Storms and Lewis Delevan—proceeded onward, destined to encounter still more trouble. They rode three days beyond Donner Lake to a trading post at desert's edge on the Truckee River, where they rested a few days before starting back.

On the morning of the second day of the return trip, Lewis Delevan, being ready ahead of the others, rode off by himself, driving the pack horse ahead of him. Montez and the others expected to overtake Delevan within a short time but, instead, they rode on all day without finding him. Since the pack horse

---

[13]San Francisco *Golden Era*, Aug. 6, 1854. James C. Delevan, a physician, was born ca. 1815 in Michigan. He was superintendant of the Rocky Bar Mining Company at Grass Valley at the time of the pack trip, although later he would be fired when his experimental mill failed to produce results. Little is known of his brother Lewis T. Delevan, except that he worked in Grass Valley as a miner and amalgamator until at least 1871. (Morse, 334, n.12; Theo Reidt, "Lola Montez' Ill-fated Trip...," p. 12). Verification that C. Richter, Lola's private secretary, arrived with Lola in the U.S. is in *N.Y. Herald,* Dec. 5, 6, 1852.

carried all the provisions, they spent a hungry night camped on the banks of the Truckee. On their way again the next morning, they fell in with a vacationing party of men and women from Nevada City, who gave them food and informed them that Lewis Delevan was not ahead of them. Lola and her friends concluded that the missing man had either taken the Downieville (Henness Pass) road, or had become lost. In either case, they thought, he would do well enough, since he had all the food, and so they returned directly to Grass Valley, arriving July 26.

James Delevan was alarmed to hear that Lewis was missing, and he was more than a little put out that his brother had been so quickly written off by his traveling companions. Intending to start off the following morning, Delevan hired twelve "fighting men" who were familiar with the Indians of the region, and also got a promise from Simon Storms that he would come along with an additional force of whites and Indians.

But Indian fighters would not be necessary. Lewis's only problem was that he had taken the wrong trail after leaving his traveling companions. The tortuous path he had chosen followed closely along the Truckee, while the more direct wagon road he should have taken ran farther from the river. "After discovering his mistake, in his clumsy attempts to get control of the pack animal, Delevan had managed to lose both it and his riding horse, and had nearly drowned himself in the process. He had eventually been required to abandon the two nags, grazing contentedly on the opposite side of the river, and walk on. Near the Donner cabins he regained the wagon road and finally, after being three days without food or blankets, another vacationing group had found him, sitting on a rock by the side of the road "looking wild and wo-begone and nearly starved...contemplating the uncertainty of all human events."[14]

---

[14]San Francisco *Herald*, July 30, 1854; also Grass Valley *Telegraph*, July 13, Aug. 3, 1854; James Delevan, *The Gold Rush*, 71-72; *Nevada Journal*, July 14, 1853.

Said a San Francisco paper of the adventure: "It is confidently asserted that his sudden disappearance with the provisions was the result of an accident and not premeditated determination to tame the spunky Countess by starvation."[15]

There seems little doubt that "Old Block" was smitten with Lola—or at least he had been before taking the pack trip. A few years later, a correspondent of *Leslie's Weekly* met Delano and perhaps heard at firsthand the story of the mountain adventure with Montez. From this, the Leslie's man concocted a romantic story poking fun at Montez and "Old Block's" renowned large nose.

The brilliant but capricious Lola, the correspondent wrote, had fallen in love with the nose—to which Delano seemed to belong, "rather than the nose to him"—and she had married "Old Block" on the strength of it. On the wedding day, in a "torrent of admiration," Lola made Delano a present of $14,000. "Never," wrote the man from Leslie's, "was there a happier man that night than 'Old Block'—the possessor of a fortune, an unrivaled nose, and one of the loveliest of women. But...The course of true love never did run smooth, and the next morning she took the money away from him, and left him to waste his sweetness on the desert air. His nose she could not take, or else no doubt she would."

Responding in another paper, Delano urged Frank Leslie to have his writer conjure back the fourteen thousand or, better yet, he said, he'd compromise and take seven thousand (fifty cents on the dollar) and give Leslie his share of Lola in the bargain.[16]

---

[15]San Francisco *Golden Era*, Aug. 6, 1854.

[16]San Francisco *Herald*, Aug. 30, 1858, and Sacramento *Union*, Sept. 10, 1858. In 1857 Delano published a two-act play entitled *A Live Woman in the Mines, or Pike Country Ahead!* dedicated to Montez. The writer was married for twenty years to a woman he left back in Ottawa, Illinois. He went East to visit her in 1851 and 1857, at which time she was very ill. She later died and, in 1871, at age 65, Delano married Marie Harmon of Ohio, who was visiting in California (Delano, *California Correspondence*, xxiii-iv; Grass Valley *Telegraph*, Nov. 24, 1853; Reidt, 11; Sacramento *State Journal*, Sept. 17, 1857).

Another result of the pack trip seems to have been the naming of some topographical features on the eastern slope of the Sierra Nevada. One tradition says that, as Lola and her men approached an unnamed lake, about fifteen miles north of Truckee, her friends accorded her the honor of naming it. She is supposed to have stood up in her stirrups, waved a hand aloft and exclaimed "Lake Independence!" The naming of 9148-foot high Mount Lola, and of Upper and Lower Lola Montez lakes, in the same vicinity, may also have been prompted by the publicity surrounding the outing.[17]

One of the enduring myths to have originated with the Dora Knapp newspaper articles concerns an encounter Montez is supposed to have had with a Grass Valley clergyman. So this story goes, a prim, old minister named Wilson sermonized from his pulpit that the presence of such a wicked and shameless dancer in Grass Valley was nullifying any good effect he might be having. When Lola heard of the accusation, she decided to set the cleric straight and, donning one of her costumes, she walked resolutely down the street and rapped loudly on Wilson's door.

The pastor and his wife were astounded to see the notorious dancer standing on their stoop, dressed only in long silk stockings, short, fleecy skirts and the most low-cut and revealing of bodices. As they stood thus transfixed, Lola marched, uninvited and defiant, into their parlor. Once there, she explained to Wilson—calling him "Meester Preacher" in her slightly foreign accent—that she had come to show him how modest her costume was, and how really sweet and innocent a dancer could be.

In his variation on this tale, old-timer Lemuel Snow embellished it at this point by having Lola offer to give Wilson an exhibition of her skill. And, when the cleric refused to allow

---

[17]Oakland (CA) *Tribune*, Sept. 14, 1941.

such lewd conduct in his home, Lola lectured him that her "Spider Dance" was "poetry of motion, and her ideal was to make the human race more artistic by her graceful dance."[18]

Unfortunately, the full enjoyment of this wonderful legend is lost when one discovers that there was no pastor of any faith named Wilson in Grass Valley during those years. And, with apologies to the memory of Dora Knapp and Lemuel Snow, this unlikely tale of saint meeting dancing sinner had been around a long time before they chose to attribute it to Lola. It had likely begun in the 17th century with Thomas Middleton's play *The Spanish Gypsy* and, certainly by the mid-nineteenth century, many people were conversant with it in Cervantes' tale, *La Gitanilla* or with its variant, Longfellow's "Spanish Student."

The Longfellow work has the Archbishop of Toledo and a cardinal being sent to Spain by the pope to put a stop to bull-fighting and lewd dances upon the stage. After disposing of bullfighting, the two send for Preciosa, a well known and enchanting dancer, so that they might see at first hand what they would be prohibiting. But Preciosa entrances the stuffy old men right from the start. She lays aside her *mantilla* and begins moving slowly to measured beats of castanet and tam-bourine. Gradually the music and dance become livelier, building in intensity to a fever pitch until the clergymen become excited, and, forgetting themselves, rise from their seats, throw their caps in the air and applaud vehemently, all the while shouting "Viva Preciosa!"

The *Alta California* made the comparison to Preciosa shortly after Lola first came to San Francisco, saying that, seeing her dance, one could understand how she had turned the head of King Ludwig, and that, like Preciosa, Montez could have also easily changed the minds of Longfellow's clerics. The Knapp

---

[18]*San Francisco Examiner*, Feb. 19, 1899; S.F. *Chronicle*, Jan. 17, 1897, and *Bulletin*, Aug. 14, 1897.

story may have been inspired by this article, or one of the several others in a similar vein that appeared during Lola's stay in California.[19]

While Grass Valley's Christian ministers may, in fact, have been uncomfortable with Lola Montez living in their town, those persons who knew her well came to recognize the redeeming qualities which we have already noted. Her faithful champion on the *Alta* staff would later remember that, although sometimes deviating from the path of virtue, Lola had also beggared herself by her extravagance and her charities to the wretched and the poor, and that she was "frequently found giving consolation to the one and substantial aid to the other."[20]

Then too, Rufus Shoemaker, editor of the Grass Valley *National*, would recall "Madam Lola...riding many miles over the hills to carry food and medicine to a poor miner," and more than once watching "all night at the bedside of a child whose mother could not afford to hire a nurse."[21]

We have seen earlier instances of how Lola demonstrated a special kindness toward children, particularly young girls. Destined to remain childless herself, perhaps the giving of attention to the offspring of others was her way of compensating for this void in her life. Or, maybe it was the result of the earlier turbulent relationship with her own mother, and the ensuing years of isolation from any vestige of family.

Long after her death, a number of seemingly-false claims would emerge to the effect that Lola had borne children. One of the earliest of these came from a woman calling herself, variously, Princess Editha Loleta, or Princess Editha Gilbert Montez. This poseur caused a minor stir by claiming to be

---

[19]*Nevada Journal*, Apr. 1, 1853; Grass Valley *Telegraph*, Dec. 22, Oct. 20, 1853, July 6, 1854; Bean, 193-94; S.F. *Alta*, June 8, 1853, Jan. 25, 1855; S.F. *Fireman's Journal*, Nov. 17, 1855.

[20]San Francisco *Alta*, July 11, 1868.

[21]Edmund Kinyon, *The Northern Mines*, 147-48.

Lola's daughter by King Ludwig. A few years later, an aspiring and beautiful actress, known as Elise Montez, claimed to have been the illegitimate daughter of Lola and her Parisian lover Dujarrier. Still later, in 1888, a spiritualist known as Madame Diss Debar swore under oath during a New York City bunko trial, against her and her lover, that she was the daughter of Lola Montez and Ludwig. Madame Debar said she had been brought by an old art dealer named Lowenhertz as a child of six to the United States, put in the care of a family that abused her, and then, afterward, she had spent time in various convents.

The third of the Dora Knapp newspaper articles credited Lola and Patrick Hull with having borne a daughter, Rosalind, whom Lola allegedly abandoned to the care of a certain Mrs. Samuel King of Sacramento, the wife of a rich gold miner. This girl, however, was supposed to have been born in 1856, which was long after Hull and Lola had divorced.

From another of those 1890's San Francisco tabloids came a still more dubious tale of a possible child. Thad Phillips, a porter on the Oakland ferry service of the Southern Pacific Railroad, laid claim in his old age that he had become Lola's valet and servant for three years beginning in 1854, when, as a mere boy, he was working as a messenger for Sacramento's American Theater. His job, Thad said, was to look after the Montez jewelry and wardrobe, and to run her errands.

Somewhat of a braggart, Phillips admitted to having read a plethora of books and articles about Lola's life, and his story seemed to be a confused blending of them. He also confessed to having forgotten many details; one of these, apparently, was that Sacramento's American Theater had burned down in 1852, before Lola even came to California. Phillips claimed that Lola had a child in Sussex, England, presumably George Heald's. He said that the English consul used to visit Lola in Grass Valley to give her 100 pounds per month from the child's father with the proviso that, to avoid scandal, she never again set foot in Sussex.

But, other than these several spurious claims, there is no evidence that Montez ever became a mother. In fact, a Nevada City newspaper editor would confirm that Lola remained childless throughout her life, asserting that there were people living in Grass Valley who had often heard her declare she would gladly give all she possessed to become a mother.

So, the children of others came to benefit from Lola's barren condition. One of these was a three-year old Grass Valley toddler named Matilda Uphoff, whose parents ran a bakery on lower Main Street. Little Matilda would come to recall with pleasure the wonderful Christmas party Lola gave for the town's few young girls, welcoming them merrily at her door, then treating them to gifts, games and good things to eat. On another occasion, when Matilda happened to be traveling to Sacramento on the same stagecoach with Lola, the dancer held the little girl and amused her for most of the trip—talking and singing as the coach rolled along—so that Matilda's grateful mother could take care of a baby sister. Uphoff believed Montez to surely be the most beautiful, kindest woman in the world, and she was certain that if Lola had been the bad influence some said she was, the mothers of Grass Valley would never have allowed their children to have anything to do with her.[22]

Susan Robinson was another little girl who may have received Lola's attention. Sue was only eight years old in the winter of 1853-54 when her father, J. B. Robinson, brought his family of itinerant players to a permanent home at the corner of Church and O'Neill streets in Grass Valley. Every member of the family—mother, father, little Susan, her brother William and sister Josephine—was a talented performer. But

---

[22]Sacramento *Union*, May 1, 1888; S.F. *Alta*, May 19, Dec. 13, 1879; Nevada City *Daily National Gazette*, July 1, 1870; S.F. *Call*, June 17, 1900; S.F. *Examinier*, June 11, 1893; Stockton *Record*, Apr. 8, 1933.

little Sue—known affectionately as "La Petite Susan," or the "California Fairy Star"—was by far the most gifted. She could twirl the banjo, dance the clog, or sing, while performing numbers such as "Black Eyed Susan," "A Kiss in the Dark," or the "Shawl Dance." As one observer noted, Susan appeared to "understand all the fascinating qualities of her sex," despite her tender age.[23]

Susan and her brother had danced in San Francisco just before Lola arrived in California, and they played there once again on the same bill with Billy and Caroline Chapman while Montez was in town. But it was in the interior towns and mining camps that the Robinsons and their children were best-known. After locating in Grass Valley, the parents taught ballroom dancing at Masonic Hall, and the family performed occasionally at Alta Hall, as well as in the nearby villages of Nevada City and Rough and Ready. When the three children played Nevada in December, Susan was repeatedly encored, and a golden "shower of dollars" was rained on the stage by the enthusiastic miners in her audience.[24]

Child performers were all the rage at the time. The H.L. Bateman children—Ellen and Kate—had become enormously famous touring the eastern United States and Europe under P. T. Barnum's aegis. Longtime California actor Walter Leman thought that Susan Robinson could have attained the same sort of fame, had she been properly trained. Sue, however, was destined for a less-enchanting future. She was severely burned while playing El Dorado County in June 1854, when her dress caught fire from the footlights. After recovering, she became a much-beloved performer in California, but never achieved any national fame. She had two children in a brief, unhappy mar-

---

[23]Grass Valley *Telegraph*, Nov. 24, 1853; Marysville *Herald*, Nov. 14, 1853; Sacramento *Times and Transcript*, May 4, 1853; S.F. *Herald*, June 29, 1853.

[24]*Nevada Journal*, Dec. 9, 1853; also Dec. 16, 1853; Grass Valley *Telegraph*, Nov. 17, Dec. 15, 1853, Apr. 20, 1854; Dempsey, 7, 97-99, 109.

riage, then died tragically in 1871, when only twenty-six years of age.

Although there is only legend and the recollection of old-timers to rely upon, there may have been still another little girl in Grass Valley who took the fancy of Lola Montez. In the spring of 1853, Mary Ann Crabtree and her feckless husband, John, came with their daughter Lotta to Grass Valley, where Mary Ann opened a boarding house only a few doors down from Lola's cottage on Mill Street. Six-year old Lotta, a precocious redhead with fetching black eyes, is supposed to have skipped one day through Lola's yard, whereupon Montez—immediately recognizing the tot's genius—took Lotta under her wing and spent countless hours teaching her the social graces, diction, dancing and how to ride.

Some have also given Lola credit for the first public appearance of "La Petite Lotta." Montez is supposed to have taken her little prodigy to W. H. Fippen's blacksmith shop in Rough and Ready, where the girl displayed her steps upon an anvil in front of a delighted crowd, to the accompaniment of Fippen's hammer strokes. A variation of this story has Lola clapping her hands to provide the rhythm.

The original tie between Lola and Lotta seems to have been made by the Cincinnati *Chronicle* in 1868. At the time, however, the California portion of the story was denounced as false and, in fact, another source has Lotta learning to dance in 1853-54 at a school conducted by a fellow named Bowers in the annex of his Grass Valley tavern. In this version, it is Bowers who is given the credit for taking Lotta to dance in Rough and Ready, where he wanted to open a second school. Another, more likely story has a certain troubadour, Mart Taylor, teaching Lotta to sing and dance at Rabbit Creek (La Porte), California, where Lotta and her family moved in late 1854.

Howsoever she got her start, the cute, lively Lotta became a huge success, dancing and singing her way through California's

Lotta Crabtree
Courtesy, California State Library

mining camps beginning in the late 1850s, accompanied by
her mother. After leaving for the East, in 1864, she would go
on to attain worldwide fame and wealth on the American stage
for fifty years, outshining both Lola Montez and Sue Robinson.[25]

But, while living in Grass Valley, Lola Montez did more
than entertain the town's little girls, ride in the mountains, and
help nurse sick miners. Unable to give up her role as social

[25]Sacramento *State Journal*, July 30, 1857; Sacramento *Union*, July 13, 1858, May 28,
1868, June 19, 1871; Leman, 355; Grass Valley *Telegraph*, Feb. 16, Mar. 2, 30, 1854; *Nevada Journal*, June 9, 1854; S.F. *Examiner*, Sept. 23, 1888; Andy Rogers, *A Hundred Years of Rip
and Roarin' Rough and Ready*, 80-81; Dempsey, 7, 97-99, 109.

luminary, she continued to entertain frequently. Rufus Shoemaker called her one of the lions of the town, saying that visitors from below, "clerical as well as lay," while taking a look at
the quartz mills, "invariably sought an introduction to her, and
always returned delighted from an hour's chat at her hospitable
cottage."[26] As had always been the case, her guests were mostly
men, and apparently many of them were potential investors
being wooed by Johnny Southwick and his mining partners.

State legislators were also her frequent guests. Lola, in fact,
was cited by a San Francisco newspaper as being one cause of
the poor quality of legislation enacted during the 1854 ses-
sion, the implication being that Sacramento law makers were
wasting too much time with long lunches, theatricals, balls and
dinners, and in traveling to Grass Valley to pay her homage.

The welcome mat at Lola's cottage was, of course, always
out for artistic personalities who might be passing through
town. One of this class to visit was Stephen C. Massett, the
itinerant, sometime musician and variety performer who, in
June 1849, had given one of the first musical entertainments in
California. At the time he visited Lola in 1854 he was co-edi-
tor of the Marysville *Herald.* Writing of it long after the event,
Massett recalled that Lola and John Southwick received him
very hospitably for what was a pleasurable evening with a
merry group which included Gil Meredith.

Perhaps the most noted artist to be feted at the Grass Valley
cottage was the famed Norwegian violinist, Ole Bull, during
his highly-successful tour of California in the summer of
1854. Bull and the pianist, Maurice Strakosh, played in Nevada City and Grass Valley in late August, and it was undoubtedly then that Lola held her evening musicale honoring them. It
is likely that Lola had met the large, handsome violinist when
they both were touring the Eastern states.

------

[26]Kinyon, 147-48.

Ole Bull
Courtesy, California State Library

Bull had the reputation of thrilling members of the opposite sex who heard him play, just as Lola thrilled the young men who saw her dance. A liberal thinker, the violinist had in his lifetime worked in support of the Norwegian national movement; he had spoken at every opportunity on behalf of religious toleration and the free school system, and had tried unsuccessfully in 1853 to establish a Norwegian agricultural colony in Pennsylvania, losing a great deal of money when the project failed.

Although Edwin Morse had not attended the public concert, nor had he been invited to Lola's fete, he later told of sitting on the porch of his boardinghouse across the street from the Montez cottage and listening to the strains of the great master's violin. He also vividly remembered the raw-boned and vigorous Bull, with the long, fair hair, as he came swinging down Mill street with great strides, Johnny Southwick trotting at his side trying to keep pace.

Extensive as it may have been, Lola's entertaining was greatly exaggerated in the Dora Knapp and Lemuel Snow articles and in the several plagiarisms of them. These fanciful tales have Pat Hull still in the picture, with he and Lola holding regularly scheduled, ultra-Bohemian soirees at the cottage, usually attended by the several married couples in the town who were friends of Montez, and about a dozen convivial bachelors and "genial spirits." At these supposed parties, each new cocktail and every new story or song was tried out as soon as anyone in the group heard of it. The best of food—cake, fruit—Spanish dishes—was always available, sometimes brought in specially from Sacramento.

The countess, so the stories said, was the central figure at each of these salons, and occasionally she would array herself in her "old stage gown and prove to her visitors that she had not forgotten how to dance, and, at the close, would pass the hat for contributions for the refreshments for the next meeting." Sometimes, Knapp and Snow maintained, these "experience meetings,"[27] as they were called, would last until daybreak, the sound of singing voices, guitars, accordions and violins resounding through Grass Valley's otherwise tranquil early morning streets, much to the displeasure of some of the town's tongue-wagging Puritans.

Just as Montez seemed incapable of living a totally reclusive

[27]San Francisco *Chronicle,* Jan. 17, 1897; also *Bulletin,* Aug. 14, 1897; *Examiner,* Feb. 19, 1899; S.F. *News and Picayune,* Apr. 22, 1854; Morse, 340; Massett, 247; Gagey, 17-18; S.F. *Picayune,* Jan. 10, 1852; Hauser, "Adventures," 59: 5, p.5; Sacramento *Union,* June 16, 1853; S.F. *Golden Era,* July 9, 1854; *Nevada Journal,* July 21, Aug. 24, Nov. 3, 1854. The legislature met at Benicia during the winter of 1853-54 until about March 6, when it moved to Sacramento.

life in Grass Valley, she also seemed unable to make do with the attentions of just one man. Besides John Southwick, there was a shadowy figure named Adler, who has been variously identified as a handsome German baron or as a doctor. One biographer says Lola met him when she played Downieville, that the two rode together in the mountains and that Lola enjoyed telling about the time a masked highwayman surprised them while they were bagging pheasants along a mountain trail. This same writer has Pat Hull still on the scene, seething with jealousy over the affair, until, at length, Adler went out hunting by himself and was mysteriously shot dead, perhaps by his own hand.

The only known contemporary reference to Adler is that of Gil Meredith who wrote to his sister Emma on January 29, 1854, that Lola had "a Crazy German" who followed her all over the country—listing the man along with Lola's extensive menagerie of animals.[28] The role of Gilmor Meredith in Lola's life is somewhat less obscure than that of Adler, but nonetheless contains an aura of mystery. After selling his cottage, Meredith moved into a small cabin for a time and then, later on, he lived in the Beatty House hotel. He had originally hoped to leave for the East within a few weeks, but ended up staying on in Grass Valley for another ten months. Ostensibly, the delay was because Meredith was waiting for the proceeds from the sale of his shares in the Gold Hill Mine. But perhaps there was more to it. One suspects that at least part of the reason might have been his fascination with Montez. Maybe they were lovers for a time; perhaps just good friends.

Meredith wrote his relatives that he was a great favorite of Lola, able to talk and do as he chose, and that he often paid her "a flying visit." He maintained that the principal attractions for him were her player piano—which played melodies from

---

[28]Meredith Papers, vol. 29; also Ishbel Ross, *The Uncrowned Queen*, 239, 246; D'Auvergne, *Lola Montez*, 201.

his favorite operas—and her excellent brandy. He remembered that sometimes, when the mood struck her, Lola—who played both piano and guitar—would sing "a plaintive Spanish air," or enlighten her guests upon her life in Bavaria. He also noted that she spoke nearly every language, and could, when she desired, make herself exceedingly agreeable.[29]

It may have been Gil Meredith who took Lola for a sleigh ride in mid-January of her first winter in Grass Valley. The region had been blanketed by a rare heavy snowstorm, and temperatures had plummeted to ten degrees below zero. With the quartz mills all frozen up and closed, many residents amused themselves with snowball fights and by sleighing in homemade, horse-drawn "pungs," fashioned out of packing boxes with pine slabs for runners. Lola was briefly seen recklessly driving such a rig—perhaps the one Meredith had built the previous winter—through the streets of nearby Nevada City. Delighted citizens in the village watched her disappear "like a meteor through the snow flakes and wanton snowballs" in the direction of Grass Valley.[30]

Further credence to a possible Meredith-Montez liaison is given by the fact that one of the few times Lola is known to have traveled to San Francisco during her residence at Grass Valley was on May 30, 1854, the day before Gil Meredith sailed from there for his home in Baltimore. Just after, or perhaps shortly before, Meredith departed, Lola may have taken another lover. On May 25, 1854, Henry Shipley, a twenty-six year old native of Massachusetts, and Amherst graduate, took over editorial duties at the Grass Valley *Telegraph*, having just come from James Allen's Marysville *Herald*. Shipley was a

---

[29]Letter to sister Emma, Jan. 29, 1854, in Meredith Papers; also letters of Aug. 3, Sept. 15, Oct. 3, Nov. 14, 1853, and Jan. 29, 1854; Grass Valley *Telegraph*, June 1, 1854.

[30]*Nevada Journal*, Jan. 20, 1854; also Jonas Winchester, Scrapbook of Clippings on Mining, Travel and other Subjects, 1851-1887; clipping from *California Courier* containing Winchester letter of Dec. 18, 1852; S.F. *Golden Era*, June 4, 1854.

handsome, good-natured but indolent fellow who had, sadly, fallen victim to demon rum. But he was a talented writer who came to enliven considerably the little Grass Valley sheet for its owners. Too much, in fact, to suit the Countess of Landsfeld.

California at the time was noted for its newspapermen who, because of their free-wheeling editorial opinions, had been called onto the field of honor by insulted men, to die or be maimed with pistol or rifle. Until Lola came along, however, none had been required to do battle with a woman.

According to Montez, shortly after he arrived in town, Shipley called on her and introduced himself as the future editor of the *Telegraph*. Lola said she received him politely, despite finding him to be of common intellect and appearance; she told of the unsavory reputation Shipley quickly gained as a besotted, pugnacious and "shoulder-striking editor" who bragged incessantly about his wealthy, high-toned family in the East, and of how fearful other townsmen were of tangling with him. Sobering up after one drunken revel, wherein he had thrown a glass of wine into the face of one man, and had called another a coward, Shipley had been obliged to write humble letters of apology.

Lola said that the vain and foul-mouthed editor came uninvited so frequently to her house in a beastly state of intoxication, that she eventually ceased showing him any consideration. On one occasion, sitting drunk in her parlor, he had pulled a letter from his pocket and, with a face full of importance, told her it was from a friend and admirer, begging him "as the only man that could save the country" to let his name be placed in nomination for U. S. senator. Shipley implied that he was really only in California for a "spree," while waiting to run for that office. He had also told Lola other wondrous tales, she said—how he had fled Cincinnati after killing one man and wounding several others; of his running off with a clergyman's wife; of how a Spanish lady had sworn to kill herself for him; and how, at Marysville, for love of an ungrateful woman, he had swallowed poison, but was saved by a stomach pump.[31]

But Lola may have been protesting too much about Shipley. We know of her fondness for good-looking young newsmen, as well as for unwashed mountebanks, and this editor fit tidily into both classes. Indeed, Stephen Massett or another writer for the nearby Marysville *Herald* hinted that something was going on when he good-naturedly said, shortly after Shipley took over, that the *Telegraph* was "presumed to be Lola's organ."[32] It is entirely likely Shipley may have briefly held an appeal for her. We know that he was a part of her coterie at the time of Ole Bull's visit. He and Bull—no mean drinker himself—had swapped stories over cocktails and no doubt Bull had given Ship his well-known demonstration at a local bar of how violin playing had developed the muscles of his right arm.

Montez would say that Shipley liked to put down any performers of lesser talent than that of a Jenny Lind. Thus, in early November, when an actress and two actor friends of Lola came to see the mines at Grass Valley and stayed on to give two performances at Alta Hall, which failed to suit Shipley, he told her that he was going to give the players "fits" in his paper. Lola thought that she had talked him out of this course, but nevertheless, in the November 14, 1854, edition of the *Telegraph*, Shipley criticized what he called the "barbarous performances" of the whole party. Calling them "strolling itinerants," he said he hoped to see the time come when "actors, too illiterate to serve as wood sawyer's clerks, and songsters, excelled by every barmaid," would stop paying Grass Valley unwelcome visits.

---

[31]San Francisco *Examiner*, Sept. 23, 1888; also *Telegraph*, May 25, 1854; Marysville *Herald*, Nov. 17, 1853.

[32]Marysville *Herald*, May 22, 1854; Nevada City *Democrat*, May 24, 1854.

Later, on the same day that Shipley's attack appeared in print, came the next act of this unfolding drama. Lola had been ill and bedridden for a week, with a lady companion ("Mrs. R.") in attendance, when the editor burst unannounced into her bedroom—or at least so said she, in an accusation reminiscent of one she had previously made against Edward Willis. In a frightful scene, the dancer upbraided the editor for his article, and he in turn verbally abused her—even threatening to cut her throat, she said. Finally Lola got out of bed, found her pistol and told him to leave the house, and never return. Giving the rejected Shipley a kick to get him started, Lola said she couldn't help laughing heartily at the exit of the "hero of a thousand imaginary battles—which nobody ever saw or heard of but himself."

Shipley's recounting of the bedroom incident was somewhat different. He said he remained very cool, despite Lola's verbal abuse and her brandishing of the pistol, and that "he left her in disgust and regret that a woman could so far forget her position."

Not content to let matters rest, Shipley had the further temerity to copy into his next weekly issue of the *Telegraph* an article taken from the *New York Times*, which spoke of the "Lola Montez-like insolence and barefaced hypocrisy" of the Queen of Spain. When Lola perused her paper as usual that morning, and noticed the abusive article containing her name "in good round English," she became furious. She gathered up her riding whip, which, as she said, had never been used on a horse, but would soon fall on "the back of an ASS." On went her bonnet, and out she stormed from her cottage, "strong in the principles...of Miss Lucy Stone" and the Women's Rights Convention, to avenge herself and all women against this scoundrel of an editor![33]

---

[33]Quotes are from S.F. *Examiner*, Sept. 23, 1888, and *Alta*, Nov. 26, 1854; also Grass Valley *Telegraph*, Oct. 31, 1854. Lucy Stone of Boston was a lecturer and women's rights activist.

The townspeople were thrown into a state of excitement by the sight of Lola rushing toward Main Street, with the whip in one hand, and a copy of the *Telegraph* in the other, "her eyes in fine frenzy rolling."[34] Soon, a huge crowd was trailing behind her toward the newspaper office. As she passed the Golden Gate Saloon, Montez spotted good old boy Shipley sitting inside at a table, enjoying a drink with the owner, Mrs. E. G. Smith. Early in November, Ship had joined the Sons of Temperance, but apparently had since fallen off the wagon once again.

Lola said she rushed in and, quick as a flash, cowhided Shipley four times on the head and shoulder, and that, after this, the editor got up and squared himself on "the most approved Yankee Sullivan principles," as he prepared to give her a "stunner in the eye." But, as she related, "The spirit of my Irish ancestors (I being a kind of three-quarter breed of Irish, Spanish and Scotch), took possession of my left hand and...before he could attain my eye, I took his, on which, thanks to some rings I had on at the time, I made a cutting impression."[35]

Shipley would maintain that he caught Lola's whip and took it from her before she could land a second blow, after which she scratched him a bit, but that his annoying coolness soon forced her to fall back on a woman's best weapon—her tongue. She used language, he said, "which our [printer's] devil says he will not set up." Finding all her endeavors powerless, Shipley said, Lola appealed to the "honest miners," but the only response rendered was a shout of laughter. Shipley said he mounted a box and asked if Madame Lola had any friend in the audience who wished to take up her fight—to which there

[34]Sacramento *Union,* Nov. 22, 1854.

[35]San Francisco *Alta,* Nov. 26, 1854, also Sacramento *Union,* Nov. 4, 1854. James "Yankee" Sullivan was an Australian pugilist and alleged criminal. In 1856, while a prisoner of San Francisco's second Committee of Vigilance awaiting expulsion from the state, he killed himself in his cell (Sacramento *Union,* steamer edn., July 15, 1854).

was no response—and, after this, he triumphantly retired, having by his calmness, completely worn out his fair enemy. Even when she invited everyone in the saloon to take a drink, the only response was a groan, and none stepped forward to show themselves her champion.

The chauvinistic Shipley said his friends thought he was too easy on Lola, and should have "inflicted that punishment upon her which belongs to a woman who will persist in leaving her sphere and the bounds of delicacy." After the fracas he left the whip in the hands of a disinterested party because the Countess claimed it to be her father's whip—"a sort of sabre of her sire."[36]

Shipley's version of his "editorial meeting" with Lola he published in an extra edition of the *Telegraph* later that same day, and other papers gleefully picked up the story. Pat Hull must have gotten a bitter chuckle as he set it in type for the November 23 edition of his San Francisco *Daily Town Talk*. Farther south, in San Diego, the *Herald* published this embellished version:

> Grass Valley Ring—First Fight of the Season.—Combatants: Marie, Countess de Landsfeldt, de Heald, de Hull, Lola Montez, and Henry Shipley, Editor of Grass Valley Telegraph.
>
> Time—11 o'clock, A. M. Tuesday November 21.
> Place—Golden State Saloon, Grass Valley.
> Weapons—Horsewhip, Nails and Tongue.
> 1st. Round—Countess pitching in, strikes blow with whip—Ship catches it—both close. Countess' second takes her off. Ship falls back with whip in his possession.
> 2nd. Round—Countess returns to the attack—with her tongue. Ship provokingly cool, smokes his pipe and laughs at her.
> 3rd. Round—Countess urged to desperation, strikes at Ship and spits in his face. Ship magnanimously advises her not to go too far.

---

[36]San Francisco *Examiner*, Sept. 23, 1888, quoting Grass Valley *Telegraph*, Nov. 21, 1854.

4th. Round—Countess tries on her old tactics—appeals to the crowd as "miners," etc. Crowd sensibly laughs at her.

4½ Rounds—A "gree chap" in the crowd said something, when the Countess informed him it was not his "put in."

5th. Round—Crowd greatly amused.

6th. Round—Cries of "Speech from Shipley." Ship offers the stump to Lola. Countess informed Ship her name is "mad Lola."

7th. Round—Countess reads extracts from Grass Valley Telegraph, counts number of words and informs Ship there are twenty words to be atoned for.

8th. Round—Ship remarks that the crowd has been sufficiently amused and concludes to retire in disgust.

9th. Round—Countess springs forward and demands the whip—"her father's whip." Article of dispute placed in the hands of a disinterested party.

10th. Round—Countess asks all hands to drink—Crowd laughs and refuses.[37]

In her turn, that night Lola took her rebuttal a few miles away to the editors of the *Nevada Journal*, who published it on November 22. She recounted from her viewpoint the entire history of Shipley in Grass Valley, as related above, as well as the story of the whipping. She pled sincerely and appealingly for readers not to be harsh—as Shipley had been—with hardworking and talented artists who, unlike herself, had not been lucky enough to meet with success. She spoke movingly of performers having to bravely smile, brace themselves and set aside personal tragedy, so that the show might go on.

As she had with other antagonists, in her letter Lola flatly accused Shipley of perhaps wanting "a cool thousand or two" in blackmail to stop defaming her. She said Alexander Dumas, Beranger, Mery, and all of her friends in Europe, had always told her that her fault was not in hypocrisy, but in being too frank.[38]

---

[37]San Diego *Herald,* Dec. 9, 1854.
[38]San Francisco *Examiner,* Sept. 25, 1888.

This very real encounter with Shipley would spawn a whole host of variations on what actually had happened. Pioneer merchant Thomas Othet spun a yarn wherein Lola is supposed to have used her whip in Grass Valley against a certain "Big Missourian." A Kanaka houseboy of Lola's, Othet said, was shopping in a local store when the Missourian called him a "damned nigger"[39] and shouldered him aside. When the houseboy reported the incident, Lola is supposed to have taken up her whip and accompanied him back to the store. But, seeing her coming, the "Big Missourian" fled through the back door and hid in the brush along Wolf Creek.

Dora Knapp recounted the Shipley incident, calling his newspaper the Grass Valley *Clarion,* and getting many of the other details wrong. She also told of the time Lola was supposed to have come home to find a "big, burly Irishman" playing with her two bears. When she ordered the man from the premises, he told her to go to blazes, and so she ran into the house, and came out with a loaded gun in her hand to chase him down Mill Street.[40] Knapp also said any act of cruelty to a dumb brute aroused Lola's wrath, and recalled her shaking her fist at a teamster one day and threatening to shoot him because he was mercilessly driving a poor lame mule along the road. Lemuel Snow copied this fable from Knapp, only he had Lola using the pistol to threaten a brutish teamster who was whipping a team of mules as they struggled to haul an overloaded wagon past her house on Mill Street.

Lemuel Snow would also have us believe that Shipley's humiliation at being beaten by a woman was so unbearable as to make him leave California within the month. In actual fact, the editor moved about eight weeks later just a few miles away to work for the Nevada City *Democrat.* In June 1857, he bought

[39]Kinyon, 144.
[40]San Francisco *Chronicle,* Jan. 17, 1897; and *Bulletin,* Aug. 14, 1897.

the bankrupt Sacramento *Democratic State Journal,* only to sell out
in less than a year and travel to the Fraser River in Canada, and
thence to Oregon. At The Dalles, in October 1858, he was
severely injured when thrown from a horse, and lay in a coma
for weeks. At one point, when it was thought he was dead, a
zinc coffin was brought to his room so his remains could be
sent to California.

But, though he didn't die in Oregon, poor Shipley never
recovered fully from his injuries. In the summer of 1859, he
edited the Portland, Oregon, *Times* for a few months, and then
returned to California in September with plans to go to
Hawaii for his health. Somehow he missed the sailing of his
ship and, totally depressed, in November he committed suicide at the Merchant's Hotel in Sacramento by taking strych-
nine. Some say he took his life because of his shame at having
been whipped by Lola. More likely, his suicide, the frequent
job changes and the crippling injury were all consequences of
Shipley's fondness for alcohol.[41]

One nagging mystery remains from Lola's days in Grass
Valley—a letter allegedly received by her about the same time
as the Shipley incident. In 1914, three needlework samplers—
believed to be Lola's handiwork—were sent to Memorial
Museum in Golden Gate Park, San Francisco, by the family of
Mrs. F. Roundtree of Grass Valley, who is supposed to have
worked for Lola (perhaps as the companion alluded to above
as "Mrs. R"). A faded letter addressed to "Miss Lola Montez"
was found in the folds of one of the samplers. On the face of it,
this strange missive appears to concern a Southern plot for a
revolt in California against the United States, and the forma-
tion of an independent California with Lola as Empress. It
reads:

---

[41]San Francisco *Examiner,* June 11, 1893, Feb. 19, 1899; *Nevada Journal* and *Alta* of June
9, 1855; Sacramento *Union,* Nov. 15, Dec. 1, 1858, Nov. 18, 1859; *Nevada Democrat,* Nov.
28, 1859.

Washington D. C. November 3, 1854. My Dear Lola: Since our last meeting in San Francisco I have been most actively engaged in securing aid from wealthy southern gentlemen in our project. I am fully convinced that there are sufficiently powerful men, both financial and political in California, to at once start the project and revolution.

Have T. call at once on you and tell him of my actions. The Spanish inhabitants of California are so bitter they can be depended upon to enlist themselves in our cause. C. is attending at that end. Do you remember meeting that wealthy Spanish gentleman of Los Angeles. He called at your room one evening after your performance. He had nothing but contempt and hatred for all Americans, as he called them Yankees. Let the conflict begin in San Francisco, Los Angeles, and Stockton. I will remain here. We will win—trust none but the chosen leaders. When we succeed, and we will, remember you are to be Empress of California. Have sent by this Steamer $50,000 to San Francisco. Be careful and prudent. Faithfully, J. C.[42]

Montez had, in fact, been warmly received in the South two years earlier, especially in Virginia where the governor, attorney-general and other dignitaries had fawned over her. Young and handsome bachelor William F. Ritchie of the prestigious Richmond *Enquirer* was particularly taken with the dancer. Young Ritchie interviewed Lola—one can't help wonder under what circumstances—and told his readers that she seemed to "belong to the Southern school, in her advocacy of a conservative system of checks and balances." Lola had commended John C. Calhoun's work, *Discourse on the Constitution and Government of the United States*, recently published, in which the Carolinian urged election of two Presidents, one northern, one southern, each armed with an absolute veto. Lola told Ritchie she had sent the book to Eugene Sue for translation into French, and predicted that the United States would adopt its recommendations.[43]

---

[42]Rogers, 71-72, from Grass Valley *Union* of unspecified date in June 1915.

[43]*New York Herald*, Feb. 22, 1852, also Jan. 13, Feb. 23, 1852; *Nevada Journal*, June 5, 1852.

But despite the interest in the question of Union shown by Lola on that occasion, the letter—with its patently theatrical tone and mysterious use of the plotter's initials—is most likely a hoax, or the work of a crank. Rather than helping plan a revolution, Montez seems to have by then begun turning her attention away from California. Before long, her revived restlessness would combine with financial misfortune and cause her to abandon the relatively tranquil life she had found for a time in the Sierra Nevada foothills.

CHAPTER SIX

The Idyll Ends

Three years ago I cried aloud in agony to be taken, and yet the Great All-Wise Creator has spared me in this agony to allow me to repent...My calm days at the cottage are gone.

...Lola Montez, Diary, 1859[1]

Is it true—have I existed...or is it all a dream?

...Lola Montez, 1852[2]

In mid-May, 1855, Lola Montez closed up her cottage in Grass Valley and went to San Francisco to make arrangements for an around-the-world artistic tour, commencing in Australia. A variety of theories have been expounded for this decision to abandon the bucolic life and return to the stage. Some say she had simply become bored with it all; others that she had tired of John Southwick, upon whom she had brought financial ruin. Most farfetched of all is the belief that a group of "respectable" women drove her from Grass Valley by attempting to burn her cottage.

Undoubtedly, Montez had become restless. There was a report in October 1854 that she might spend the winter in Hawaii, and another rumor surfaced about the same time saying she planned to join a theatrical group under D. V. Gates for a tour of the mines. Then too, the wrangle with Shipley in November had surely disturbed the relative tranquility she had

---

[1] In Dyer, 26. [2] *New York Herald*, Jan. 15, 1852.

achieved in Grass Valley and, by having taken her case to the press, she had revived unpleasant memories of the many similar incidents in her past. Her feeling for the town, and it for her, must surely have changed from that point onward.

But the principal cause of Lola's decision to leave her mountain home was probably the sinking state of her finances. By mid-1854, California had begun to feel the effects of its first recession, which had been brewing since the very beginning of the frenzied Gold Rush years. High interest rates, political corruption, the succession of floods and fires, and the increasing difficulties in extracting gold from the earth all worked together to bring on a slowdown.

The bad times were especially hard on the theatre business. A number of actors and singers had left for Australia, where things had been booming ever since the discovery of gold in February 1851. The fifteen-month tour "down under" of James Stark and family had netted them some $100,000, and their success had induced a whole host of others to leave in July 1854.

The recession's climax came in February 1855, with a widespread crash, triggered by news that the large banking firm of Page, Bacon and Company had failed. Throughout California, runs were made on financial institutions, many of which were forced to close their doors for a time. Depositors at Grass Valley and Sonora stormed the Adams Express Company offices in an attempt to get their money. Several firms, like B. Davidson and Wells, Fargo, paid off every demand, but Adams, Page and a few others were forced to declare bankruptcy. Hundreds of merchants failed, and many people, who had amassed considerable sums, found themselves suddenly penniless.

Although several periodicals credited Montez with profiting in her quartz-mining investments, such seems not to have been the case. Furthermore, by the time the depression hit, her dwindling funds may have been totally in the hands of John

Southwick, as this note she penned on November 22, 1854, to Southwick's partner, C.K. Hotalling, implies:

> My dear Hotalling. Johnny told me that if I needed it I was to apply to you as my banker. I do not expect him home until Friday next, and have the most perplexing need of sixty dollars. I beg you to give it to the bearer of this.[3]

Most likely, what little remained of the assets of both Montez and Southwick were lost in the February crash, and this caused Lola to once again take to the boards. Her journalist friend on the *Alta* staff implied that this was the case. But, whatever her reason may have been, it is certain that she left her Grass Valley home fully intending to eventually return. Most of her possessions were left there, and she retained her faltering mining interests.

In San Francisco, Lola assembled a rather odd collection of performers to join her world-wide tour. The troupe would include James Simmonds, a low comedian and ballad writer; John Jones, a mediocre actor-manager with some experience in staging dances—who was perhaps the same fellow of that name who had traveled with Lola in the Eastern states; a certain Mr. Daniels, likewise of dubious talent; Lola's ever-loyal violinist Eigenshenck and—to round out the company—Mrs. Harriet Fiddes and her two daughters. Fiddes, the former Miss Harriet Cawse, was an English contralto who had met with limited success in San Francisco, mainly singing operatic roles.

But the most important member of the company, for Lola, was her young and handsome new "agent," Augustus Noel Follin. Follin had come to California in 1850 at age 23, leaving his wife Caroline and two children in New York while he sought his fortune. By the time he and Lola met, this down-at-the-heels drifter had apparently "seen the elephant," and failed

---

[3]T.W. Norris Collection, Bancroft Library, Berkeley, CA.

the test. Now, like Dujarrier, Ludwig, Willis, Hull and Shipley before him, his association with Montez would assure him even more deadly troubles.

Noel Follin had worked at San Francisco's American Theater, probably in non-acting jobs, and it may have been there that he met Lola. In any case, he seems to have become totally smitten with her from the first glance. On March 16, 1854, he wrote his younger sister Miriam from San Francisco that he had met "the lawless little meteor" who had been the mistress of Ludwig, Dumas and Liszt. "Madam the Countess of Landsfeldt," he told Miriam, "thinks your daguerreotype the most beautiful one she ever saw. She says, 'una cara tan intelegente tan linda.' She is in love with you, and actually kept it for two days: She lives in Grass Valley...with a pet bear, a dozen dogs, birds, a summer house filled with the rarest flowers, all sorts of musical instruments...there is all the remnants of a lovely woman about her, her nose appears chisseled [sic] out of marble and her conversational powers are fascinating to a degree: I talked with her in English, French & Spanish, she speaks German Italian Portuguese and Russian in addition."[4]

Within a few months, perhaps with Lola's help, Follin had become an itinerant actor, doing mostly low comedy parts and using the stage name T. Folland. He joined a troupe organized by Lola's friend from the Sacramento Theater, Charles A. King, and toured the mountain towns that summer, including Downieville, Nevada City and Grass Valley. With the same group, Follin helped open the new Marysville Theater that fall, and, by January 1855, he was playing in Nevada City on the same bill with Mr. and Mrs. Barney Williams.

---

[4]Madeleine B. Stern, *Purple Passage: The Life of Mrs. Frank Leslie*, 18; also S.F. *News and Picayune*, Jan. 18, July 19, 1854; S.F. *Golden Era*, Apr. 30, 1854, June 3, 1855; *N.Y. Herald*, Sept. 3, 1852; Grass Valley *Telegraph*, May 18, July 6, 1854; Hubert H. Bancroft, *California Inter Pocula*, 341; S.F. *Alta*, Aug. 31, 1853, Feb. 25-26, Mar. 1, 6, 20, May 21, 28, June 2, 1855; *Alta*, Aug. 31, 1853, Feb. 25-26, Mar. 1, 6, 20, May 21, 28, June 2, 1855; S.F. *Bulletin*, Sept. 23, 1916; Grass Valley *Union*, Dec. 22, 1856; *Nevada Journal*, May 18, 1855; *Nevada Democrat*, Oct. 11, 1854; Delevan, 77; Ewer, 4:54.

Although Follin seems to have been a sensitive person, he unhesitatingly abandoned his family when Lola proposed that he join her Australian tour. He wrote a melancholy letter to his mother and sister from Sacramento before leaving, asking them to tell his wife of his plans:

> I hardly have the heart to write. I have tried to do so twenty times during the last week but could not. Now that the moment has arrived in desperation I send a few lines...in three days I leave California. I am going to Honolulu, Sidney [sic], Australia—China— Calcutta—Bombay—Constantinople and England, and so on to Paris and New York. I shall be gone two years or more. I go with the Countess Landsfeldt, Lola Montes, as agent—if successful I shall make twenty-five thousand dollars. I have nothing to lose and all to gain; things are and have been very dull in California for months...I dare not trust myself to say more. I should die if I did. God bless you. I love you. Noel.[5]

Longtime California actor Walter M. Leman was playing at the American Theatre during the week of Lola's departure from San Francisco. On the night before she sailed, he, Laura Keene, J. W. Thoman and others of his company went to Lola's hotel to drink a glass of wine and say good-bye to her after their performance. Leman recalled that she was in the highest of spirits, and full of pleasant and gracious words for all of her guests. Based on his observations that night, he expressed the opinion that the notorious Montez recklessness and imperious manner had begun to abate a bit. But, as events would prove, nothing could have been further from the truth.

The press was generally kind to Montez upon her departure. The Grass Valley *Telegraph*, with Shipley gone, admitted that there were many in town who could attest to her intellect and kind nature, and the paper wished her well despite her not being a proper exemplar in many other respects. Even Daggett and Foard's San Francisco *Golden Era*, ever cynical where it came

---

[5]Cannon, 54; Stern, 18-19; Grass Valley *Telegraph*, June 22, 1854; S.F. *Alta*, July 30, 1854, July 28, 1854; S.F. *News*, Nov. 15, 1854; *Nevada Democrat*, June 21, July 5, 1854, Jan. 24, 1855; Marysville *Herald*, June 22, 1854; Leman, 249-50.

to the dancer, dropped its usual animosity long enough to admit that Lola's kind nature and many courtesies had made her a host of friends in California.[6]

Lola, her performers, a maid and a young male servant left San Francisco on June 6 in the *Fanny Major*, a sailing ship in regular service to Australia. A large crowd of her friends and admirers, and many of the just-plain curious, assembled at Cunningham's wharf that afternoon to see the celebrated woman on her way. The ship's rigging, its boats and the throng of people on deck made it necessary for some of the gawkers to stretch on their toes to get a glimpse of the famous woman. One impassioned man was heard to exclaim, "There's Lola! That's her, with the green parasol! See, quick! Hurrah for Lola! J—s, look at her, there!"

Lola's pink ribbons and green parasol could be seen fluttering and glistening on deck as *Fanny Major* cleared the wharf at 5:30 P.M., then all sight of them disappeared as the ship warped into the stream, loosed her wings and sped westward through the fog-shrouded Golden Gate to begin that sparkling passage to the antipodes. "All that's bright must fade," lamented one San Franciscan. Said another: "With a stock of cigaritos, and in a cloud of smoke, she is once more following her name around the world. How long the bond of union between...[Lola and her troupe] will last, time will prove. A tedious sea voyage, we ween, will put harmony severely to the test."[7] Unlike Walter Leman's, this prediction would prove to be right on the mark.

As *Fanny Major* plied her way to Sydney, via Honolulu, Tahiti and Apia, Samoa, the close-quartered boredom of a long sea voyage indeed seems to have brought out the worst in the eccentric woman, upsetting the Australian venture from the

---

[6]Leman, 251; S.F. *Alta*, June 1, 1855; Kinyon, 147, from Grass Valley *Telegraph*, June 6, 1855; S.F. *Golden Era*, June 3, 1855.

[7]San Francisco *Chronicle*, June 7, 1855; Ewer, 4:54; *Golden Era*, June 10, 1855.

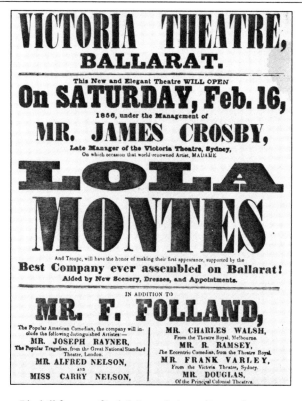

Playbill for one of Lola Montez's Australian performances
From the author's collection.

very outset. The first news to filter back to California told of
her attempt to stab one of the ship's crew who had kicked her
favorite dog—a huge terrier—for its "unmannered habit."[8]
Following this, disgusted with her fellow cabin passengers, she
is supposed to have taken up quarters in the steerage.

And, not surprising to anyone, the entire tour of Australia
was a turbulent one, following much the same pattern of
squabbles, tantrums and sensational publicity as had been the

[8]Grass Valley *Telegraph*, Nov. 6, 1855; S.F. *Alta*, May 12, 1855; *Bulletin*, Nov. 2, 1855.

case since Lola's first coming into the public eye. Not long after arriving in Sydney, she discharged her entire company—except Follin—and used local actors for her first appearance at the Royal Victoria Theater on August 23, 1855.

The disenchanted band of American thespians, led by Mrs. Fiddes, quickly got up lawsuits which charged Lola with firing them because she had learned that touring beyond Australia wouldn't prove profitable. According to them, they had been engaged for a full year with a promise of return passage to San Francisco at the end. For her part, Lola alleged that they were very poor actors, engaged at enormous salaries and paid large advances, and she maintained that, despite this, they had insulted her and refused to either perform their duties or cancel their agreements on reasonable terms.

Whatever the truth might have been, one of the suits—a claim for 100 pounds—was lodged in time for a writ of attachment and an arrest warrant to be issued just as Lola and Follin were boarding the steamship *Waratah* for Melbourne on September 8. A sheriff named Brown came aboard with the warrant, but was unable to locate Lola until just after the steamer had sailed. She offered 500 pounds as a deposit to meet her actor's claims, but the lawman refused it, insisting that she pay the whole amount of their demands, even though he held no warrants or writs for the balance.

Determined not to leave the steamer with Brown, Montez somehow excused herself long enough to go to her cabin, where she stripped off her clothes and jumped into bed. When the impatient sheriff came after her, she shouted through the locked door that she was stark naked, and challenged him to come and get her by force if he dared. Naturally enough, Sheriff Brown backed off.

Next, Brown asked the captain to return his ship to the pier. When this was refused, the frustrated man tried to hoist a signal to summon the water police, only to find that a Montez partisan had cut all the halyards. Thus, the red-faced sheriff was obliged to disembark empty-handed at the headlands, to be received with gales of laughter upon returning to Sydney.[9]

Lola and Follin went on to Melbourne, Geelong and Adelaide, and thence to the Ballarat and Bendigo goldfields, causing trouble and excitement at every stop. At Melbourne, as had been the case in San Francisco, a rival theater capitalized on the Montez peculiarities by staging a burlesque of her "Spider Dance." In it, George Coppin, the manager, flounced about in a short skirt with a huge spider hidden under it, while singing verses of ridicule.

It was in Melbourne, as well, that Lola did journalistic battle with a local editor who had decried the immorality of her dancing and, subsequently, she was cheered mightily for her pluck, when Noel Follin defended her from the stage. Also, while playing that city, she was confronted at the conclusion of a performance by a frightful-looking, drunken old man who rushed on stage, gun in hand, and pursued her backstage before he could be seized and arrested. This wild-eyed fellow excused his actions by declaring his passion for Lola, saying he had only intended to "make an impression upon her heart" with his unloaded pistol and, by frightening her, induce her to return his love.[10]

Yet another anecdote sprang from Lola's Melbourne engagement. The prominent American owner of a local shipping firm, George Francis Train, said he called on Montez at the Theatre Royal, and was shown to the green room, where he sat for a time waiting for her. Suddenly a great ball of feathers burst through the door toward him and, before he could react, he found himself smothered by deliciously-scented lace petti-

---

[9]*Nevada Journal,* Nov. 23, 1855; Cannon, 55-57; D'Auvergne, *Lola Montes,* 243; Joseph N. Ireland, *Records of the New York Stage,* 2:8, 595.

[10]Marysville *Herald,* Apr. 23, 1855; also Dec. 18, 1855.

coats as the audacious dancer tossed her foot over his head. The eccentric Train was well known for his extravagant tales.[11]

Montez was performing in Adelaide when news was received that Sebastopol in the Crimea, so long besieged by the Allied armies of France, Great Britain and the Turks, had finally fallen. Three days later, despite having recently become seriously exhausted, she gave a benefit for the widows and orphans of men who had fallen in that battle. She won many Australian hearts by her kindness.

Lola's first stop in the goldfields was at Ballarat, where she opened February 16, 1856, in the new Victoria Theater, which had been built especially for the occasion. Here, as everywhere else, her male admirers adored her for her courage. When given tours of the mines she never failed to descend without hesitation into the deepest of holes. Invited to christen the Victoria Reef, an armchair was "gorgeously rigged" to allow her to descend the shaft in comfort, but Lola dismissed this effeminate arrangement out of hand, and, "thrusting her pretty foot in the noose, she laid hold of the rope with one hand, and with a glass of champagne in the other, descended amidst a wild tumult of delight."[12]

A much-publicized tussle resulted after Henry Seekamp, editor of a Ballarat newspaper, published an anonymous and derogatory letter concerning Montez. The two of them engaged in a ferocious, extended fight in the bar of her hotel, lashing with whips at one another and pulling hair and clothing. Seekamp even managed to land a blow to Lola's chops before Noel Follin finally arrived on the scene to separate the opponents. In the aftermath, Follin threatened to shoot Seekamp, and Lola made a curtain speech in which she dis-

[11]Jay Monaghan, *Australians and the Gold Rush*, 231-32. Train was still in Melbourne at the time Lola was. He left Australia on Nov. 8, 1855, and in 1902 wrote his autobiography, from which this story was taken.

[12]Cannon, 66; also S.F. *Alta*, July 5, 1856.

Carte de viste of Lola sold
during her Australian tour.
Courtesy, Nevada County,
California, Historical Society

closed that she had offered to meet the editor with pistols, but
that "the coward who could beat a woman" had "run from a
woman."[13] Subsequently, the antagonists continued their warfare in court—Seekamp charged with slander, and Lola with
assault—before the matter finally fizzled out.

Not long after doing battle with Seekamp, Montez quar-
relled over finances with James Crosby, her manager in the
goldfields, and verbally abused him so badly that Crosby's
overbearing, mannish wife whipped and beat Lola most bru-
tally. The dancer's wrist was broken and her face scarred and
bruised such that she and Follin fled to Bendigo, where she was
obliged to take a month off to recover. At times she required
two doctors in constant attendance, according to the story
Follin told one disappointed theater audience.

---

[13]Brereton, 7; also Oroville (CA) *Butte Record*, Aug. 2, 1856.

When the battered Montez was finally able to open at Bendigo on April 1, she showed that the beating had not caused any loss of spunk. With a fierce thunderstorm raging outside, the play she was doing was dramatically interrupted when a huge flash of lightning struck at the stage end of the theater. The bolt exploded open a three-foot diameter hole near the eaves—injuring two actors with flying splinters—then shot between Follin and another man to set fire to some gauze scenery on the opposite side. Despite the total confusion and the screaming of other women, Lola was said to have remained completely cool. As the smoke cleared, she told her audience of delighted "diggers" that there was supposed to be a little thunder and lightning later in the play, but should this sort of thing continue, they wouldn't need "any sham affair—only a little brandy."[14]

Montez and her lover, Noel Follin, returned to Sydney in early May and spent nearly eight weeks there without once performing. She was totally exhausted. There had been recurrent and severe headaches ever since arriving in Australia, and one attack had kept her confined in her room for two weeks. Reports reaching California months earlier indicated that the tour would be abandoned and she would soon return to Grass Valley to spend the rest of her life. So, having finally given up any thought of proceeding farther, she and Follin took passage on the bark *Jane A. Falkinburg*, from Newcastle, New South Wales for San Francisco, via Tahiti and Honolulu.

On the morning of July 8, one day out of Honolulu, Follin was lost at sea, under mysterious circumstances. Several accounts, written long after the fact, have surmised that he was jealous over an affair Montez had in Sydney with Major-General Charles Wellesley. They portray a moody Follin throwing himself into the sea, the victim of Lola's rejection and his own remorse for having abandoned his family. Reports at the time,

---

[14]Cannon, 74.

however, say only that the young actor's birthday was being celebrated with a supper, during which he stepped up on deck to
empty a glass, and, being somewhat under the influence of
champagne, a sudden lurch of the vessel pitched him overboard.

When Lola disembarked in San Francisco a few weeks
later—totally alone, save for her maid and usual menagerie of
animals—she seemed emotionally battered. Follin's death
affected her profoundly for a time; much of her insolent
courage and fire was missing, and there was, outwardly, a
noticeable change in her appearance since leaving for Australia
eighteen months earlier. The cynics at the *Golden Era* noted that
the tragic death of her so-called "agent"—the first and only
man she professed to have ever loved—had nearly unseated her
reason. She refused to be comforted in her grief, was gloomy
and indifferent to everything, and had even lost her taste for
cigaritos and "cobblers."[15]

Follin's death was undoubtedly a factor in Montez's growing
interest in Spiritualism. At the time, there were as many as a
million people in the United States who had experimented
with this uniquely-American fad which had begun in 1848 in
upstate New York. Seance groups gathered to converse with
departed spirits, using a system of raps to answer simple yes
and no questions; the tables they sat around sometimes rose,
dipped and turned without apparent agency. At one particularly notable "knocking" or "rapping," as they were called, the
table was even reported to have danced to the tune of "Yankee
Doodle."

Lola had been interested in the new "science" for at least
four years. In Connecticut, a salacious writer had reported that
she had invited a New Haven medium and some other gentle-

---

[15]San Francisco *Golden Era*, Aug. 3, 1856; *Bulletin*, July 27, 28, 1856, Aug. 14, 1897;
Alta, July 27, 28, 1856, Mar. 29, Apr. 4, 1861; *Chronicle*, Jan. 17, 1897; *N.Y. Times*, Apr. 26,
1856.

men to her rooms, but that no spirits could be induced to appear until some of the more "uncongenial" minds had left the room, after which, it was said, there were plenty of "rappings."[16] At Grass Valley, she had read Andrew J. Davis's book, *The Principles of Nature, Her Divine Revelations*, which expounded the theory that information from other worlds and higher intelligences could be obtained from persons in the sleep-waking state.

Now, in its contumely, the *Era* noted that Lola had cast aside the foolish vanities of life, and would henceforth "gather jewels which rust not." If the fit were to continue, the editor said, people could next expect to see the countess dressed in drab-colored clothes with a "long Quaker poke bonnet."[17]

Her friend on the *Alta* staff would later recall that when Lola arrived in San Francisco she rented a small iron house where she received a select circle of her oldest friends—editors, lawyers, poets and doctors—but seldom females. He said she was never without her Australian birds, one of which was a magnificent talking white cockatoo, and her pack of dogs, whose only merits were their rough coats and devotion to her. In spite of having known the *Alta* man since she had arrived in the United States, it was not until this time that Lola seemed at all willing to discuss her past life, which she now did, but still only sparingly.

The newsman said that Follin's suicide made a marked change in Lola, since she undoubtedly considered herself the cause. He told of her falling for a time under the influence of a down-at-the-heels fellow named Underhill, who was creating a stir at the time as a "trance lecturer."[18] Lola sought him out, provided for his means and kept him in her house, much as one would a dog. Although she soon discovered that he was a char-

[16]*New York Herald*, Apr. 17, 1852; Sacramento *Times and Transcript*, Mar. 23, 1853.
[17]San Francisco *Golden Era*, Aug. 10, 1856; *Alta*, Sept. 29, 1856; Sacramento *Union*, Feb. 26, 1861, Mar. 15, 1865.
[18]San Francisco *Alta*, Apr. 4, 1861.

latan, and threw him out, it was not before he had relieved her of a considerable amount of her money. The experience, however, failed to shake her belief in the Spiritualist doctrine.

This more subdued and otherworldly Lola played to crowded houses for two weeks beginning August 7 at the new, gas-lighted American Theatre, at Sansome and Halleck Streets. The old American, where she had performed in 1853, had been torn down to make room for the new hall. Oddly, the company supporting Montez included Lola's erstwhile satirists, Caroline and William B. Chapman. While Caroline only appeared once on same bill, and that in a different play, Billy frequently played opposite Lola in such pieces as *Charlotte Corday, Eton Boy, The School For Scandal*, and even in *Lola Montez in Bavaria.*

The critic of the *Alta* was astonished at how much Lola's acting had improved since she had first come to California. It was deemed to be spirited and refreshingly-free of affectation, and the "clap-trap of the stage" which some of the great actresses used to cover up their faults. Her *Charlotte Corday* he called "a true and earnest portrayal of the...girl determined to free her country from a tyrant's grasp;" and he said he had never laughed harder than he did at her Cleopatra in the farce *Anthony and Cleopatra.*[19]

Despite the improvement, on this second go-around Montez could no longer command the high ticket prices she had upon first coming to California. Tired from the traveling and the emotional crisis brought on by Follin's death, she didn't begin dancing until well into the engagement. Even then, she begged off when asked for an encore of "El Olle" on the first night she danced.

Of the engagement, the *Era's* critic would only concede how singular it was that Lola had gotten through it without a single pugilistic encounter, other than "slapping the chops" of a young gentleman, whose gallantry had prevented him from

[19] *Ibid.,* Aug. 14, 1856; also Aug. 9, 10, 16, 20, 21, 23.

returning the blow. San Francisco's second Committee of Vigilance was just then winding up its business and, just two days after Lola's arrival, had strung up the alleged murderer, Joseph Hetherington. The *Era* writer thought Lola's failure to indulge in her "favorite pastime" of fighting might have been caused by its being in bad favor with the Committee.[20]

Thus, although the weary dancer had done nothing to provoke them, there were still attacks on her character. Twice, on Lola's night off, Caroline Chapman dusted off her role as Catherine Klopper in the well-worn Montez satire. And, what would prove to be Lola's last journalistic skirmish in California resulted when a subtly vitriolic reader—or, more likely, an editor—of the *Evening Bulletin* attacked the morality of her "Spider Dance." It started with a letter from a purported Alameda County resident calling himself "Country Joe," who had just seen a Montez performance. Writing in the bumpkinish style then so popular, "Joe" described his adventure in the big city:

> I came to town on some little business, and my young friend Spriggins got me to go to the theatre with him. Spriggins is a fast young man, Mr. Editor...so I relied considerably upon his judgement...He said the Spider Dance was worth seeing, and all the folks would ask if I had seen it when I got back...I've seen considerable dancing in my time...But that Spider Dance...Weel, I ain't a married man yet and if I was ever to catch Sarah Ann a dancing Spider Dances I don't think I ever would be...
>
> Spriggins said the Spider Dance was to represent a girl that commences dancing and finds a spider on her clothes and jumps about to shake it off. If that's it, Mr. Editor, then in the first part of the dance I guess she must see the spider up on the ceiling and it's in trying to kick the cobweb down she gets the spider on her clothes. She kicked up and she kicked around in all directions, and first it was this leg and then it was the other, and her petticoats were precious short, Mr. Editor on purpose to give her a fair chance. Then she was

---

[20]San Francisco *Golden Era*, Aug. 24, 1856; *Fireman's Journal*, Aug. 2, 9, 1856.

just a going to stoop down and take a rest, when she saw the spider a
dropping right on her, and she got excited like, and she worked her
body round and round, and squirmed like a snake, and then she
jumped up again and she kicked so high! Well, Mr. Editor, I put my
hat over my face, and just peeped over the brim and looked at Spriggins—there he was with his neck stretched out and alooking right at
her with a double-barreled spy glass!...

Just then...a man up stairs hollered out "hey, hey!" and people all
over the house commenced hollering "hey, hey!" and "hi! hi!" and I
took my hat down away from my eyes to see what was up. If the
Countess wasn't crazy, I don't know what on earth was the matter
with her. She seemed to get so excited like, that she forgot there was
any men at all about there, and didn't see the fiddlers right under her
nose, once. She was going on like mad, lifting her petticoats right
up! and shaking them! and whirling round! Why the little girls when
they are a "making cheeses" don't begin to turn around like she did.
The people hollering at her seemed to excite her more and more,
and she really did seem to be so earnest like in shaking it off of her,
that once I really thought I saw the spider drop from her clothes
onto the floor. Just then that fellow upstairs hollered right out
again, "hey! hey! hi! hi!" and the folks up stairs and down stairs all
commenced yelling like Indians, and astamping so hard I was afraid
the galley would come down on top of me. I puts on my hat, and
jumping over the back seat I made a break for the door, and didn't
feel safe until I was on the other side of the street. I was just getting
my breath again when I heard another yell inside and a great noise
and then the people commenced a rushing out of the door. I was
afraid some accident had happened, when I heard Spriggins singing
out, "Hellow, Joe!" "Hellow Spriggins" said I, and he came up to
me. "Why on earth did you get up and leave!" he said. "I couldn't
stand it," says I; "I was afraid the house would come down, or she'd
take her dress right off, and I couldn't stand it." "Why, it is nothing
to be afraid of when you get used to it," says Spriggins, "and you
went away before you saw it all."

But, Mr. Editor, I saw more than I wanted to, and I ain't used to
it—that's a fact.

A response from Lola appeared the following day, in which
she accused "Joe" of being a Jesuit. Her dance, she said, was

merely an allegory in which the spider was the Jesuit, and the dancer, Lola, the Jesuit-hater. Since its fame was world-renowned, and it had been performed a thousand times in front of the ladies of America, she was astounded that the "slightly verdant" Joe would insult them so by implying that it was immoral. Lola advised her country cousin to go home and see the country shows, or his mother might give him "a good sound drubbing."

But "Joe" refused to be bullied by the Montez letter, and insisted upon the final word several days later. This second letter, from "Broadhorn Ranch" in Alameda County, was written in a style slightly more sophisticated:

Dear Mr. Editor. I went to the Post Office on Sunday morning, to see if Mr. Jones in the Washington Market had sold that last lot of eggs and how much he had got for that tall pair of Shanghaies that he had let me have the .15 on, that took me to the American. By the way, Mr. Editor, if ever you are buying anything in the chicken and egg line, I always send mine from the ranch to Jones, and he gets them from me, fresh three times a week, so you will know when to go. (We must inform our correspondent, that we always charge for advertisements—Ed.)

Wee, I didn' get nary a word from Jones, but there I saw a newspaper for me, with my name on it, as large as life in Spriggins hand-writing...right up at the top of the page I saw a mark with a pen, and right under it in big letters it said, "Card from Lola Montes, The Jesuit Hater! 'The Spider Dance' and 'Country Joe.'" Ha! Ha! I thinks, that's me—and Spriggins wanted me to see this.

Well...I read it...[and] I can't hold a candle to the Countess at calling names...you know I ain't no Jesuit, and there ain't a Catholic priest anywhere's near where I live...She says the Spider Dance is an allegory. Well...Mr. Editor, if such things is allegories, then as Spriggins says, "I'm down on them..."

I leave it to you...if it ain't kind of unnatural for a woman to show off before folks like I told you she did the other night...Mr. Editor, as the Countess is a friend of yours...you just hint to her like, that such dancing may suit in San Francisco, but it wouldn't do in Alameda! and she says all the ladies in the United States have seen the Spider Dance. No, Mr. Editor, I know one that hasn't and Sarah Ann never shall if I can help it...Spriggins told me the other night she said she was a Spanish woman, and there ain't no such in Illinois, so she ain't no cousin of mine...If she wasn't a Countess, and a lady...I would say, "I don't want nothing more to do nor to say with no such cattle;" and I'm surprised you let them write to your paper. Yours, till death. Country Joe.[21]

It seems clear that Montez initially intended to remain in California upon her return from Australia. Having become deeply interested in SPIRITUALISM and religious subjects, she plainly indicated her desire to perform for just a few months, then retire from the stage to Grass Valley, where she still had mining interests.

Lola was scheduled to open in Sacramento soon after finishing in San Francisco but, for some reason, remained on in the Bay City for an additional two weeks. She made arrangements with Duncan and Company, auctioneers, for the sale of most of her extensive collection of diamonds and valuable jewelry, the proceeds to be sent by B. Davidson and Company to Noel Follin's stepmother, Mrs. Susan Follin, of 13 Stuyvesant Street, New York City, for the care and education of his two orphaned children.

The emotionally-battered Lola became the butt of still more spoofing when a new five-act burlesque, called *A Trip to Australia, or Lola Montez on the Fanny Major*, opened September 1 at the American Theater. The play depicted a supposed series of shipboard scenes from Lola's voyage to Australia, and had been written by a San Francisco woman, E. M. Spangenburg, who said she had been a passenger on that trip. Its characters included the countess, played by Caroline Chapman, the countess's friend Rhoda, Mrs. Fidides (Fiddes) and her daughter Ella, Neptune, and Tommy (Noel Follin), played by Billy

---

[21]The Country Joe letters are in the S.F. *Bulletin*, Aug. 22, 23, 25, 1856; also see *Alta*, July 28, Aug. 17, 23, 28, Sept. 28, 1856.

Chapman. The piece's buffooneries included a "Spider Dance" by Caroline, a scene wherein Lola tries to stab the mate with a bowie knife, and gets locked in her stateroom for it, and sundry other sketches involving a dog, a monkey and Billy Chapman minus his pants. Each night the burletta concluded with the entire cast singing "A Yankee ship and a Yankee crew...And a fightin, swearin Countess too—I'm going home"—interrupted by the countess arriving with a horse-whip in hand to drive the other actors from the stage.[22]

But ragging Lola was no longer as fashionable as it once had been. It seemed that, due to her remorse over Follin and her concern for his family, many in San Francisco were just now discovering that she also had a compassionate and vulnerable side. So, although it initially drew good crowds of the curious, this latest mockery of Lola ran a mere three days. It was generally condemned as being a coarse and vulgar exaggeration of Lola's peculiarities. Even the *Era*'s editor called it "dull" and "absurd," adding that "were not the author a lady, [he] would speak of the play with severity." He revealed that Spangenburg had visited his office to accuse several newspaper critics and the actors in the play of having conspired—through Lola's influence—to kill the production.[23]

The impressive Montez jewelry collection, the greatest portion of which had been presented to the dancer by admiring individuals and organizations, was sold on September 8. Solitaire diamond rings, watches, crosses, gold chains, medallions, nuggets, brooches, massive Australian gold work and numer-

---

[22]San Francisco *Bulletin*, Sept. 3, 1856; also Edith M. Coulter, "California Copyrights, 1851-56," 39; S.F. *Herald*, Sept. 1, 1856; *Alta*, Aug. 31, Sept. 2-7, 1856. Although his sister would live longer, Billy Chapman died in San Francisco on Nov. 8, 1857, at age 70, after being run over by a buggy, severely injured, while crossing from his hotel to the theater in Marysville a few months earlier. Inasmuch as he had left his large family unprovided for, and his Telegraph Hill properties had been mortgaged off, San Franciscans gave his survivors a monster benefit shortly after his death (*Fireman's Journal*, Nov. 4, 1857; Sacramento *State Journal*, Sept. 17, Nov. 13, 1857).

[23]*Golden Era*, Sept. 6, 1856; *Bulletin*, Sept. 1, 2, 1856; *Fireman's Journal*, Sept. 6, 1856.

ous other ornaments comprised the 89 lots for sale. One evening, before the jewelry was sent to Duncan, Lola brought it out to show a few friends, and recounted for them the history of each article. The display was also made available beforehand for inspection by prospective buyers, prompting the *Alta* to suggest that all should go and "feast their eyes."[24]

Although attendance at the sale was large, and the bidding spirited, only about $10,000 was realized—not nearly as much as expected for the possessions of such a notorious woman. The highest bid, $600, was for a pair of diamond earrings. Some thought that offers might have been higher had Lola been there to personally present the items to their new owners, but she had left two days earlier for her Sacramento engagement.

Old-timer George E. Barnes, reminiscing in 1895, said Duncan took advantage of her absence by making quaint references to the different pieces. "Here's a beautiful ornament," he said in one instance, "The Madame says it is one of the most remarkable she has ever seen in her life, and you know, ladies and gentlemen, she has seen many remarkable objects."[25] If the story is true, Duncan was perhaps fortunate Lola didn't hear of it, else he might have joined that illustrious group who had felt her whip.

Montez performed at Sacramento's Forrest Theatre from September 8-13 to overflowing houses, doing her usual fare. She was to have played longer but, reportedly ill, she unexpectedly interrupted the engagement and traveled to Grass Valley. It was about this time that something or someone made her decide to leave California. The reason may have been—as her friend on the *Alta* staff revealed in later years—that a man had failed to respond in an *affaire du coeur*, causing her to attempt

[24]San Francisco *Alta*, Sept. 4, 1856; also *Bulletin*, Sept. 5, 1856.

[25]*Bulletin*, Nov. 9, 1895, also Sept. 8, 1856; Duncan and Co., Catalogue of the Auction Sale...; *Alta*, Sept. 7, 9, 1856.

suicide by swallowing oxalic acid. The diary entry cited at the beginning of this chapter certainly adds credence to such a theory.

In any case, Lola began settling her affairs in order to leave for the East. A will was prepared which provided for her property at the time of her death to be converted to municipal bonds, and for Noel Follin's stepmother to administer them in trust for Follin's children. The children were to be educated in the calling for which they seem best suited, and in the "knowledge and love of God, and His character and attributes as revealed in His word." It was also Lola's wish that they be thoroughly instructed in the principles of that "class denominated Spiritualists."[26]

At Lola's further request, Duncan and Company disposed of a house and five vacant lots she owned on San Francisco's Stockton Street. She also sold the cottage in Grass Valley, along with its furnishings, to Solomon D. Bosworth, the future postmaster. Edwin Morse would accuse her of selling the place with a heartless disregard for her former lover, John Southwick, by then, he said, a sick and ruined man. Morse further claimed that Southwick had deeded the cottage to her, and Lola sold it, just as it stood, for a mere song. But, as we have seen, Gil Meredith was very specific about having sold it to Lola, not Southwick.

Whether or not Lola was the proximate cause, Southwick did, in fact, battle financial problems and bad health for the next few years, made worse by a fall from a horse. He eventually moved to Kern County, California, whence he was committed to the Stockton Insane Asylum in December 1871 for about a year before being returned to his relatives in New York.

Montez interrupted her stay in Grass Valley on September 20 for just one day to perform in Sacramento for the benefit of

---

[26]*Alta*, Apr. 4, 1861, also Sept. 14, 15, 19, 20, 29, 30, 1856; Morse, 340; *Golden Era*, Sept. 14, 1856; Van der Pas, 21; Sacramento *Union*, Sept. 9-12, 1856.

Joseph Dunlop, manager of the Forrest Theater. She left Grass Valley for good and returned to Sacramento again on the twenty-ninth to resume her engagement, playing with the support of J.B. Booth, Jr. to pitifully small audiences. It was here, in a curtain speech on October 2, she finally revealed her intention to leave in a few weeks for New York City to provide for the future care and education of Follin's children.

On Saturday, October 4, which was to have been her final night in Sacramento, a mere handful of patrons was kept waiting long after the usual hour for the curtain to go up, before finally being told that the evening's entertainment was to be cancelled. One report said this was because Lola was indisposed; another that members of the company had not been paid and refused to perform.

After this pathetic closing, Lola and Booth returned to San Francisco where he organized a company to support her, which included her old friend Charles A. King. Here she played what would prove to be her final engagement in California from October 13 through 17 at the Metropolitan Theater. She had been scheduled for a benefit on the eighteenth but, instead, one was held there that night for Billy Birch and his wife, both of the San Francisco Minstrels.

Montez might have played longer, but Julia Dean Hayne had been scheduled into the Metropolitan from October 20 through November 8, and the American Theater was similarly booked. There was a report saying she would return after Hayne left, and another—which gave further weight to the idea that she had consumed oxalic acid—that she would, after recovering from her severe hoarseness, proceed on a professional tour of Marysville and other interior towns, where engagements had been for some time awaiting her.

But Lola's plans to leave the state were firm. She sailed from California for a second and final time on November 20, 1856, on the new steamship *Orizaba*. Her maid, Periwinkle, remained behind to marry the man of her choice and, in her place, Montez hired a destitute young male servant who was anxious to return to New York City.

The *Bulletin's* theater critic, "Dress Circle," sat amongst one of the sparse audiences attending Lola's final performances. As he watched her do the "Spider Dance," he penned an epitaph to the former glory of this woman who had so sensationalized California. "It is very plain," he said, "to all but herself, that properly 'her dancing days are over.' Though yet rather graceful in her posturing, she does not display, nor is it to be expected at her age, that degree of elasticity and life which is required to maintain a high position as a danseuse...the exertion appears somewhat painful."[27]

---

[27]San Francisco *Bulletin*, Oct. 17, 1856, also Oct. 13-16; Sacramento *Union*, Sept. 29-Oct. 6, 1856; *State Journal*, Oct. 6, 1856; *Golden Era*, Oct. 19, 1856; *Alta*, Sept. 25, Oct. 8-20, Nov. 8, 1856; *Nevada Journal*, Mar. 30, 1855. Charles A. King would fall ill while touring with his performers in the interior, and die of dropsy at Sonora, California, on Feb. 5, 1857, after a severe illness of three weeks. The Metropolitan, on the west side of Montgomery Street, between Jackson and Washington, was completed in late 1853. It was initially known as the new San Francisco Theater, and was the first theater to use gas lighting after it became available in the city in February 1854 (Gagey, 37, 38; S.F. *Herald*, Sept. 27, 1852).

Steamship *Orizaba*
Courtesy, California State Library

CHAPTER SEVEN

Death of a Magdalen

Is there anything sadder in the world than the old age of vice, especially in woman? She preserves no dignity, she inspires no interest.
                                                    ...*Camille*, Alexandre Dumas, fils.

Is not this a brand plucked out of the fire?   ...Zechariah 3:2

T he aging Lola Montez may have been depressed—per-
    haps even suicidal—before leaving San Francisco in
    the *Orizaba*. However, once at sea, she again displayed
her remarkable resiliency and ability for getting on with life.
Her steamer was bound for San Juan del Sur on the
Nicaraguan isthmus, by now the preferred location for crossing to the Atlantic. And, as chance would have it, she had as fellow passengers some 200 recently-recruited, virile young
freebooters, hurrying to join William Walker's army of fili-
busters which had invaded Nicaragua a year earlier.

Although some have said cholera broke out on the voyage,
and that Lola selflessly devoted herself day and night to nurs-
ing the sick, in actual fact there was no such epidemic, and she
seems to have rather enjoyed the journey, playing cards and
taking part in "rappings" with others interested in SPIRITUAL-
ISM. As one Californian observed, her mood at this time seems
to have fluctuated "between religion, spiritualism and cham-

pagne sprees" and, in his opinion, champagne would carry the day.[1]

A newspaper correspondent who was on board identified Captain Tinklepaugh, commander of the steamer, as conductor of the seances, and noted that Lola had acquired a handsome filibuster colonel as a protector. She was totally engrossed day and night with the seances, he said, during which her circle had managed to communicate with spirits from the "vasty deep," including those of the "old gentleman," King Ludwig, and his body guard.[2]

While still in San Francisco, Montez had indicated she would return to New York City via Havana. Although she may have stopped in Cuba enroute, she certainly did not travel to Europe as some have suggested. By January 23, 1857, she had established residence in New York City. There were indications that she was quite well off financially and was making plans to invest in local real estate. She was also supposedly preparing for a theatrical engagement in the city, and had offered $12,000 per year for the rights to manage a new theater being built on Broadway. While nothing would come of these latter plans, she did find a fresh, new toy as the focus of her attention.

The repentant dancer's generosity was apparently spurned by Noel Follin's widow, Caroline, when her offer was made to educate Noel's orphaned children. But Follin's stepmother, Susan Danforth Follin, it would seem, had no such compunction about dealing with her stepson's former lover. Tradition has it that when Lola first met Susan, she threw herself at the woman's feet crying, "I have killed your son!" Whether this little vignette actually took place can't be said, but Susan was seemingly quick to forgive Montez, since she invited the

[1]*New York Times,* Nov. 14, 1856.

[2]San Francisco *Bulletin,* Dec. 20, 1856, also Nov. 21, 1856, and Nov. 9, 1895; *Alta,* Nov. 11, 18, 20, 1856, Apr. 4, 1861; *Fireman's Journal,* Aug. 2, 1856.

dancer to live in her house at 13 Stuyvesant Place, and allowed her to take charge of Noel's young half-sister, Miriam, the same girl whose daguerreotype Montez had so admired while still in Grass Valley.

When Lola first met her, twenty-one year old Miriam Florence Follin had already been around the block. She was a girl who was more than a match for Montez in the field of amatory conquest. At age 17 she had been seduced by—or had herself seduced—a jeweler's clerk, whom she had been forced to marry after her mother, Susan, brought a lawsuit against the young man. But the pair had never lived together and, because of Miriam's "misdeeds" which her husband later discovered, the marriage had been annulled about a year before Lola returned to New York. Despite her dubious morals, however, Miriam was a bright and very beautiful young woman. And, although her father, Charles Follin, had never actually married Susan Danforth, he had seen to it that Miriam had received a good education.[3]

Lola probably knew nothing of the girl's past; perhaps she didn't care. In any case, she took Miriam under her wing and taught her some rudimentary theatrical skills and then, palming her off as a younger sister, "Minnie Montez," the two went on tour. This unusual pair made a successful debut at the Green Street Theater in Albany, New York, doing Edward Stirling's two-act drama, *The Cabin Boy*. Next on their schedule was Providence, Rhode Island, but a great inundation in the Albany region on the night of February 8, 1857, caused the ice to break up and water to rise rapidly on the Hudson. By the following day, Albany's streets were flooded and houses could

---

[3]Virginia City (NV) *Daily Territorial Enterprise*, July 14, 1878, reprint, 4-6; also *Golden Era*, Mar. 8, 22, May 3, Aug. 23, 1857; *Alta*, Feb. 17, Mar. 29, Apr. 4, 1861; *N.Y. Times*, Jan 23, 1857. *Enterprise* editor, Rollin Daggett, wanted to revenge himself on Miriam Leslie for her insults toward the ladies of Virginia City in her book describing the cross-country journey of the Leslie party. He had someone, perhaps Miriam's former jeweler's clerk husband, dig up evidence concerning her past.

been seen floating bodily down the river. Communication with the outside world was seemingly cut off; all railroad tracks were submerged, and canal boats, barges and steam tugs were sunk or damaged.

Ever sensitive to an opportunity for publicity, the indomitable Lola, nothing daunted by the fearful danger before her, challenged some boatmen to take her and her "sister" across the ice-choked, swollen river in a rowboat. In a scene evocative of little Eliza on the ice floes, the two women made the perilous journey and were safely landed, being the first persons after the storm to accomplish the crossing. Never mind that a part of their theatrical wardrobe had been lost, and that their exhausted boatmen were washed downstream and nearly drowned on their return trip—the daring Montez sisters were rewarded for their feat with a splash in a leading New York weekly.

But the affiliation of the two women was a short-lived one. In just a few more weeks, Miriam was back in Albany performing without her mentor. It seems she had been fornicating with a former congressman from Tennessee, William M. Churchwell, and it may be, as one vindictive reporter later said, that Lola had had an "ocular demonstration that Miriam was not an innocent miss." A more likely explanation of the breakup, however, is that Lola had, by then, simply grown tired of dealing with such a strong-minded "sister."[4]

Like Lola, her prototype, Miriam-Minnie would go on to have relationships with many celebrated men, most notably the publisher, Frank Leslie. As his widow, she would for many years run the huge publishing empire which Leslie had created. Some of the other male scalps Miriam collected during her lifetime were those of the poet Joaquin Miller, a certain mar-

---

[4]*Enterprise,* July 14, 1868, p. 4; also N.Y., *Frank Leslie's Illustrated Newspaper,* Mar. 7, 1857; Stern, 20-23; *Golden Era,* Mar. 22, 1857; Ross, 269.

quis, a prince and a Spanish grandee. In the 1890s she also briefly married, then divorced Oscar Wilde's brother William. When this remarkable woman died in 1914 she left two million dollars to the cause of women's suffrage.[5]

After ridding herself of Miriam, Lola went on alone to play St. Louis, Cincinnati, Louisville, Cleveland and Chicago. The old standby dramas and comedies comprised the bulk of her repertoire, augmented by several new works: *Margot, or the Poultry Dealer*, a comedy written especially for her by Thomas De Walden; *Rosalie Bouquet*; and *The Knave of Hearts*, in which she portrayed the Chevalier De Follicourt. As for dancing, on occasion, "El Olle," "Spider Dance" or "La Tyrollean" would be trotted out for an audience. And, to spice up her role as Julian in *The Cabin Boy*, Montez incorporated two sailor's hornpipes into the play, one by herself and another by a certain Mr. D. W. Leeson. But Lola's dances were pallid and lifeless compared to those of her earlier years.

Still, it was a profitable and successful tour, despite the infrequent, uninspired dancing and the resultant lower admission prices. Montez had no train of admiring camp followers now to distract her, and she pushed herself hard, often doing the lengthy *Lola Montez in Bavaria* and another play in the same evening. Perhaps as a consequence of having overdone it, in St. Louis she was reported to be lying dangerously ill.

As always, the senescent sinner was abused by newspapers that didn't care for either her acting, her reputation, or her temper. A fierce argument at the end of her engagement in Louisville, on April 10, gave rise to still another story of her tearing her dress open and threatening to horsewhip a man.

That evening Lola was scheduled to play *Margot*, but arrived late at the theater, reportedly in a churlish mood. Before she was even fully dressed, she came out of her room to demand

---

[5]Stern, 3, 5, 155, 182, 164.

that the green baize which covered the stage floor be removed, since it affected her eyes. The stage manager, Bradley, refused to do so, arguing that to take up the covering would further delay the play, but he promised to remove it at the end of the first act. Unsatisfied, Lola rushed on stage to present her case directly to the audience. They, of course, couldn't refuse a woman, and their support caused George Mellus, the lessee of the theater, to come out and announce that the offensive baize would be removed, not to satisfy Lola, but to comply with the wishes of the audience.

Meanwhile, behind the curtain, Lola was verbally abusing Bradley—calling him an "old fool," whom she could "lam out of his boots,"[6] having whipped much better men than him. Accounts of the affair in the local papers say she ripped the front of her dress to ribbons to prove her strength, and then had to be conveyed, hysterical, to her dressing room. The baize was removed, and word of it was sent to Lola, but she flatly refused to go on, making it necessary to cancel the evening's entertainment.

Sometime during that spring, Montez decided to act on advice she had been given by James Gordon Bennett and others in recent years, and become a lecturer. She abandoned her theatrical tour and returned to New York City, where she bought a house at Third Avenue and 90th Street. Once settled, she divided her time between planting flower beds and preparing a series of lectures and, when she took the road again later in the summer, it was to begin this new career.

Her year-long lecture tour drew large audiences throughout the Atlantic states and eastern Canada. For a mere fifty cents a seat, the former seductress gave audiences the opportunity to see her close-up, and to hear her opinions, as well as choice tid-

---

[6]Louisville (KY) *Courier*, Apr. 11, 1857, also Mar. 30-Apr. 10; *N.Y. Times*, Apr. 11, 1857; *Leslie's*, Apr. 4, 18, 1857; St. Louis *Missouri Republican*, Mar. 12-21, 1857.

bits from her turbulent past. Women, in particular, could now come to see the notorious former courtesan without fear of wagging tongues.

Lola's lecture on "Beautiful Women" was a collection of beauty tips, combined with tales of famous European beauties. Anecdotes about personalities Montez had met during her Paris years—Dumas, George Sand, Mery, Lamartine, and such—comprised another discourse which she called "Wits and Women of Paris." Her "Heroines of History" dealt with women who had acquired great power during their lives, such as Queen Isabella of Spain, Mary Queen of Scots, Catherine II of Russia, Joan of Arc, and George Sand.

A speech entitled "Comic Aspect of Love" proved a great favorite with men, and it never failed to bring a bit of a blush to the cheeks of women in her audience. While its principal thesis was that the novelty of love soon wears off, it also touched on the free love sects in ancient France, as well as some recent ones which had sprung up in the United States. She considered Mormonism, then the subject of much discussion and controversy, one of these free love establishments, declaring that Joseph Smith's followers and other such "modern religionists" gave proof of the ridiculous results which could spring from a "combination of fanaticism and love."[7]

In her talk on "Gallantry," Lola spoke at length of her friend King Ludwig, and of what she called their platonic love. She offered him as a shining and noble example of what a truly gallant man should be. American businessmen, on the other hand, she thought were dull fellows who had no time for gallantry. They "made love in a truly business like manner," she said, and managed the heart of a pretty woman as "they did the stock on 'Change.'"[8]

---

[7] Montez, *Lectures*, 224; also *N.Y. Times*, Mar. 19, 1858; *Golden Era*, May 3, June 28, 1857.

[8] *Alta*, Mar. 31, 1858.

Two other lectures were devoted to the latest version of Lola's life story. By this time she had dropped all pretension of having been born in Spain but, still unable to give up Latin origins entirely, she now claimed to have been born the daughter of Elizabeth Oliver of "Castle Oliver," a descendent of the noble Moorish-Spanish family of the Count of Montalvo. Her father, she said, was Edward Gilbert, son of an English lord.

While Montalvo is a valid Spanish surname, and there is an old town of that same name in Cuenca province of east-central Spain, it is most unlikely that Lola's forebears on her mother's side came from that region or had any trace of Moorish blood. And, while there was indeed a Captain Robert Oliver who had come to the Limerick, Ireland, region in 1645 and went on to become a wealthy landowner, there is no evidence that Elizabeth Oliver was among his descendants.

Another of the many fictions contained in Lola's autobiographical lectures is her promotion of stepfather Patrick Craigie to the rank of general when, in reality, he never rose above the local East Indian rank of major before dying at Dinapore in 1843.

One other lecture—more a harangue, actually—dealt with "Rome and Civilization." By now more intolerant of Catholicism than ever, Lola told her audiences that the religion was the product of an effete civilization, and would eventually succumb to the progressive spirit of the age. She theorized that, had the Mayflower brought Catholics to America rather than Puritans, the country would never have advanced. Protestants, on the other hand, she said, had given the United States the five great facts of the time: steamboats, railroads, the telegraph, freedom of the press and the American republic.

There was general agreement that the novice lecturer's manner was prepossessing, and that she delivered her talks with feeling and clear, sweet elocution. One Bostonian who saw her at the lectern, her burgeoning figure disguised in a loose, white gown, conceded that she still retained a striking countenance, highlighted by her bold, brilliant eyes. But—he thought, uncharitably—there was, nevertheless, "something low and ugly in the *tout ensemble.*" This man, who could find neither beauty nor grace in a woman who had been "so degraded," correctly predicted her future: "Hurried on by her own power, by her own passion, she will yet pause somewhere, perhaps on the verge of the grave, for the sacrament of repentance and her baptism will be one at which our hearts will all be present, and at which the heroic poets she has so nobly interpreted may fitly stand sponsors."[9]

The lectures proved profitable and, encouraged by her success, in 1858, Montez published three books, all of which sold well. The first is a 292-page work comprising several of the lectures and her autobiography. The second book, entitled *Anecdotes of Love,* contains over 125 love stories down through the ages, including those of Pericles, Caesar, Louis XIV, John I, Henry IV, Caligula, and Agememnon.

While the others are well-written, Lola's third opus is far and away the best—a witty and cleverly-written little satire called *The Arts of Beauty or, Secrets of a Lady's Toilet With Hints to Gentlemen on the Art of Fascinating.* Its first part contains what one admiring Californian called "valuable information on subjects which are generally considered too delicate to be discussed in print." But then—as this reviewer noted—one always could count on Lola to remorselessly tear away "the veil from the sanctum sanctorum of female artifice and prudery."[10]

Arts of Beauty contains many common sense suggestions for improving the figure, complexion, eyes, hands, hair and voice. Some of these tips might even be considered quite modern: following a good diet, use of moderation in everything, getting plenty of sleep and open-air exercise, and maintaining strict

[9]San Francisco *Bulletin,* Dec. 23, 1857.
[10]Sacramento *Union,* Sept. 18, 1858.

cleanliness. But there are also some suggestions which are uniquely nineteenth century in nature, such as one which recommends bathing in tepid water and bran as a remedy for skin disorders. *Hints To Gentlemen* contains fifty rules for young men to use in wooing their ladies fair. These bitingly-sarcastic tips reveal the full depth of the diseased and aging Lola's bitter disappointment in men. Proficiency in the art of fascinating women is a man's duty, Lola said, since every "lord of creation" seems to think he was born exclusively for this purpose, and zealously devotes most of his time to it. But, Lola conceded, she had seldom met a man who didn't already consider himself skillful in the art.

A few samples will suffice to give the tenor of the work. From Rule the 1st: "Women prefer triflers to men of sense, and when you wish to make one of the sex tremendously in love with you, you will of course make yourself as big a fool as possible..." Then this, from Rule the 19th: "There are four things which always possess more or less interest to a lady—a parrot, a peacock, a monkey, and a man; and the nearer you can come to uniting all these about equally in your own character, the more you will be loved."

Many critics thought the lectures and books to be brilliant, entertaining and instructive—even literary. Lola's benevolence and magnanimity were held out as bright examples in the columns of certain dailies and ladies' magazines; editors who began by attacking her became her warm, personal friends and lauded this new Madame Montez as a pattern of taste and elegance.

But there were plenty of others who thought someone else had done the writing; that while the books and lectures were indeed brilliant, they were far beyond the capability of a person of such low character; that Lola's only skill was in retaining a smattering of information on a variety of topics and in being

quick to catch up the ideas of the clever people who surrounded her. The Reverend Charles Chauncey Burr—publisher of
the New York monthly, *Old Guard*—has often been named as
the real author of both the lectures and books, with Lola supposed to have furnished only the historical data for her autobiography. And, while indeed one of the editions of her lectures
and autobiography, also published in 1858 at Philadelphia,
lists Burr as editor, this may have been the only role he played.

Lola always staunchly defended her authorship, as did
admirers such as Rufus Shoemaker of the Grass Valley *National,*
who said he thought Lola to be the real author, inasmuch as he
had repeatedly heard her "converse on European politics, the
Jesuits, and other topics touched in her lectures."[11] Then too,
James Gordon Bennett mentioned several times that she was
working on lectures concerning the public men of Europe.

Further substantiation of Montez's authorship comes from
a bachelor of the *Alta California* staff who attended one of her
Sunday soirees at her Third Avenue and 90th Street home in
1858, and reported that she was devoting her mornings to the
writing of *Arts of Beauty.* This newsman had only met Lola once
before, briefly, but she recognized him immediately when he
entered. The house was jammed with a polyglot group of
guests—French, German, English, American, Cuban, and Italian—and Lola spoke to them all in their own tongues as she
sat in an easy chair at the center of the room. Her repartee
incessant, she welcomed all newcomers without once inter-
rupting the stream of dialogue. The fragrant fumes of choice
tobacco filled the rooms, and Lola's hands were constantly
busy in the preparation of fresh supplies of "the weed" for herself and those around her. She asked her California guest if he
would like a cigarette, and he said yes, mainly so that he could

[11]Kinyon 148; S.F. *Bulletin,* Feb. 14, 1861; *Fireman's Journal,* Nov. 21, 1857, Jan. 3,
1858; *N.Y. Times,* Jan. 22, 1861; Sacramento *Union,* Feb. 18, 1861; *N.Y. Herald,* Mar. 31,
1852.

watch her manufacture it. He stared in amazement as Lola took from the arm of her chair a reticle containing tobacco and silk paper and, within less than 20 seconds, rolled, twisted and lighted a smoke.

The *Alta* man couldn't help noticing that Lola's aging hands were almost transparent, and that, despite all her vivacity and sparkling wit, she was "but a wreck." Her face was drawn and haggard, and only her wonderful eyes retained their beauty— eyes, he said "that never ceased till the last hour of her life to express the force and passion of her nature."[12]

There was only one other woman at dinner that evening, whom Lola placed to her left. At her right hand sat a cashiered Zouave officer, the dashing Captain Henri de Riviere, who, like Lola, was lecturing in New York that summer. Across Riviere's face an old sabre cut had left a sinister scar. When the dinner conversation turned to a recent sensational murder, the captain left the table and, showing his familiarity with Lola's house, helped himself to a pair of scissors in a drawer so that he might demonstrate his theory of how the murder had occurred.

Known as a "lady killer," de Riviere had himself recently made headlines by abducting for a few days a young girl, Miss Blount, and trying to marry her over the objections of her frantically-worried father. The captain, it seems, was already married to, or had as a mistress, a woman he had brought with him from France. Ironically, a few weeks after Lola's dinner party, de Riviere would be arrested for viciously assaulting a well-known Nicaraguan filibuster, Captain Lewis E. Grant, just as the Frenchman was entering New York's Hope Chapel to deliver a lecture on "Love."[13]

Given her continued association with the likes of de Riviere, it is understandable that Montez was despised by many per-

---

[12]San Francisco *Alta*, Apr. 15, 1872; Sacramentio *Union*, Aug. 17, 1858.

[13]Sacramento *Union*, Nov. 3, 1858.

sons for daring to lecture and write on morals and religion in the fashion of an Emerson or Theodore Parker. They were offended that the many-mated adventuress, who had led such a sinful life, hadn't had the good grace to simply sink into obscurity after her stage career faltered. To some, like the editors of San Francisco's *Golden Era,* she remained a total enigma. On the one hand, when hearing of her latest "freak," they might label her a "female Lucifer"—"half-woman, half-man and half-untameable wild beast." At other times these same men conceded that she appeared to be a "much-abused, well-meaning" woman.[14]

Even in her new, more subdued role of authoress-lecturer, Montez continued to generate reams of copy for the papers. While enroute from Niagara to Buffalo, she went to smoke in the baggage car of her train and fought with the conductor over her right to be there. It was said that the man "dried up" in an instant when she looked archly at him and said she had "horse-whipped bigger men." In a Montreal confectionery, after being brazenly ogled by several young army officers, Lola paid for their candies, telling the proprietor "she didn't wish the gentlemen to lose a copper" in satisfying their curiosity by staring at her. In Lancaster, Pennsylvania, it was reported she had turned up her nose at her hotel room, saying, "I would not cut my throat in a place such as this!"[15]

But, such accounts notwithstanding, Montez had, in fact, become less combative. When the Montreal *Witness* chose to attack her moral character, her response was surprisingly muted; there was no challenge, as in earlier years, asking the editor to choose "Pistols or Pizzen." Lola could only accuse her tormentor of un-Christian behavior, and admit that her own life had not been without error.

And, pathetically, Lola's love life was now in disarray. This

[14]*Golden Era,* Mar. 28, 1858; also Oct. 10, 1858.
[15]San Francisco *Wide West,* Sept. 5, Nov. 15, 1857; *Nevada Democrat,* Mar. 10, 1858.

woman who, in her prime, had caused hundreds of men to fall at her feet, now seemed incapable of attracting a single male of any stature or stability. In December 1857, she announced her engagement to marry a forty-year-old Austrian prince named Schulkoski, whom she had known in Dresden, and who now lived in up-state New York. Lola planned to travel to France for this brilliant marriage, or on business connected it, and not return until spring.

But something went awry, and Montez bolted suddenly and prematurely for Europe. The day after Christmas, she was seen by a reporter at an American banking and shipping house in Paris. She had just arrived the day before by steamer from New York, and already was seeking a passage back by the January 2nd Cunard steamer from Liverpool. To the reporter, Lola looked disappointed and feverish, and connecting this fact with her hurried return to the United States, he concluded that her planned marriage had failed. A contemporary newspaper account had the prince denying any marriage plans, saying that he already had a wife and five children, with whom he was perfectly satisfied. In her autobiography, Lola would claim that it was she who ended the engagement upon learning that Schulkoski was traveling through the South with a celebrated singer, as husband and wife, while at the same time "telegraphing kisses three times a day" to her in New York City.[16]

Not long after her experience with Schulkoski, Lola appeared as a witness in a New York city lawsuit, and made sensational headlines when testimony hinted that her past had been more unsavory than she would care to admit. The suit was brought by David W. Jobson against Norman B. Griffin to obtain compensation for Jobson's services as an adviser and witness in a case in which Griffin had been the defendant. Lola

---

[16]Montez, *Lectures*, 83, *Nevada Journal*, Jan. 22, 1858; S.F. *Wide West*, Jan. 24, 1858; *Bulletin*, Jan. 29, 1858; *N.Y. Herald*, Dec. 12, 28, 1857; S.F. *Chronicle*, Mar. 21, 1903; *N.Y. Times*, Sept. 7, 1857, Feb. 1, 1858; Sacramento *Union*, Feb. 8, 1861.

was called by the defense as a character witness against Jobson. Jobson, an obvious charlatan, had posed variously as a doctor, lawyer or dentist. His attorney, C. R. Schermerhorn, in questioning Lola, insisted that she had been born in 1815 at Montrose, Scotland, the illegitimate offspring of a certain Mary Watson. Jobson testified that in Lola's early days in London he had given her money to prevent her being taken to the watchhouse or having to take to the streets for a living. He said she was an assistant chambermaid to the "Strain"—a slang term for gonorrhea—before she ran off with James.

Ignoring this thinly-veiled reference to prostitution, Lola said she would have considered herself a better woman had she been born a chambermaid. Insulted by all this unwanted delving into her past, she retaliated by testifying that she had first met Jobson while living in London in 1849. He had called on her, she said, and told her he was an attorney and wanted to write her memoirs. But Jobson was known as a jailbird in England, Lola claimed, and he had twice tried to blackmail her and her husband, George Heald.

Eventually the defendant's counsel and Jobson argued and came to blows. Lola sat and watched, delighted, as the police broke up the fight, and the referee was obliged to adjourn the proceedings. As Jobson was leaving the courtroom, Montez— not yet fully satisfied—stood up and shouted "Stop that fellow! He's stealing a hat!" Jobson, it seems, had become so muddled that he was carrying off the referee's hat by mistake.[17]

Not long after Jobson lost his case, the vengeful man lectured at Stuyvesant Hall to a small audience on the subject of Lola's early life. The talk, which was generally adjudged to be exceedingly vulgar, seemed an effort on his part to show that she had often thrown herself at him, and that he had just as often been able to resist her charms. The only two women to attend his lec-

---

[17]San Francisco *Bulletin*, Mar. 22, 1858; *Alta*, Mar. 21, 1858; *N.Y. Times*, Feb. 27, 1858.

ture were quick to leave it in disgust. A short time after this, Lola was again called to testify as to Jobson's bad character in a libel suit, which Jobson had brought against the owners of the *New York Times* for accusing him of being a swindler.

For most of 1858 Lola remained in New York City. Early in the year she lectured frequently both at the Brooklyn Athenaeum and Hope Chapel on Broadway. In March, a translated version of *Lola Montez in Bavaria* was done by German players at their theater in the Bowery to a crammed house. After the play, Lola delivered her lecture "Comic Aspect of Love" from a desk on stage and was so enthusiastically received as to be called three times before the curtain. Montez had several times announced that she would leave for Europe that spring, but nevertheless she remained in the city. In late May and early June, she lectured at the Broadway Theater, and on occasional evenings also played Mrs. Chillington in *Morning Call* opposite a former Californian, A. W. Fenno.

One day during this period, Lola was standing on the rear platform of a crowded Third Avenue streetcar when a young pick-pocket grabbed her purse. The conductor succeeded in grabbing the thief and he dropped the purse, but was able to slip out of his coat and escape. Montez confessed that she was as pleased at the smartness of the little fellow in getting away as she was at the recovery of her money.

That spring Lola was also reported to be intensely interested in the two daughters of the notorious Mrs. Emma Cunningham, who had been acquitted in May 1857 of murdering her lover, Dr. Harvey Burdell. It was said that Montez was visiting the girls almost daily, even though Mrs. Cunningham was well off enough so that they couldn't have been wanting for anything.[18]

---

[18]*New York Times*, Feb. 21, Mar. 19, Apr. 20, May 25-June 4, 1858; Sacramento *Union*, May 1, June 3, 1858; S.F. *Wide West*, Mar. 28, May 30, 1858; *Fireman's Journal*, Mar. 27, 1858; *Leslie's*, May 16, 1858.

There were rumors later in the year that Montez was involved in the establishment of a large "free-love" association near New York City. The free-love movement was another of those strange fads to emerge in mid-nineteenth century America, and many of its supporters were also devotees of Spiritualism. Their cause centered around women's rights, including the freedom of a woman—as proclaimed by the Rutland Free Love Convention in England—"to love whom she will."

A free-love league begun in New York City in 1855 had soon died out but, later, another which sprang up in Erie County, Ohio, flourished for over a year before its leaders, of both sexes, were arrested on charges of adultery. By the fall of 1858, the movement was once again in full bloom, given considerable impetus by a convention held in Utica, New York, in September. Knowing her history of involvement in such causes as we do, it is reasonable to assume that Montez may have indeed contributed to the movement in some way.[19]

For certain, she had by then become quite active in the Protestant faith. She delivered her caustic lecture on "Rome and Civilization" at Hope Chapel on October 13 to raise money for rebuilding Reverend Ralph Hoot's free Episcopal church for the poor, which had been demolished in a gale. That evening, after dealing with Catholicism, Lola lambasted Dr. Horatio Potter, bishop of the Episcopal diocese of New York City, and other clergymen who disapproved of Hoot having accepted her offer to lecture. Mincing no words, she accused them of the multiple sins of bigotry, cruelty to the poor and a lack of Christian spirit.

Soon after this, Lola finally sailed for the British Isles. She was greeted by a few friends when she landed at Galway, Ireland, and told reporters she was most anxious to visit her birthplace at Limerick, which she had left as a mere child. She

---

[19]Sacramento *Union*, Sept. 4, 18, Oct. 19, 1858; S.F. *Golden Era*, Oct. 10, 1858; *N.Y. Herald*, Dec. 6, 1857.

Lola Montez and dog,
ca. 1858
Courtesy, California State
Library

was described as being a very prepossessing but agreeable
woman, who was dressed handsomely in a black silk dress,
adorned with an expensive fur mantle and a richly-jeweled
Maltese cross. Montez spent about a year in Britain, traveling
under the name Mrs. Heald. Most of her time was spent in
London, where by April 7, 1859, she was lecturing at St. James
Hall, and where an edition of her autobiography and lectures
was published.

Spiritualism had by then come to England, where it had
taken on a marked religious connotation. Lola evidently
became more and more involved with both it and Christianity,
and was supposedly influenced, while in London, by Stephen
Pearl Andrews, the reformer and eccentric philosopher. That
summer, an acquaintance came across her in Regent's Park,
reading to several children from her Bible. Plainly dressed, and

with her dog Gyp nearby, she said she was devoting most of her time to helping the poor and in distributing religious tracts.

It was also in London that Montez renewed her acquaintance with Mrs. Augustus Thistlethwayte, the former Laura Bell, a notorious Irish beauty who had created a sensation a few years earlier by attempts similar to Lola's to snag for herself a head of state. Lola had undoubtedly met Bell in Paris in the fall of 1850 when, as a nineteen-year-old, Laura was plying her charms on Louis Napoleon. Now, much like Montez, Laura had become exceedingly pious, and she and her husband were preaching the gospel. Laura helped Montez obtain a lease on a boarding house near Hyde Park, which Lola hoped would augment her income. Montez reportedly invested some 900 pounds in this venture before going broke and becoming ill with a nervous problem diagnosed as brain fever. An old Methodist couple is supposed to have taken her to their home in Derbyshire to convalesce.

After Lola's return from England, about November 1859, she lectured for a time at Mozart Hall on Broadway in New York City, then afterward in Washington, D. C., Louisville and other cities. She had as new subjects, "Fashion," and "John Bull at Home." The latter dealt with both the humorous and darker sides of the English character, as compared to that of Americans. It also belittled the gallantry of Englishmen, and criticized them for their treatment of the Chinese and West Indians.[20]

A former acquaintance of Montez from the staff of the *Alta California* saw her lecture in Washington on February 3, 1860, to a hall full of foreign ministers, senators and congressmen and their ladies. This is one of the last personal descriptions we have of the fast-declining Montez.

---

[20]Sacramento *Union*, Aug. 17, Nov. 3, 18, 1858, Feb. 26, 1861, Mar. 15, 1865; *Alta*, Nov. 18; D'Auvergne, *Lola Montes*, 219; Montez, *Lectures*, 292; *N.Y. Herald*, Oct. 12, 1850; Ireland, 2:8, p. 594.

When Lola caught sight of the journalist just before her lecture ended, she sent her agent to ask him to remain so that she might speak with him. When the program was over, the Californian and a few of his friends were led into a small anteroom, where Lola was chatting with several of the diplomats. She gave him a warm, demonstrative reception in the presence of her other guests, and then, later, invited him to her hotel, where she kept him up until dawn answering a barrage of questions about men, events and things in California.

Before he left, Lola insisted upon giving him a letter of introduction to Ned Wilkins of the New York *Herald*, which she wrote on her lap "in a bold clear hand, so representative of her character." She asked Wilkins to take her old California friend—a "knight of the pen"—and "show him the elephant and make a Bohemian of him." The "knight of the pen" who left this reminiscence was probably *Alta* reporter E. D. Knight. One suspects it was he who had been Lola's longtime and constant defender on the staff of that newspaper.[21]

On this same tour, Lola lectured before a large crowd at Cook's Hall in Springfield, Illinois. The following night, Abe Lincoln's friend, Bill Herndon, lectured at the same place to a minuscule audience. The *State Journal*, in comparing the two houses, railed against the "woman who has violated every known rule of life, mocked at the sacredness of the marriage relation and publicly set at naught all that is beautiful and modest in womankind." During this period, Lincoln had also been lecturing, without much success, at 25 cents admission.[22]

Sometime after returning to America, Montez unexpectedly met a certain Mrs. Buchanan, the wife of a wealthy New York seedsman and florist, who had been her schoolmate in Montrose, Scotland. Buchanan was a devout Christian and,

[21]*Alta*, Apr. 4, 1861; *Bulletin*, Feb. 14, 1861. The newspaperman could also have been drama critic John A. Durivage who had joined the *Alta* about 1851, and had formerly worked for the New Orleans *Daily Picayune* (Sacramento *Record-Union*, Jan. 1, 1888).

[22]Carl Sandburg, *Abraham Lincoln: The Prairie Years*, 2:238.

although she may have been shocked to discover that the schoolgirl she had known thirty years earlier had become the notorious Lola Montez, she nonetheless allowed their friendship to rekindle.

By now, Lola herself was possessed of a full religious fervor, fueled, no doubt, by dark forebodings about her poor health. Shattered by syphilis and excessive smoking, she began to live very quietly, studying scripture, and expounding her beliefs to anyone who would listen. A strange turnaround in the same woman who, only eight years earlier, had written her friend Joseph Scoville that she would never stop at the Albany Temperance House again since it contained "nothing but bed-bugs and Bibles."[23]

In the summer of 1860, the syphilis spirochetes which had been working inside Lola Montez's body for some ten years finally completed their work, causing her to suffer a severe stroke. As a consequence, she was paralyzed in her left side and lay unconscious, close to dying, for many days.

A story, which could be taken as apocryphal, would somehow later arise to the effect that the stroke had been brought on as a result of an accidental meeting with Noel Follin's orphaned daughter, while walking down Broadway. The impulsive Montez was said to have rushed to embrace the girl—whose education she is supposed to have financed—only to be coldly rebuffed by the object of her charity, who not only denied ever having known her, but also threatened to call a policeman if Lola persisted in bothering her. Lola was said to have gone home in sorrow, and that same day suffered the destructive attack of paralysis.

Howsoever Lola's stroke may have occurred, soon afterward she was taken to the Buchanan home at Astoria, Queens, on Long Island. A man who visited her there in September was shocked and saddened to see the transformation in body and

---

[23]Sacramento *Times and Transcript*, July 1, 1852.

mind of the once-beautiful and vibrant dancer. Lola sat dressed in a morning robe in the Buchanan garden, her hollow cheeks, sunken eyes and cadaverous complexion forming a stark contrast to the surrounding gay flowers. She was unable to speak a word, except spasmodically, and only after repeated efforts as, unconsciously, she wiped at her frothing mouth with the sleeve of her dress. Her visitor said she had acquired a strange, wild appearance and had evidently lost all further interest in the world around her. He could only comment, "What a sermon on human vanity!"[24]

Montez remained at Astoria until early November 1860, when she improved enough to be moved back into the city. Perhaps sensing the opportunity for an important victory over sin, two prominent Episcopalian clerics, Rev. Francis L. Hawks and Bishop Horatio Potter (the same whom Montez had berated two years earlier for lacking Christian spirit), placed Lola in a boarding house at 194 West Seventeenth Street, not far from Hawk's church, and began ministering to her spiritual needs. Here she apparently lived under the pseudonym "Fanny Gibbons," cared for by a practical nurse. Charges—perhaps unfounded—would later come to light to the effect that the now-helpless Montez had been moved there only after she had signed over all of her possessions to Mrs. Buchanan, and that the nurse was a hateful old woman who starved and treated Lola abusively.

Many of the alleged details of Lola's last days come from a little tract called *The Story of a Penitent*, written by Rev. Dr. Herman Dyer, editor of the *Episcopal Quarterly Review*. It portrays a contrite Lola—a sort of super-Magdalen—yearning eagerly for Christ's forgiveness and salvation. She received the best of medical care, the book says, but still the shattered and chastened woman's condition gradually grew worse.

---

[24]San Francisco *Bulletin*, Oct. 15, 1860; Marysville *Appeal*, Sept. 2, 1860.

Reverend Hawks was said to have visited her frequently to pray and read with her, and he credited her with a particular fondness for the Magdalen story, which portrays Christ's forgiveness of that fallen woman. Hawks said Lola even made a few visits to the asylum of the Magdalen Society, to instruct the outcast women and girls sheltered there from their former lives in New York's numerous houses of prostitution. Hawks declared that in his entire life he had never seen deeper penitence and humility, or more bitter self-reproach than he saw in Lola, whom he found to be a "woman of genius, highly accomplished...and of great natural eloquence."[25]

The Story of a Penitent also contains fragments of a diary supposedly begun by Lola while she was still in England. An entry for September 10, 1859, confirms the repentance Hawks observed which had totally changed Montez's life. She wrote: "How many, many years of my life have been sacrificed to Satan, and my own love of sin! What have I not been guilty of, either in thought or deed, during these years of misery and wretchedness!...I only lived for my own passions..."[26]

Another diary entry is couched in language which provides some insight into Lola's long-term estrangement with her mother, Mrs. Patrick Craigie. In it, Lola blames her dam for the course her life had taken, implying that Mrs. Craigie had exposed her to evil company as a young girl, and then turned her back on her. It isn't known whether Lola had communicated with her mother during the year she lectured in England, but it seems unlikely that the two ever got together. However, when news of Lola's stroke reached Europe, Mrs. Craigie is said to have written Mrs. Buchanan to inquire about her daughter, and then to have traveled to America hoping to see her. When she arrived at New York City in November, Craigie

[25]Dyer, 39.
[26]Ibid., 20.

contacted Mrs. Buchanan, as well as Lola's physician, Dr. John Cooper.

In later years, Dr. Cooper would confirm Lola's intense hatred of her mother, and her fear of seeing her again. According to the doctor, Montez told him that Mrs. Craigie had always been jealous of her, had never loved her, and could only now be interested in anything she might inherit. Consequently, Cooper said, Lola asked him and Reverend Hawks to help her hide from the mother, who was thus obliged to return to England, unsatisfied.[27]

On Christmas day, 1860, Lola went for a walk, took cold, and was seized with pneumonia. Still partially paralyzed and suffering greatly, she began to sink. Now her whole time was occupied in devotions, preparing for death. There were more frequent visits by Hawks and those members of his congregation who had befriended her, and whose esteem she had won by her sincere repentance. On one occasion when Hawks was about to leave, he said, Lola grasped his hand, and, with a child-like eagerness of manner, exclaimed: "Tell me, tell me more of my dear Saviour!"[28]

And so, the once-cocky, one-of-a-kind woman died in exceedingly humble circumstances on Thursday, January 17, 1861, far from any of her remaining family, and long since abandoned by the friends of her early days of reckless notoriety. At the moment of her death, Hawks was at her bedside, reading from the Bible. He related that, by then, she was unable to speak, but, when he asked her to let him know by a sign if she thought she had found full forgiveness and salvation through Christ for her past life, Lola promptly "fixed her eyes" on him and "nodded her head affirmatively."[29]

Reports were conflicting, but Lola's Christian friends seem

---

[27]Ross, 299, 301, 305; D'Auvergne, *Lola Montes,* 223.
[28]Dyer, 116.
[29]Ibid., 40.

to have given her a decent burial. As one observer remarked, it was "all that an event of this peculiar nature could be."[30] Reverend Hawks conducted an Episcopal funeral service at the Buchanan house, during which Isaac H. Brown, the undertaker and sexton of Grace Church, was seen to wipe the tears from his eyes as he heard the clergyman admit that he had never known a case of more sincere penitence than was evinced by poor Lola. After this, what was described as a large cortege of some of New York's most respectable citizens and their families proceeded to Greenwood Cemetery, Brooklyn. There, sexton Brown read the committal service and then, having spent his grief, turned aside to speed the work of the grave diggers: "Hurry up with that dirt, damn you," one observer heard him mutter.[31]

Although her lecturing had been profitable, Lola apparently had continued to spend so freely, with her characteristic improvidence, that at the time of her death she had only some $1,247 to her credit in two savings banks. Just what had become of her New York City house is not known. Three hundred dollars of what remained was given to the Magdalen Society, and the rest was used to pay her debts and bury her.

A plain Italian marble slab was erected over Lola's grave, bearing the name Mrs. Eliza Gilbert. Whose choice the inscription was can't be said. Most likely Hawks and Mrs. Buchanan made this decision, determined to dignify their ward's final resting place by giving her an unremarkable married name; or, perhaps, the choice was that of a repentant but still not totally truthful Lola who had no desire for the name that had made her so notorious to be placed upon her tombstone.

The first news of Lola's death was sent in haste over the wires in all directions. From Missouri it sped across the west-

[30]Sacramento *Union*, Feb. 18, 1861.
[31]Ross, 304.

ern half of the continent by Pony Express to Fort Churchill, Nevada—the western terminus of the soon-to-be-completed transcontinental telegraph—and from there it was transmitted to San Francisco. A spate of articles appeared in California papers, but an impending great Civil War and the press of other matters soon crowded out stories of the last days, redemption and death of the former courtesan. Still, those reminiscences of her years in the Golden State, written by those who had known and admired her, were generally of a warm and sentimental nature. One sorrowful Californian wrote this epitaph:

> Pause by the coffin's haft!
> Speak a kind word for the fair penitent,
> Who for her sins atoned ere life was spent,
> And Death had hurled his shaft!
>
> Gaze on that pallid face!
> Closed are the dreamy eyes that years agone
> Made a king vassal, and usurped a throne!
> Closed—closed for endless space!
>
> A few scant feet of earth
> Suffice for her! Grave-clothes of snowy white,
> Where once the dance-dress was with spangles bright!
> Sadness, where once was mirth;
>
> Have we not erst been bid
> That we forgive as we would be forgiven,
> Though the offence be seventy times a seven?
> Nail down the coffin's lid![32]

The poem's author and many of his fellow California pioneers could perhaps best understand the reason why, for a time,

---

[32]San Francisco *Golden Era*, Mar. 31, 1861; also Marysville *Appeal*, Feb. 9, 1861; Ledger Book of Deaths, 1861, N.Y.C.; *Alta*, Feb. 4, 17, Apr. 4, 1861; *Bulletin*, Feb. 14, 1861; Sacramento *Union*, June 17, 1858, May 22, 1861; San Jose *Pioneer*, Mar. 15, 1895; *Golden Era*, Aug. 5, 1860.

Lola had found happiness in the golden foothills of the Sierra Nevada. Although such men had cared not a whit for her pretentious airs and use of titles, Montez had been a kindred spirit amongst them. Such spirited flamboyance and panache as she possessed held great attraction for men who had had the grit to uproot themselves and make the long and hazardous journey to California and, once there, grub for gold or fight to build new homes and businesses. Never mind that Lola's acting and dancing were less than artistically ideal, or that her behavior and sentiments were not always impeccable—they were never dull, nor uninspired.

Lola, like these enterprising adventurers, had long since made a choice to forge her own destiny, rather than submit to it, as she might easily have done after that London court failed to give her a real divorce from Lt. James. And, like many of these Westerners, along the way she had acquired a lightsome and outlandishly-humorous acceptance of life's hard realities.

So, those Californians who reminisced about her life didn't simply dismiss the enigmatic woman as a flaming whore or as a shrewish, lying virago. They perhaps remembered that she had fought troglodytic notions wherever she had encountered them, and that it had always been her eccentric action, not her careless bounty, which was most often and most speedily reported wherever she went. Perchance they recalled as well that, though she had run higgledy-piggledy though life, she had always been motivated by a fierce desire to live it to the fullest, and that, indeed, this she had done, packing more excitement into her brief existence than any mere mortal might reasonably expect.

Today, the only tangible evidence of Lola Montez's presence so long ago in California, other than a few obscure place names, is a replica of her house at 248 Mill Street in Grass Valley. The little cottage was painstakingly rebuilt in 1975 so as to resemble the original single-story structure just as she had left it in 1856. Aside from this, there remains only the legend, but it should serve to brighten the lives of those who happen to hear of it for so long as there is a California.[33]

---

[33]Sacramento *Bee*, July 7, 1975; S.F. *Morning Call*, June 17, 1900; San Jose *Pioneer*, Aug. 15, 1900. The Bosworths, who bought Lola's house and eventually added a second story, sold it in 1898 to W.S. Berriman; it was sold again in 1933. Having been condemned in 1975, the house was torn down beginning that year, and rebuilt by the local Lion's Club as a single-story cottage, using as many materials from the original building as could be salvaged. It is now a state historical landmark. Lotta Crabtree's house still stands, two doors away, at 238 Mill Street.

Select Bibliography

BOOKS, MONOGRAPHS, PAMPHLETS AND ARTICLES

Altrocchi, Julia C. "Paradox Town," *Calif. Hist. Soc. Quar.*, 28:3.

Ayers, Col. James J. *Gold and Sunshine; Reminiscences of Early California.* Boston: Richard G. Badger, 1922.

Bancroft, Hubert Howe. *California Inter Pocula.* S.F: The History Co., 1888.

Bean, Edwin F., comp. *Bean's History and Directory of Nevada County, California.* Nevada City, CA, 1867.

Brereton, Roslyn. "The Glamorous Gold Rush." *Pacific Historian*, 13:3 (Summer 1969).

Buck, Franklin A. *A Yankee Trader in the Gold Rush; The Letters of Franklin A. Buck.* Boston: Houghton Mifflin Co., 1930.

Cannon, M. *Lola Montes; the Tragic Story of a "Liberated Woman."* Melbourne, Australia: Heritage Publications, 1973.

Corti, Count. *Ludwig I of Bavaria.* Trans. by Evelyn B. Graham Stamper. London: Eyre and Spottiswoode, 1938.

Coulter, Edith M. "California Copyrights, 1851-1856." *Calif. Hist. Soc.Quar.* 22: 39.

D'Auvergne, Edmund B. *Lola Montes, An Adventuress of the 'Forties.* 1909. Reprint, NY: Brentano's Publishers, 1925.

_____. *Adventuresses and Adventurous Ladies.* NY, J. H. Sears and Co., ca. 1920.

Delano, Alonzo. *A Live Woman in the Mines, or Pike County Ahead!* NY: Samuel French, 1857.

_____. *Alonzo Delano's California Correspondence.* Ed. by Irving McKee. Sacramento Book Collector's Club, 1952.

_____. *Pen Knife Sketches or Chips off the Old Block.* 1853. Reprint, S.F: Grabhorn Press, 1934.

Delevan, James. *The Gold Rush; Letters of Dr. James Delevan from California to the Adrian, Michigan, Expositor, 1850-1856.* Mount Pleasant, MI: Cummings Press, 1976.

Dempsey, David with Raymond P. Baldwin. *The Triumphs and Trials of Lotta Crabtree.* NY: William Morrow and Co., 1968.

Derby, George Horatio [John Phoenix, pseud.]. *Phoenixiana; or, Sketches and Burlesques, by John Phoenix.* N Y: D. Appleton and Co., 1865.

Duncan and Co., San Francisco. *Catalogue of the Auction Sale of the Jewelry of Lola Montez.* S.F., 1856. 6 pgs. Bancroft Library, Berkeley, CA.

Dyer, Dr. Herman. *The Story of a Penitent: Lola Montez.* NY: Protestant Episcopal Society for the Promotion of Evangelical Knowledge, 1867.

Ewer F. C., ed. *The Pioneer: or, California Monthly Magazine.* 4 vols. 1854-55. Reprint, NY: AMS Press, 1966.

Gagey, Edmond M. *The San Francisco Stage; a History.* NY: Columbia Univ.Press, 1950.

"G. E. C." *The Complete Peerage.* London: St. Catherine Press, 1945.

Hale and Emory. *Marysville City Directory.* Marysville, CA 1853.

Hauser, Miska. "The Adventures of Miska Hauser." Trans. by Arthur M. Abell. NY, *The Musical Courier,* 59: 4-10 (July 28-Sept. 9, 1909).

_____. *The Letters of Miska Hauser, 1853.* History of Music in San Francisco Series, Vol. 3, May 1939. Ed. by Cornel Lengyel. Works Progress Admin., Northern Calif. Reprint, NY: AMS Press, 1972.

Hittell, John S. *A History of the City of San Francisco, and Incidentally of the State of California.* S.F: A. L. Bancroft Co., 1878.

Holdredge, Helen. *The Woman in Black; the Life of Lola Montez.* NY: G. P. Putnam's Sons, 1955.

Ireland, Joseph N. *Records of the New York Stage from 1750-1860.* 2 vols. NY, 1867.

Kinyon, Edmund. *The Northern Mines.* Grass Valley, CA: Union Pub. Co., 1949.

Leman, Walter M. *Memories of An Old Actor.* S.F: A. Roman Co., 1886.

A List of the Officers of the Army and of the Corps of Royal Marines on Full, Retired and Half Pay. London: War Office, 1819, 1849 and 1850.

McMinn, George R. *The Theater of the Golden Era in California.* Caldwell, ID: Caxton Printers, 1941.

Massett, Stephen C. *'Drifting About,' or What Jeems Pipes of Pipesville Saw and Did.* NY: Carleton, 1863.

Megquier, Mary Jane. *Apron Full of Gold; The Letters of Mary Jane Megquier from San Francisco, 1849-1856.* Ed. by Robert Glass Cleland. San Marino, CA: The Huntington Library, 1949.

Monaghan, Jay. *Australians and the Gold Rush.* Berkeley: Univ. of Calif. Press, 1966.

Montez, Lola. *Anecdotes of Love; Being a True Account of the Most Remarkable Events Connected with the History of Love in All Ages and Among All Nations.* NY: Dick and Fitzgerald, 1858.

_____. *Lectures of Lola Montez (Countess of Landsfeld), Including Her Autobiography.* NY: Rudd and Carleton, 1858.

_____. *The Arts of Beauty or, Secrets of a Lady's Toilet. With Hints to Gentlemen on the Art of Fascinating.* NY: Dick and Fitzgerald, 1858.

_____. *The Lectures of Lola Montez with a full and complete autobiography of her life.* Ed. by Rev. Charles Chauncey Burr. Philadelphia: T. B. Peterson and Bros., 1858.

Morse, Edwin F. "The Story of a Gold Miner." *Calif. Hist. Soc. Quar.,* 6: 205-37; 334-41

Myers, Gustavus. *The History of Tammany Hall.* 1917. Reprint, NY: Burt Franklin, 1968.

Neville, Amelia Ransome. *The Fantastic City. Memoirs of the Social and Romantic Life of Old San Francisco.* Ed. by Virginia Brastow. Boston and NY: Houghton Mifflin Co., 1932.

Ostini, Fritz von. *Wilhelm von Kaulbach.* Leipsig, 1906.

Pendleton, Harry C. *The Exempt Firemen of San Francisco.* S.F: Commercial Pub. Co., 1900.

Pratt, Helen Throop, "Souvenirs of an Interesting Family," *Calif. Hist. Soc. Quar.,* 7: 282-85.

Ramey, Earl. *The Beginnings of Marysville.* S.F: Calif. Hist. Soc., 1936.

Reidt, Theo. "Lola Montez' Ill-fated Trip to the Truckee River." *Nevada County Hist. Soc. Bulletin,* 37: 2, p. 12.

[Richardson, John ?] *Lola Montez; or A Reply To The 'Private History and Memoirs' of That Celebrated Lady, Recently Published by The Marquis Papon, Formerly Secretary to the King of Bavaria, and for a Period, the Professed Friend and Attendant to the Countess of Landsfeldt.* New York, 1851.

Robinson, David G. *Comic Songs; or Hits at San Francisco, by Dr. D. G. Robinson, and sung by him at the San Francisco Theatre.* San Francisco, 1853.

Rogers, Andy. *A Hundred Years of Rip and Roarin' Rough and Ready.* 1952.

Ross, Ishbel. *The Uncrowned Queen; Life of Lola Montez.* NY: Harper & Row, Publishers, 1972.

Sandburg, Carl. *Abraham Lincoln; The Prairie Years.* NY: Charles Scribner's Sons, 1926.

Stern, Madeleine B. *Purple Passage; The Life of Mrs. Frank Leslie.* Norman: Univ. of Okla. Press, 1953.

Vandam, Phillip. *An Englishman in Paris.* NY: D. Appleton and Co., 1892.
Van der Pas, Peter W. "The Lola Montez Home." *Nevada County Hist. Soc. Bulletin,* Vol. 34, No. 3 (July 1980)
Werner, George S. *Bavaria in The German Confederation, 1820-1848.* Cranburg, NJ, 1977.

NEWSPAPERS

Auburn, California, *Weekly Placer Herald,* 1852-1853.
Benicia, *California Gazette/California State Gazette,* 1851-1852.
Bidwell, California, *Record,* 1853-1855.
Boston, *Daily Evening Transcript,* 1852-1853.
Boston, *Daily Advertiser,* 1853.
Boston Post, 1853.
Charleston, South Carolina, *Daily Courier,* 1852.
Cincinnati, Ohio, *Courier,* 1853.
Cincinnati, Ohio, *The Daily Enquirer,* 1853.
Columbia, California, *Gazette,* 1852-1854.
Downieville, California, *Mountain Echo,* 1852-1853.
Grass Valley, California, *Daily National,* 1853.
Grass Valley, California, *Telegraph,* 1853-1858.
Grass Valley, California, *Union,* 1856.
London Times, 1843-1849, 1853.
London, *The Illustrated London News,* 1847, 1849.
Los Angeles, *Star,* 1851-1854.
Louisville, Kentucky, *Daily Courier,* 1853; 1857.
Marysville, California, *Daily Evening Herald,* 1851-1855.
Marysville, California, *Appeal,* 1860-1863.
Montgomery, Alabama, *The Daily Alabama Journal,* 1852-1853.
Nevada City, California, *Daily National Gazette,* 1870.
Nevada City, California, *Nevada Journal,* 1851-1858.
Nevada City, California, *Young America/Nevada Democrat,* 1853-1862.
New Orleans, *The Daily True Delta,* 1849-1853.
New Orleans, *The Daily Picayune,* 1845-1849; 1852-1853.
New York, *Daily Tribune,* 1853, 1855.
New York, *Frank Leslie's Illustrated Newspaper,* 1857-1858.
New York Herald, 1849-1857.
New York Times, 1852-1861.
Oakland, California, *Tribune,* 1941.
Oroville, California, *Butte Record,* 1856.

Panama City, Panama, *The Daily Panama Star*, 1853.

Philadelphia, Pennsylvania, *Public Ledger*, 1852-1853.

Placerville, California, *Herald*, 1853.

Saint Louis, Missouri, *The Missouri Republican*, 1853, 1857.

Sacramento, California, *Bee*, 1975.

Sacramento, California, *Daily Democratic State Journal*, 1852-1857.

Sacramento, California, *Sacramento Daily Union/Daily Record-Union*, 1851-1888.

Sacramento/San Francisco, California, *Placer Times/Transcript/Placer Times and Transcript/Daily Placer Times and Transcript*, 1849-1855.

San Diego, California, *San Diego Herald*, 1851-1855.

San Francisco, *Daily Alta California*, 1851-1882.

San Francisco, *Daily California Chronicle/Daily Chronicle*, 1853-1939.

San Francisco, *Daily Evening Bulletin/Morning Call/Call-Bulletin*, 1855-1916, 1933.

San Francisco, *Daily Evening Journal*, 1852-1854.

San Francisco. *Daily Evening News/Daily Evening News and Picayune*, 1853-1854.

San Francisco, *Daily Evening Picayune*, 1851-1854.

San Francisco, *Daily Herald*, 1850-1856.

San Francisco, *Daily Pacific News*, 1851.

San Francisco, *Daily Public Balance*, 1850-1851.

San Francisco, *Daily Whig and Commercial Advertiser*, 1852-1853.

San Francisco Examiner, 1888-1899.

San Francisco, *Fireman's Journal/ Fireman's Journal and Military Gazette*, 1855-1859.

San Francisco, *The Golden Era*, 1852-1861.

San Francisco, *The Pacific*, 1851-1856.

San Francisco, *The Sun*, 1853-1854.

San Francisco, *The Wide West*, 1854-1858.

San Jose, California, *Sunday Mercury*, 1867.

San Jose, California, *The Pioneer*, 1877-1883; 1893-1901.

San Jose, California, *Tribune*, 1857-58.

San Jose, California, *San Jose Weekly Visitor/Santa Clara Register/ Telegraph-Register*, 1853.

Stockton, California, *Journal*, 1850-1852.

Stockton, California, *Record*, 1933.

Stockton, California, *San Joaquin Daily Republican*, 1851-1854.

Stockton, California, *Weekly Times*, 1850-1851.

Virginia City, Nevada, *Daily Territorial Enterprise,* July 14, 1878, reprinted as a 24-page pamphlet.

UNPUBLISHED MATERIAL

Birth Record Registers, Churches of Limerick, Ireland. Genealogical Library, Church of Jesus Christ of Latter Day Saints, Salt Lake City, Utah.

Broadway Theater of New York City, Advertising Broadside for Thursday, January 8, 1852. California History Center, Sacramento.

Christening Records, St. Mary Church, Marylebone Road, London County, England. Genealogical Library, Church of Jesus Christ of Latter Day Saints, Salt Lake City, Utah.

Jonas Winchester, Scrapbook of Clippings on Mining, Travel and Other Subjects, 1851-1887. California State Library, Sacramento.

Jonathan Meredith Papers, vol. 29, Gilmor Meredith letters, 1853-54. Library of Congress, Washington, D. C.

Record of Deaths, 1853, Death Certificate of Edward P. Willis. Massachusetts State Archives, Boston.

T. W. Norris Collection, note, Lola Montez to C.K. Hotalling, dated November 22, 1854. Bancroft Library, Berkeley, California.

Ledger Book of Deaths, 1861, Death Certificate of Mrs. Eliza Gilbert. Municipal Archives, New York City.

INDEX

Lola Montez:
The California Adventures of Europe's Notorious Courtesan
has been produced in an edition of 1000 copies,
Printing by Cushing-Malloy, Inc., Ann Arbor, Michigan.
Designed by Robert Clark.
The typeface is Centaur.